CANINE SPORTS & GAMES

GREAT WAYS TO GET YOUR DOG FIT AND HAVE FUN TOGETHER!

Kristin Mehus-Roe

Storey Publishing

The mission of Storey Publishing is to serve our customers by
publishing practical information that encourages
personal independence in harmony with the environment.

Edited by Lisa H. Hiley and Deborah Burns
Art direction and book design by Jessica Armstrong

Illustrations by © Kathryn Rathke

Indexed by Nancy D. Wood

Printed in the United States by Versa Press
10 9 8 7 6 5 4 3 2 1

Library of Congress Cataloging-in-Publication Data

Mehus-Roe, Kristin.
  Canine sports & games / Kristin Mehus-Roe.
     p. cm.
  Includes index.
  ISBN 978-1-60342-083-9 (pbk. : alk. paper)
  1. Dog sports. 2. Games for dogs. I. Title.
  II. Title: Canine sports and games.
SF424.M44 2009
636.7—dc22
                    2008031839

Contents

Everything You Ever Wanted to Know About Canine Sports

All the Sports That Are Fit to Print

FOR DESI

By the time I began writing this book, my Australian cattle dog, Desi, was long past her prime. Her days of doing agility and hiking had been over for several years and even swimming and walks around the block had become more than her arthritic knees could handle. Just short of her 16th birthday, Desi tumbled down a short set of stairs and broke her leg. At the emergency veterinarian's office, I was told that she probably had bone cancer. The only treatment options were amputation or major surgery involving bone grafting; neither was viable for a dog of her age and health status. So I made the difficult decision to have her put to sleep.

When I left her on the floor of the vet's office, she looked like she was sleeping her deep, heavy, old-dog sleep, which was nothing like the way she had slept for her first 12 or 13 years of life. Then, her sleep was light and almost jumpy; she was always ready to spring awake to protect the house or to pester me for a walk or run. During her life, Desi must have run a thousand miles, swum a hundred more, and hiked dozens of hills. She did agility, experimented with herding, and was a world-class dock jumper before dock jumping became a sport.

Desi was the inspiration for much, if not all, of my dog writing, including shelter stories, pet-care articles, and my first book, Working Dogs. Desi probably would have been happier living on a ranch than in our urban home, but she was game to try anything I presented her with and always made me proud. This book first began bubbling in my mind as I watched her run laps around the many other dogs she encountered on our walks, runs, hikes, and swims. She was game to try new sports into her teens (although she never did learn to catch a Frisbee — despite hours and hours of attempts she'd always stand stock still, staring the Frisbee down until it smacked her in the face). I'd always wanted to write a book about canine sports for Desi, for all the miraculous experiences she gave me and for what she taught me about the world of dogs. So this book is for her, and for all the other athletic, smart, courageous dogs out there.

WHY DO DOG SPORTS?

People come to dog sports for many reasons. Most are just looking for something fun to do with their dogs, but many turn to dog sports as a last resort when dealing with behavioral issues.

One hundred years ago, most dogs were doing the jobs that they were bred for. Herding dogs herded, guard dogs guarded, and hunting dogs hunted. These dogs spent their days hard at work and their nights curled up in the barn or on the porch, exhausted. Family dogs routinely ran free — leashes were uncommon and crates were unheard of. At most, a dog might be kept in a fenced yard or tied up outside of the house, but generally they ran loose in the streets, fighting and playing with other dogs, visiting neighbors, and getting into mischief. Most slept in doghouses and ate table scraps for dinner. Routine veterinary care was unusual; dogs saw a vet only in the case of a catastrophic injury or when close to death. Strays were ignored or rounded up and put to death.

Today, life has changed dramatically for American dogs. It's no longer acceptable for dogs to roam loose, and the number of dogs euthanized each year has dropped dramatically. There are hundreds of commercial dog foods and nutritional supplements available, consumers spend billions of dollars on pet care, and most dogs sleep inside the family home, if not in a family bed.

Rather than being working partners, dogs are now considered members of the family. But for all the emotional investment that people have in their pets, there is often something missing in many of these dogs' lives: *the chance to run and jump and play and work as they were bred to do.*

The simple fact is that dogs who were developed to do intense work are not equipped to hang out in the house while their people work for eight hours a day, five days a week. They become bored and frustrated, often causing damage to themselves or to their owners' property. Some dogs develop separation anxiety, while others can neither relax nor focus. They roam from room to room whining and crying, looking for an outlet for their pent-up energy.

Taking up a dog sport isn't the cure-all for dog behavior issues, but it's certainly a good place to start — particularly when you are dealing with a young dog of an energetic breed. Strongly motivated herding breeds, high-energy pit bull types, and driven Labs are prime candidates for landing in animal shelters. Full of vim and vigor, they can become stir-crazy without structured exercise and training.

There's little doubt that doing canine sports can help almost any dog to become more balanced, better behaved, and happier. Most dogs benefit from having an outlet for their energy and intelligence, from the discipline required for training for a sport, and from the confidence that comes with success. An added bonus is that your high-energy pooch will sleep all night.

But the best and most common reason to become involved in dog sports is that it's simply a lot of fun. The dogs love it, the people love it, and you will never feel quite so fulfilled as a dog owner as when you see your dog's open mouth and sparkling eyes as he tears through a tunnel or leaps off of a dock into the water.

You just can't beat the feeling of your dog's adoring eyes meeting yours as you teach him a new trick. Just as canine unit police officers often comment that their police dogs are the best partners they ever had, being part of a dog–handler team will help you to appreciate your four-legged friend like never before. Your bond will become immeasurably stronger as you work together, train together, travel together, and play together.

People might ask, "Isn't it easier to run or bike or ski without your dog? And isn't it a little silly to be spending all that time and money to play with your dog?" Well, yes and yes. It is easier to do many sports without a dog, and sometimes it does seem a little silly to put a lot of effort into playing a game with a dog. But it's also far more fun to do almost any sport with your dog, and there really isn't anything wrong with being silly, is there? In fact, participating in dog sports takes as much humor as it does dedication and energy. If you can't jump up and down and look like a fool encouraging your dog to catch a ball or a Frisbee or to pull a cart piled with giant bricks — well, then, neither of you is going to have much fun.

It's not all fun, of course. Dog sports are hard, exhausting, and trying at times. Sometimes you will want to throttle your dog (but of course you won't), and other times you will feel like this is something neither of you will ever figure out. But if you stick with it, eventually you will have a moment that will make it all worthwhile.

You might be in the middle of a dark snowy wood, with the only light coming from the blue reflection of the moon on the snow and the only sound being the panting of your dog's breath and the quiet shushing of your skis over the snow. Or you might be at the center of a roaring arena with your dog nailing every jump and hitting every contact, and doing it with a swish and a flair that makes your heart burst with pride. Either way, you'll think for a minute about what it took to get you there, and you'll be grateful that you and your dog stuck around for the ride.

CHAPTER 1

Finding the Right Sport

WELCOME TO THE WONDERFUL WORLD of canine sports, where there is an activity for every dog. Whether your dog is a water-loving Lab who can't contain himself the moment he spies a bit of blue (or even muddy brown!) water, a livestock-happy cattle dog who is compelled to herd everything from kids to cats, or a nose-to-the-ground beagle whose sniffer leads him everywhere he goes, there is a way to put that energy and those instincts to work in a way that is fun for both of you.

A Sport for Every Dog

The variety of canine breeds reflects the many jobs that dogs were originally bred for, but as those jobs have changed or disappeared, dog sports have arisen to provide a way for dogs to practice those skills so intrinsic to their nature. Just because your dog was bred to be a herder doesn't mean that he'll love moving sheep from the moment he steps into the paddock, but the chances are pretty high that he'll at least know what is expected of him.

The fact is that not every dog likes every sport, or is suited to every sport. Some sports can even be dangerous for some dogs. And even if *you* adore a sport, it has to be a good match for your dog if both of you are to have fun and be successful.

The beauty of dog sports is that all but a few are open to any dog, and dogs of any level of athletic ability are welcome to try them out. Looking for the right sport for your dog is part research and calculation and part trial and error. Spend some time reviewing the canine sports, read some books, and talk to some handlers. Then visit an event or two. If it looks like something that you and your dog would enjoy, sign up for a class. It's not a lifetime commitment, so feel free to push your boundaries a bit — you'll be glad you did.

The Right Match

Sometimes an owner and dog aren't suited to doing a particular sport together. Dog enthusiasts Barbara and Jarred Reisinger, for example, thought that agility would be an excellent sport for their fiery papillon, Tiffany, but Tiffany and Barbara just didn't click together. "It became obvious that Tiffany and I worked better at flyball. I think it's just the dynamics of the sport. She gets riled up in flyball in the way I wanted her to get riled up in agility."

It's also important to remember that your dog will change. Even if she adores flyball today, after a while you might find that she prefers to catch a disc. In 5 or 10 years she may have arthritis or other age-related disorders that make an active sport less enjoyable or even painful; perhaps switching to obedience trials then would make sense.

Take the cue from your dog. If she has always *loved* flyball but now seems unenthusiastic or reluctant, there's a reason. She might be ill, or she might have had a bad experience that you didn't catch. Maybe a new dog in the class or on your team is giving her the stink eye, making her ill at ease.

Reisinger adds that as Tiffany ages, they are looking toward new sports better suited to a slower, older dog. "She's shown good interest and solid dependability in tracking. She loves being outdoors, and I think she would really love it."

Experienced sportspeople caution that although picking out a breed traditionally suited to a particular sport gives you a better chance of having a stellar disc dog or agility champion, it's certainly no guarantee. Never adopt or buy a dog without the willingness to adjust your expectations if she doesn't turn out to be the superstar you'd longed for. She may be better suited to a different sport, or she may simply not be an athlete. Instead of a skijoring champion, your new husky may turn out to be an excellent therapy dog or an enthusiastic freestyle dancer.

It's important that a sport is something you like and want to participate in as well. If your dog falls in love with a sport that you find yourself unwilling or unable to participate in, however, consider asking a dog-less friend (or a friend whose dog doesn't want to do the sport she wants to do!) to handle your dog in that particular sport.

Figuring Out Your Dog

Every dog is different, but certain types of dogs tend to enjoy one sport more than another. For example, herding breeds, such as Border collies and Australian shepherds, often excel in agility and flyball. Hunting dogs, such as Labradors and pointers, tend to do well in dock jumping, field trials, and hunt tests.

When deciding what type of sport you and your dog might want to participate in, there are many factors to consider, including his personality, activity level, and athletic ability. Dogs who are extremely high-energy, love to jump, and have boundless enthusiasm may prefer an extreme sport like disc to a more sedate sport like obedience. Mellow, older dogs will probably take to tracking more easily than to flyball.

And don't forget to consider your own likes and dislikes and fitness level. You want to find a sport that suits both of you!

SPORTS IN THIS BOOK

- Agility (p. 106)
- Canine Freestyle (p. 152)
- Carting (Drafting/Driving) (p. 232)
- Disc Dog (p. 126)
- Dock Jumping (p. 134)
- Dryland Pulling (Canicross/Scootering/Bikejoring) (p. 224)
- Earthdog (p. 180)
- Field Trials & Hunt Tests (p. 174)
- Flyball (p. 118)
- Herding (p. 160)
- Lure Coursing (p. 188)
- Obedience (p. 142)
- Rally (p. 148)
- Schutzhund (p. 200)
- Skijoring (p. 216)
- Sledding (p. 208)
- Tracking (p. 168)
- Water Rescue (p. 194)
- Weight Pulling (p. 238)

ABOUT CONFORMATION CLASSES

Conformation, the judging of purebred dogs against a written breed standard, is the granddaddy of organized dog sports. It has been popular for 150 years and has in large part driven the establishment of most other organized dog sports. The first modern dog shows were held in Great Britain during the mid-1800s. By the end of the century, a number of annual dog shows had been established; some, such as Crufts (established in 1891), continue to this day.

American dog fanciers were quick to embrace the idea of dog shows. The Westminster Kennel Club Dog Show was established in 1877, followed by the American Kennel Club (AKC) in 1884. The AKC is the largest governing body of American conformation. It was the first dog registry to sanction dog shows in the United States and continues to be the largest registrar of purebred dogs and sponsor of canine sports. Most American dog shows are held under the sanctioning of the AKC. The United Kennel Club (UKC), established in 1898, places more emphasis on showcasing sports that test breed skills, such as hunting and going to ground.

Evaluating dogs by conformation provides "a systematic way to evaluate each breed against its own standard of appearance," explains the American Kennel Club's vice-president of event operations, Robin Stansell. "A sled dog moves differently from a toy dog, for example. As fewer dogs are actually performing the tasks they were bred for, the sport of conformation has evolved and breed standards have changed. Judges have to consider the basic function of the breed and evaluate dogs based on an ideal that has developed over time."

Everything You Ever Wanted to Know About
DOG GAMES

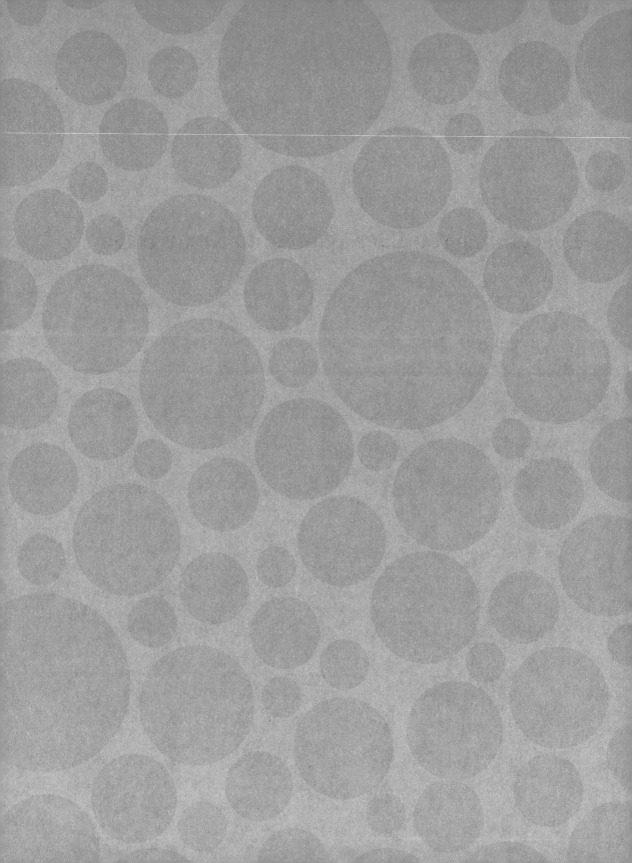

In conformation shows, purebred dogs are judged on how well they meet a detailed written breed standard. The standard describes the ideal dog, and the dog who best meets that ideal wins. Show dogs must be sound without any "faults," which might be floppy ears when the standard calls for erect ears, the wrong color, or an actual genetic disorder, such as albinism, hip dysplasia, or blindness.

Winning show dogs are bred to uphold the standard and further refine the breed. For this reason, show dogs cannot be neutered or spayed. In order to be eligible for sanctioned shows, dogs must be registered with the sanctioning body — only dogs registered with the AKC can compete in AKC shows, for example.

While competitors vary in the degree of seriousness they bring to showing, conformation is especially popular among breeders who want to match their dogs against other representatives of the breed. It helps them to hone their breeding programs and allows them to advertise the quality of their dogs. Nonbreeders involved in the sport may include the owners of purebred dogs who enjoy showing, or someone who made an agreement with his dog's breeder to show the dog if he proved to be an excellent example of the breed. And there are some wealthy owners whose dogs don't even live with them! They see dog showing as an investment. The dogs typically live with their handlers, who often care for them as though they were their own.

Whether conformation is a sport or not is a subject of great debate among dog people. For the purposes of this book, because involvement in most conformation activities is limited to dogs who are bred for conformation, we have chosen not to include it as one of the canine sports. For more information on showing, consult the resources section.

Personality Type

Take a look at the sports and the doggy personalities listed on the next page and see how your pooch matches up. Is he smart, focused, and full of energy? Agility might be his thing. Or maybe he has the grace of a ballet dancer and loves a crowd. Your dog may well be the next canine freestyle star.

Of course, dogs thrive in sports for different reasons. Your bumbling Rover might love disc, despite the fact that he drops every toss. That's okay, too. If he loves the sport but will never win any prizes doing it, it's still perfect for him.

Breakdown by Breed

This chart, on pages 16 and 17, lists the breeds most commonly seen participating in various canine sports, but it is in no way intended to discourage any particular breed from trying out any given sport. All dogs are individuals, regardless of their breeding, and many of them march to their own drummers! Except for a few sports that are restricted to certain breeds by the sponsoring organizations — earthdog and lure coursing, for example — most of these sports are open to any dog who has the right aptitude and attitude. Mixed breeds often excel at a variety of activities.

Physical Characteristics

Although your dog doesn't need to be an athlete of Olympic caliber to participate in any of these sports, some physical traits are needed for particular sports. See the chart on page 18.

Any dog also needs to have a level of fitness that will ensure he isn't injured while playing. For instance, if your dog has bad hips or arthritis, sports that involve jumping are not for him, although he may be able to enjoy agility for years — as long as the jumps are set low and he's not pushed too hard.

Some sports, such as canine freestyle and rally, are ideal for dogs with physical limitations. The beauty is that they're also perfect for super athletes — most sports can be whatever you make of them.

The most important thing is to keep your dog's safety in mind. Never push him beyond his limitations and always take training and increases in activity level slowly. While you can introduce a puppy to the basics, don't allow him to pull or jump before he is a full year old and has stopped growing (for larger breeds, this may take more than a year). Beginning these activities at too early an age can lead to a lifetime of pain.

Find the Right Sport for Your Dog's Personality

SPORT	PERSONALITY TRAITS																	
	Confident	Outgoing	Curious/Adventurous	Dependable in crowds	Amenable to new situations	Independent/Free spirit	Intelligent	Trainable	Biddable/Eager to please	Focused	Enthusiastic	High energy/lively	Loves to pull	Loves water	Loves jumping	Courageous	Determined/Tenacious	Closely bonded to handler
Agility	●		●		●		●	●		●	●	●			●	●		●
Canine Freestyle	●	●		●	●		●	●	●	●	●							●
Carting	●		●	●	●			●					●			●	●	
Disc Dog	●	●	●	●	●			●		●	●	●			●			●
Dock Jumping	●		●	●	●					●	●	●		●	●			
Dryland Pulling	●		●	●	●	●				●	●	●	●			●	●	
Earthdog	●		●		●	●	●			●	●					●	●	
Field/Hunt	●		●		●		●	●	●	●	●							
Flyball	●	●	●	●	●					●	●	●			●		●	●
Herding	●	●	●		●		●	●		●	●	●				●	●	●
Lure Coursing			●		●	●				●	●	●					●	
Obedience	●	●		●	●		●	●	●									●
Rally	●	●		●	●		●	●	●									●
Schutzhund	●		●	●	●		●	●		●	●					●	●	●
Skijoring	●		●			●				●	●	●	●			●		
Sledding	●		●			●				●	●	●				●		
Tracking	●		●				●	●	●	●							●	
Water Rescue	●	●	●	●	●			●	●	●	●		●	●		●	●	●
Weight Pulling	●			●					●	●			●			●	●	●

Find the Best Sport for Your Breed

SPORT \ BREED OF DOG	Alaskan husky	Alaskan malamute	Australian cattle dog	Australian kelpie	Australian shepherd	Bearded collie	Belgian Malinois	Bernese mountain dog	Border collie	Border terrier	Bouvier de Flandres	Canaan dog	Collie	Corgi	Chesapeake Bay retriever	Doberman pinscher	Fox terrier	German shepherd dog	Golden retriever
Agility			●	●	●	●	●		●	●		●	●	●	●	●	●	●	●
Canine Freestyle			●	●	●	●	●	●	●	●	●	●	●	●	●	●	●	●	●
Carting	●	●						●			●								
Disc Dog			●	●	●		●		●			●	●		●				●
Dock Jumping															●				●
Dryland Pulling	●	●						●			●				●				●
Earthdog										●									
Field/Hunt															●				●
Flyball			●	●	●		●		●	●			●		●			●	●
Herding			●	●	●	●	●		●		●	●	●					●	
Lure Coursing																			
Obedience			●	●	●	●	●		●	●	●	●	●			●	●	●	●
Rally			●	●	●	●	●	●	●	●	●	●	●	●		●	●	●	●
Schutzhund							●				●						●	●	
Skijoring	●	●						●	●						●			●	●
Sledding	●	●						●											
Tracking			●	●	●		●		●	●	●	●	●	●	●	●		●	●
Water Rescue															●				
Weight Pulling	●	●						●											

BREED OF DOG

Gordon setter	Irish setter	Jack Russell terrier	Labrador retriever	Leonberger	Newfoundland	Pointer	Poodle	Portuguese water dog	Rat terrier	Rottweiler	Saint Bernard	Samoyed	Shetland sheepdog	Siberian husky	Springer spaniel	Whippet	Mixed breed	Pit bull type	Scent hound	Sight hound	Terrier
●	●	●	●			●	●	●	●			●	●		●	●	●	●	●	●	●
●	●	●	●	●	●	●	●	●	●	●	●	●	●		●	●	●	●	●	●	●
				●	●					●	●	●		●			●				
		●	●						●				●		●		●	●			●
●	●		●	●		●	●	●									●	●			
●	●		●	●		●				●		●		●			●	●		●	
		●							●												●
●	●		●	●		●	●								●						
●	●	●	●			●							●		●	●	●				●
											●		●								
																				●	
●	●	●	●	●		●	●	●	●	●		●	●	●	●	●	●	●	●	●	●
●	●	●	●	●	●	●	●	●	●	●	●	●	●	●	●	●	●	●	●	●	●
																		●			
●	●		●	●		●	●		●	●		●		●		●	●	●		●	
												●		●							
●		●	●	●														●	●		
				●	●			●													
					●				●	●				●				●			

Find a Sport that Matches Your Dog's Abilities

SPORT	PHYSICAL CHARACTERISTICS																		
	Small	Small to medium	Medium to large	Any shape or size	Any level of physical ability	Agile	Fast	Flexible	Strong	Athletic	Powerful	Good catcher	Good jumper	Good runner	Good swimmer	Physically sound	Sound hips and joints	Excellent nose	Good eyesight
Agility		●	●			●	●	●		●			●	●		●	●		●
Canine Freestyle				●	●														
Carting			●						●		●					●	●		
Disc Dog		●				●	●	●		●		●	●	●		●	●		●
Dock Jumping		●	●			●		●		●		●	●		●	●	●		●
Dryland Pulling			●						●	●	●			●		●	●		
Earthdog	●					●		●		●								●	
Field/Hunt			●							●				●		●	●	●	●
Flyball		●				●	●	●		●		●	●	●		●	●		●
Herding			●							●						●	●		●
Lure Coursing			●				●			●				●		●	●		●
Obedience				●	●														
Rally				●	●														
Schutzhund			●			●			●	●	●		●	●		●	●	●	●
Skijoring			●			●			●	●	●					●	●	●	●
Sledding			●						●	●	●				●	●	●		
Tracking				●	●													●	
Water Rescue			●						●	●					●				●
Weight Pulling				●					●		●					●	●		

Discovering Your Options

The following is a general guide to the kinds of sports that different types of dogs and their handlers may enjoy. As a rule, dogs who participate in any of these sports should tolerate the nearby presence of other dogs and people. This doesn't mean that a dog needs to be exuberantly outgoing with new faces or that he must interact with them, but that he accepts the presence of other leashed dogs in close proximity and tolerates being approached and/or examined by unfamiliar people.

Agility

Dogs navigate a course consisting of obstacles such as an A-frame, dogwalk, and teeter-totter, as well as jumps and weave poles. The handler runs alongside the dog giving him directions but is not allowed to touch or lead him. The goal is for the dog to run the course as quickly and with as few faults as possible.

Agility is an excellent sport for dogs who are intelligent and energetic and need plenty of mental and physical activity. The sport has a very steep learning curve, and it can take a long time before a dog masters the skills — some dogs (and some people) simply don't have the focus for it.

Patience and commitment are key for agility handlers as well as for the dogs. Athleticism in a handler is a bonus since handlers must move through the course with their dogs; however, there are many elderly handlers and handlers with physical disabilities.

Canine Freestyle

Dogs and their handlers perform choreographed routines in time to music, sometimes with props and costumes. Sometimes called doggy dancing, canine freestyle incorporates elements of many dog sports, including the commands and tricks of obedience, the flash of Frisbee, and the footwork of agility.

Many dogs and dog breeds enjoy canine freestyle, regardless of age, size, and mobility, as the routine can be adjusted to a dog's physical ability. To do well in canine freestyle, dogs must enjoy training and be closely bonded with their handlers. They should also be friendly or at least tolerant of other dogs and love to be around large groups of people. A fearful or shy dog will rarely thrive in canine freestyle.

Many handlers are drawn to the sport because of a background in dance. Canine freestyle is as physically demanding as the routine you create.

Even a wheelchair can easily be integrated into a doggy dance routine. The main commitment is the time that it takes to develop a bond with your dog and painstakingly train him step by step. If you love to train your dog in obedience and love to dance, this may well be the sport for you.

Carting
(Drafting/Driving)

Although most people who enjoy drafting or driving with their dogs do it as a noncompetitive hobby, some breed clubs sponsor draft tests that follow a course or driving races that are similar to those in dryland pulling. Drafting, also called carting, recreates the original work of a number of dog breeds, including Saint Bernards, Bernese mountain dogs, and Newfoundlands. Until the invention of the automobile, these dogs were commonly used to pull carts and to haul freight. Driving literally puts the handler in the driver's seat — the handler sits in the cart and actually directs the dog much as she would a horse. There are many types of carts used for driving, but for speed most people choose sulkies, which are lightweight two-wheeled carts.

Drafting and driving are excellent sports for almost any powerful working dog who loves to pull. In addition to the traditional drafting dogs, this includes pit bull types, huskies, and Rottweilers. Drafting requires a patient handler who doesn't mind taking the time to introduce a dog to the cart slowly and with care. This isn't a swashbuckling, adventurous type of sport, so it often appeals to older handlers who enjoy the opportunity to see their dogs do what they were bred to do. The only physical requirement on the handler's part is to be able to manage the equipment.

Disc Dog

Handler–dog teams compete in two events: distance and accuracy, and freestyle. In distance and accuracy the team has one disc and 60 seconds in which to make as many catches as possible. Each catch is awarded points based on distance and on whether the dog catches the disc with all four feet in the air.

In freestyle, dogs and handlers perform a choreographed routine to music using five discs and a number of tricks and jumps. Dogs are awarded points based on their success in catching the disc and completing tricks, their athleticism, the difficulty of the routines, and the "wow factor."

If your dog loves to run, jump, catch, and retrieve, there's a very good chance he'll love disc. Disc is one of the few sports in which dogs and people truly participate equally. If you're a rotten Frisbee player, you and your dog won't be winning any tournaments (although you'll probably still have fun!). Handlers need to be willing to practice their sport as much as their dogs do. As a rule, athletic handlers tend to do best in this sport. Frisbee events are typically fun and rollicking affairs with lots of music and enthusiasm.

Dock Jumping

Dogs jump off of a dock, leaping for distance (measured by where the base of the tail hits the water). Vertical jumping is another option for dogs who get more air than distance. Water-loving dogs often love dock jumping, but jumping from a height of two feet into clear blue water in front of a crowd, with rock music blaring, can be intimidating. Dock dogs need to be confident and adaptable.

The sport has become a venue for the owners of hunting dogs to test their dog's instinct for retrieving. It's one of the rare canine sports to attract more male handlers than female. Dock jumping requires little in the way of formal training or time commitment. You need to socialize your dog to lots of situations and be willing to seek out water for him to enjoy. Dock jumping tends to attract outgoing folks who enjoying hanging out with other dog people.

Dryland Pulling (Canicross/ Scootering/Bikejoring)

Dryland pulling is essentially skijoring (cross-country skiing combined with sledding), but on land; it includes bikejoring, scootering, and canicross. In bikejoring, one to three dogs pull a rider on a bike. In scootering, the handler rides a scooter with 16- to 20-inch mountain bike wheels. In canicross, the handler is on foot and wears a padded belt or harness to which a single dog is attached. These are all great sports for young, high-energy dogs who love to run and pull. They are often jokingly called the perfect sports for dogs who can't learn to heel.

As with skijoring, in dryland pulling the handler is often doing as much work as the dog. Handlers who are athletic and physically active will enjoy these sports most. Successful handlers are willing to get outside with their dogs daily, or at least several times a week, and tear up the trail.

Earthdog

Earthdog was specifically developed to test the innate going-to-ground hunting instincts of the smaller terriers (20 pounds or less); hence, it is one of the sports exclusive to a certain type of dog. Terriers run through a narrow tunnel in the ground that has wooden sides and ceiling and a dirt floor. At the end of the tunnel are caged rats, which the terriers must "work."

Working the prey may mean barking, growling, or scratching at the cage, though individual judges define working the prey in various ways; one judge may pass a dog who scratches or even just stares at the cage, while another will pass only a dog who barks.

A newer, as-yet-unsanctioned version of earthdog, called strongdog, has been created for larger breeds such as American Staffordshire terriers and Airedale terriers. In this version, modeled after Irish events, dogs enter tunnels to retrieve the "prey," usually a badger skin stuffed with about 20 pounds of sand or rocks, and bring it back to the surface.

Most people who participate in earthdog and strongdog only attend the trials and do little if any training otherwise, so the time commitment is minimal. Trial attendees, however, should commit to the weekend, as tests usually take two days. And because the trials tend to be group efforts, it's highly likely that you'll be recruited to help out.

Field Trials & Hunt Tests

Dogs are tested on their ability to hunt, flush game or point, and retrieve. In field trials, dogs compete against other dogs at the trial, whereas in hunt tests dogs compete against their own records rather than other dogs. Most field trials and hunt tests evaluate the skills of the gun dogs, though there are also trials for coonhounds and other hunting dogs.

Field trials and hunt tests were created as a way to assess the hunting skills of the many dogs used for hunting. Dogs who participate don't have to be the best hunters, but they should enjoy being outdoors, running, retrieving, and, possibly, swimming.

Many handlers who participate in field trials and hunt tests also hunt; many others simply participate as a way to see how well their hunting dogs do. In field trials and hunt tests, the skill of the handler is often as important as the skill of the dog. To be competitive, you will have to commit long hours to training your dog and developing your own hunting skills.

Flyball

Teams of four dogs compete by sending a single dog at a time down a track, jumping over four hurdles to reach a flyball box at the end of the lane. The dog hits the flyball box with all four paws, triggering a ball to shoot out. He catches the ball, returns over the hurdles, and hits the start/finish line, prompting the next dog to go. An entire team typically finishes its run in less than 30 seconds. Teams usually consist of three larger dogs and a "height dog" — a smaller dog whose height determines the height of the jumps.

Flyball practices and competitions are noisy and chaotic. Any dog who participates must be energetic and enthusiastic but not so intense that he can't calm down when necessary. Dogs should be physically sound, as the repeated jumps and high-velocity turns can be hard on joints.

This sport provides opportunities for adult handlers of any age and level of physical ability. It is the quintessential team sport — the relay can't be run without all the dogs participating. If you join a flyball team, your team will count on you to attend regular practices and competitions. It's an intense sport, with lots of rowdy and high-pitched barking, so people who are sensitive to such things probably won't enjoy it.

Herding

Dogs exhibit their ability to herd livestock (ducks, sheep, or cattle) through a set course. Originally organized by farmers to show off their working dogs' prowess with stock, most trials today are dominated by herding dog owners who are attracted to a rural lifestyle without necessarily wanting to live on a farm.

Although most herding organizations will allow almost any dog to compete in herding, the dogs who excel come from breeds developed over centuries to handle livestock. Many non-herding breeds may enjoy herding, but they are rarely competitive, and the steep learning curve can be trying for their handlers. Not all herding dogs take to the sport, however. In addition to a strong interest in livestock, a dog needs intelligence, agility, and a deep bond with his handler.

Handlers must be patient, motivated people who can be firm but enthusiastic with their dogs. They also must be willing to drive long distances to train and compete. Because herding requires livestock, you can't train your dog just anywhere.

Lure Coursing

Dogs chase an artificial lure, usually a piece of white fur or a white plastic bag, that is pulled along a course by means of a motorized pulley system. In trials, dogs race three at a time but are titled based on their individual times instead of on their race placement. Lure coursing is a sport exclusively for the sight hounds, including greyhounds, whippets, salukis, and Rhodesian ridgebacks.

Lure coursing requires no formal training other than exposure to the lure, and owners usually come to the sport with an interest in testing their dogs' innate coursing instincts. Owners of rescued racing greyhounds are often especially interested in the chance to see their dogs in action. The sport is also helpful for sight hound breeders who are trying to maintain dogs with a strong drive in their bloodlines.

Lure coursing does not necessitate much in the way of training or expense, as it is mainly about the dogs' instinctive behavior. However, because lure coursing requires a somewhat complicated coursing pulley system even for practice, you will probably have to join a club in order to participate.

Obedience

A natural extension of basic dog training, obedience refines and develops the traditional commands such as *heel* and *stay* by incorporating long-stay commands and heeling in a figure eight, among other requirements. Dogs must also exhibit skills in scent discrimination, fetch and retrieve, and hurdles.

Handlers are not allowed to encourage or touch their dogs throughout the exercise. The pair begins a trial with 200 points and loses points each time a command isn't done precisely right. While this rigidity appeals to many handlers, it has been blamed for a recent downturn in interest in the sport.

Obedience requires a dog who loves to learn and is highly bonded to his handler. The trick is that he must also be enthusiastic, confident, and independent enough to perform in front of a crowd with little communication from his handler.

Although handlers can have any level of physical ability, they must be highly motivated to train their dogs. Training in advanced obedience takes a great deal of time and patience, and successful handlers view the rigidity of obedience as a challenge rather than a detriment.

Rally

Dogs follow a course with a number of stations; at each one is an instruction to perform a specific command. The course may be timed. The command may be simple, such as *sit* or *down*, or more complex, such as heeling in a figure eight. As in obedience, the team begins the rally course with a certain number of points and loses points if they make a mistake; however, the point deductions are more forgiving than in obedience.

Rally, sometimes called rally obedience or rally-o, was developed to make obedience less staid and more fun for both dogs and handlers. Detractors say that it's also less challenging. Handlers are allowed to communicate freely with their dogs, encouraging, whistling, even clapping.

Rally doesn't require a lot in the way of physical ability, but dogs who participate must be highly bonded to their handlers and eager to please. For dogs who require lots of ongoing enthusiasm and praise from their people, it's a good alternative to obedience.

Like obedience, rally requires a lot of training time, even though it doesn't require the same rigidity of training. It's a good sport for enthusiastic handlers who have a hard time stopping themselves from cheering their dogs on.

Schutzhund

Despite its perception as solely a "protection" sport, Schutzhund consists of three areas: obedience, tracking, and protection. The obedience and tracking events are similar to traditional obedience and tracking, although far more rigid. In obedience, dog–handler teams are tested in following commands, tractability, and handler skills. In tracking, dogs must detect and follow a scent over a variety of terrain. The protection component centers on "bite work." Dogs are trained to bite (and release) a protective sleeve on command. Part of the key to protection work is that the dog is never aggressive and always follows the commands of his handler.

This is among the most difficult dog sports to train for and is surely the sport that requires handlers to take on the most responsibility. A well-trained Schutzhund dog is protective but obedient. A poorly trained Schutzhund dog, however, can be dangerous. Schutzhund handlers must be willing to spend huge amounts of time training their dogs in a highly regimented manner.

Skijoring

Skijoring combines cross-country skiing and sledding, with one to three dogs attached by a towline to a cross-country skier who skis behind the dogs as they pull. To minimize the risk of injury to both skier and dogs, the skier wears a padded belt that attaches to the towline while the dogs wear pulling harnesses.

Any dog who enjoys running and pulling can do skijoring. Nordic dogs such as Siberian and Alaskan huskies enjoy it, as do the setters, retrievers, and hounds of the world. Dogs of all sizes and shapes participate; the only qualification is that they love to pull and run and that they are big enough and physically sound enough to do it.

Although there are some skijoring competitions, skijoring is largely a hobby sport. Many of the people who take up skijoring love the sport of sledding but are unwilling or unable to devote the level of time and commitment to a team of dogs required of a musher. In skijoring, the handler must be as athletic as the dog, so this is a sport for a fit person who is at least an adequate skier.

Sledding (Mushing)

Teams of 4 to 24 dogs pull lightweight basket sleds or heavier toboggan sleds with a musher directing them. In competition, there is a preordained course and a time limit. While many mushers sled only for fun, competition is a big part of this sport, with mushers and their teams often traveling long distances to compete.

For the most part, dogs who love sledding are the ones you'd expect: huskies and other Nordic dogs who have been bred for it over centuries. Sled dogs are unusual among canine athletes because sledding is really more of a job than a hobby. Sled dogs generally live outdoors in kennels or on tie outs rather than as house dogs.

Sled dog handlers, or mushers, are a special breed of person. Most mushers are outdoorsy, athletic, competitive people who love winter sports and are devoted to their dogs. Exercising, feeding, and housing four or more very active, high-energy dogs takes a huge amount of time as well as money. Most mushers live in rural areas in order to have enough land for their dogs and their sport, and many travel hours to and from their day jobs to maintain this lifestyle.

 ## Tracking

Dogs follow a predetermined scent trail over distances of several hundred yards, through a series of turns. At advanced levels, cross tracks are laid in an attempt to confuse and distract the dog. Unlike search and rescue, the goal is to follow the track itself, rather than find a person or object at the end of the track. A search and rescue dog may, for example, search the air for a more direct scent of the missing person. A tracking dog, however, is penalized for leaving the track, even if leaving it means that he finds a more direct route to the goal.

Tracking can be done by any breed but requires a dog with a great sense of smell and the single-mindedness to focus on a scent trail. Tracking may be the only sport in which you truly rely on the dog to lead the way, so the dog must be self-confident and intelligent.

Tracking is an exacting and time-consuming sport, but one that also brings great satisfaction to dogs and owners who love to spend long hours in the outdoors. Patience is an important factor in training a tracking dog. Handlers must be prepared to go through the steps slowly and be willing to let their dogs ultimately call the shots.

 ## Water Rescue

Dogs are tested on their ability to save multiple victims, take a boat line from one boat to another, tow a drifting boat to shore, and rescue an unconscious victim from under a capsized boat. Water rescue tests are most popular among Newfoundland dog clubs, but Leonbergers sometimes test with Newfoundland clubs for the same skills. Portuguese water dog clubs test for slightly different skills.

These breeds have centuries of history as water rescue dogs and nearly all of them are born with a deeply ingrained love of water. An all-breed club has been established, however, giving any water-loving dog the opportunity to participate in water rescue.

Training for water rescue takes a significant commitment. It requires a team of people and a lot of equipment, including a boat. Many newcomers to the sport are surprised to realize that the handlers must love water as much as their dogs do. To practice, most people must join a club, and because water tests require a number of stewards to be in the water acting as victims, everyone is expected to take a turn — which means donning a wet suit and jumping into the water, even when the weather is miserable.

Weight Pulling

Dogs pull sleds or carts on wheels or tracks laden with weights are increased incrementally. Dogs are given a set length of time to pull the weight a prescribed distance. Each time the dog manages to pull the weight during the time allotment, he advances to the next level. Classes are divided into weight categories, so even very small dogs can compete.

Although originally developed as a sport for large northern dogs such as Alaskan malamutes, weight pulling has come to be dominated by the power-houses of the dog world, like American pit bull terriers and American bull-dogs. Plenty of smaller dogs participate, however, and at almost any weight-pulling event there will be a smattering of nontraditional dogs as disparate as golden retrievers, corgis, and minia-ture poodles. Because he competes only within his own weight class, a success-ful pulling dog doesn't have to be big and strong, although he must have a great deal of willpower and eagerness to please his owner.

There are no physical requirements for handlers, but you should be willing to make a fool of yourself by calling enthu-siastically to your dog while he does his thing. To many handlers, weight pulling is a fun and safe way for their brawny dogs to show their stuff, and depending on your level of commitment, you may train with your dog daily or hardly ever. Traveling to competitions may involve the most work, as they are often few and far apart.

CHAPTER 2

Other Opportunities for Fun

DESPITE THE INCREASING POPULARITY of organized canine sports, what most people like to do with their dogs is just hang out with them. Whether your idea of canine fun is a walk around the block, a five-mile run, a swim in the lake, or a trip to the dog park, your dog just loves to be by your side. Even when pursuing noncompetitive activities, it's important to be mindful of your dog's health, safety, and enjoyment. You may love to run, for example, but your dog might prefer — or need — a lower-impact activity such as walking or swimming. And not all dogs have the right personality for the unstructured, somewhat chaotic play at dog parks. Remember, it's supposed to be fun!

Swimming with Your Dog

Swimming is a favorite activity for many dogs. If you have a Lab, a Newfie, or a Portuguese water dog, chances are that it's hard to persuade him to leave the water once he's in it. But a love of swimming certainly isn't exclusive to dogs traditionally bred for water work. Many dogs love to swim, and even those who aren't interested in actual dog paddling will enjoy wading or splashing in cool water on a warm day.

Although a self-respecting water dog isn't picky about the water that he swims in, many humans are fussy about who shares their swimming spots. In many communities, it can be very difficult to find a place where dogs are allowed to swim. The owners of urban dogs in particular are challenged to find good doggy swimming holes, though some communities have established stretches of shorefront or lakeside beaches where dogs are allowed. Dog owners in Long Beach, California, for example, successfully petitioned the city for a canine beach and now enjoy a quarter mile of dog-friendly sand.

If you live in an area without a doggy swimming area you have a few options: You can petition for access to a municipal lake or pond; you can take swimming excursions out of the city; or if you have a yard, you can buy a pool.

Buying a pool may actually be more feasible than it sounds. There are many models of aboveground pools that can accommodate even the largest dog, if proper access (a sturdy ladder or steps or, better yet, a deck) is provided. Many of these have filtration systems and don't need to be emptied regularly.

For a smaller dog, a shallow wading pool makes a decent swimming hole. Some dogs just love to loll in the water, and for them even a small kiddie pool can be enjoyable. Choose the type made of hard plastic instead of an inflatable model that probably wouldn't stand up to doggy nails for more than one or two sessions.

PLAYING WITH THE OLDER OR DISABLED DOG

Not every dog was born to run. Some dogs just prefer to walk. Slowly. Others may have disabilities that preclude them from participating in most sports, or they may not have the right temperament. Some dogs don't like crowds of people, other dogs, or too much activity. Aging dogs often lose the ability to participate in sports due to arthritis or other age-related disorders. The good news is that a reluctance or inability to participate in canine sports doesn't mean that your dog can't continue to be involved in activities and to play a big role in your life.

All dogs benefit from getting outdoors and doing a little exploring. Veterinary acupuncturist Eric Hartmann calls these excursions "mental breaks" and encourages them for all of his canine clients, including those who are severely disabled. According to Hartmann, just the act of taking a dog out of his usual routine and into a new environment, such as a park you haven't visited before, is enormously stimulating. There are new scents to smell and sights to see. The activity of other dogs, kids, and wildlife, as well as the smells and textures of dirt and grass and leaves, will give your dog a welcome adventure.

In addition to parks, take your older or disabled dog with you to the local coffee shop (if you can sit outdoors) or on errands with you. For many dogs a trip in the car feels like a Disneyland ride. Turn your quick trip to the store for milk into an opportunity for your otherwise housebound pet to have a mini adventure.

Swimming Pool Rules

If you're lucky enough to have an inground pool, you have a water dog's paradise. There are, however, several important rules when it comes to allowing dogs to play in a pool, no matter what the depth of the water.

Never leave your dog in the pool alone.

Dogs can panic and drown very quickly. Don't allow access to the pool when you're not at home. The pool should be fenced, and your dog should be kept in another part of the yard when he's not actually swimming.

Teach your dog a way out.

If you have an aboveground pool, use portable stairs or build a deck around it. Your dog should know how to get out of the water by using the stairs, and this knowledge should be reinforced with a cue. When dogs panic in the water, they often become confused and unable to find the exit. If he has a cue that is triggered every single time he leaves the pool, his memory of the exit will become automatic.

Many pool-owning dog people reinforce where the exit is by always having their dogs touch a particular place with their noses as they exit the pool. For example, place a large ceramic planter next to the stairs into the pool. Every time your dog uses the stairs to leave the pool ask him to "touch" the planter. A clicker is a great way to teach this. Touch, click, treat!

Don't let your dog call the shots.

Swimming should be a bonus for your dog, not an expectation. Some water dogs become obsessed with swimming in the pool if they have unrestricted access. They may whine constantly to get to the pool or worse: bark, jump on swimmers, and generally make it unpleasant for the humans trying to enjoy themselves.

Swimming should be a special, supervised activity that you control. Teach your dog a cue that means "time to swim," and don't let him go in the pool without hearing or seeing that cue first. A cue could be a command, the sound of a bell or whistle, or the appearance of a particular toy. When it's time to end the session, end it firmly. Do not let him jump back in after you call him out. Lead him away from the pool and restrict access until the next swim.

Always rinse your dog after he swims.

Chlorine is harsh on human hair and it's also harsh on dog fur. Don't let him drink the water — keep a bowl of water available for quick gulps between laps. You may consider switching to a biological filtration system instead of chlorine, as chlorine will strip the natural oils from your dog's fur and often will lead to itchy, dry skin.

Consider buying your dog a life jacket.

While there are a number of dog life jackets on the market, none are approved by the U.S. Coast Guard, so you may have to try out a few to find one that works correctly for your dog. An added bonus is that most models have a handle, which can be helpful when teaching your dog to swim and can also be used to pull your dog out of the drink if he slips into the pool or off a boat deck. A life jacket should not be used in lieu of supervision, however. Just like children, dogs can drown in small amounts of water in amazingly little time. Even dogs who are good swimmers are at risk for drowning, especially as they become older and are more easily disoriented.

Water Caution

Never, ever, ever jump into an open body of water after your dog if he is having trouble. Dogs tend to be stronger swimmers than are humans, so if he is having trouble, you definitely will. Trying to help a dog swim to safety will likely result in his climbing on you in his panic. This phenomenon occurs in both humans and dogs and leads to many secondary drownings.

Instead, help your dog by calling his name repeatedly and running parallel to him on the shore to keep his focus on you, not on panicking. Along a river there are various points where the current eases a little, making it easier to get to the side. If he's caught in a rip current, the best thing he can do is swim parallel to the shore until he's out of the current. Encourage him to keep going.

Swimming in Public Places

Many of us do not have pools, so we have to take our dogs to public beaches to swim. If you take your dog to a public place to swim, remember that the two of you are ambassadors for the rest of the doggy swimmers out there. Rivers, lakes, and ocean beaches are fun places to spend the day with your dog. To ensure that you're allowed back (or at least not prohibited) and that you both stay safe, here are some basic rules to follow.

- **Respect the rules.** Don't take your dog to places where dogs are not allowed.

- **Don't take an aggressive or badly trained dog.** A dog who threatens people or other dogs shouldn't be off leash in areas where he'll encounter either. A dog who doesn't obey will annoy other swimmers and may put himself at risk in the water.

- **Always clean up after your dog.** Take more poop bags than you think you'll need — it's better to be safe than sorry, and you can help out another poor soul who forgot his bags. Always dispose of the waste properly afterward. Yes, that does mean trekking the bags out if there is no trash can.

- **Never let your dog swim unattended.** A small wave, rip current, or tussle with another dog can panic him quickly. Always be there to help him out if he needs you.

- **Know the water conditions.** Just as you shouldn't swim in unknown bodies of water yourself, don't let your dog swim unless you know that it's safe. Ocean waves can be deceptively powerful, and fast-moving rivers can be incredibly dangerous, sweeping your dog away in seconds. Even seemingly gentle waters can have hidden dangers such as rip currents or tides, whirlpools, and underwater snags. If possible, ask a ranger or lifeguard about the current water conditions. If there is no ranger or lifeguard, ask other folks who are swimming or strolling the waterline about water conditions. If you live near the ocean and swim there often, know what the water-condition flags mean (black means "don't swim!!").

- **Always take drinking water!** It often doesn't occur to us to take water for our dogs when they're going swimming. But this is hard play and they're going to get thirsty; they will drink the water they're swimming in if they have no alternative. Many dogs will even drink salt water, making them more thirsty and leading to stomach upset. Offer water often.

- **Bring several floatable toys.** At least one always disappears in the course of play, and don't sweat it if another dog runs away with one. It's kind of like the playground in that you may go home with a different toy than you arrived with!

HOW TO GET THE MOST OU OF WALKING YOUR DOG

Other than feeding your dog, walking him is the most basic of all chores. Even dogs with large fenced-in yards need stimulation and new experiences, whether you're strolling around the block after dinner or power-walking through town early in the morning. But in order to enjoy those daily outings, you need to teach your dog some basic manners so that you are the one taking him for a walk, not the other way around. Here are the fundamentals:

- **Train your dog** to know all his basic commands (*come, leave it, drop it, sit, down,* and *stay*) as well as how to walk politely without straining at the leash. This doesn't mean he has to walk like a robot next to your side, but he should be paying attention to you and responding to your signals, not tearing around at the end of the leash and pulling you off your feet.

- **Don't let your dog lunge at other dogs,** small children, passersby, or people on bikes. If you have an excitable dog who either loves to greet all comers or reacts aggressively to perceived threats, teach him to sit and stay while the temptations pass by.

- **Dogs shouldn't be allowed to mark repeatedly** while on walks. The best way to do this is simply not to allow him to stop and mark — call his name or offer a treat to distract him when he indicates that he is going to mark. Do give him the opportunity to relieve himself before and after your trek. Always take poop bags and clean up after your dog.

Running with Your Dog

For dogs and people, running is not only great exercise but also a terrific way to bond with each other. The look on your dog's face when you pull out your running shoes reinforces what you already know: Your dog loves this activity and loves doing it with you. Having a dog who needs a lot of exercise every day is an excellent way to motivate yourself to keep moving. Even if it starts as a chore, a daily run can become highly addictive. Running is good for the heart, tones muscles, and ensures that you both sleep well at the end of the day. But running can also be hard on knees and joints, of both the canine and human variety. One of the leading causes of running injuries is not being in good shape when you start. Too many of us think we can lace up a pair of running shoes and jump into running five miles a day. We can't, and our dogs can't either. Before beginning a running regimen with your dog, make sure both of you are in good shape and check in with your doctor and your vet.

If you're new to running, start with walking. The first week walk one mile a day, the second week walk two miles a day, and the third week walk three miles a day. If you feel as though you need more time to build up to three miles, take it. Observe your dog on your walks and make sure he is comfortable and not moving stiffly or limping.

Once both of you can comfortably walk three miles, begin running. For the first week, walk one mile, run one mile, and walk one mile. After a week or when it feels comfortable, walk one-half mile, run one-and-a-half miles, and walk one mile. Do this for another week or until you're comfortable with this distance.

Go up by half-mile increments until you reach a good distance for you and your dog. For some, two miles is just fine, while others become marathon runners and regularly run 10 miles at a time. Just make sure that your dog can keep up with you without distress if you start eating up the miles.

Rules of the Road

To keep yourself safe when running, and to ensure that your dog and you are good ambassadors, you should consider a few rules to run by.

Always clean up after your dog.

Give your dog the opportunity to defecate and urinate before you set out but never assume that he won't relieve himself on the road, even if he's just done so. A good run can stimulate his bowels and he'll often stop again. Give him the chance to go after your run as well.

Many runners dislike carrying anything when they run, but there are convenient little poop-bag holders that can go around your wrist or snap to your dog's collar. They are widely available at pet supply stores and over the Internet.

Other options include tying plastic bags to your dog's collar or leash or wearing a sweatshirt or running pants with pockets. If there isn't a trash can nearby, you'll have to carry the poop along with you. Yes, it's gross but it's necessary. You might want to map out a route where there are trash cans.

Keep your dog on leash when running.

It's tempting to let your dog off leash to run alongside you, but even a dog with very good recall can be distracted when another dog runs by or when a squirrel crosses his path.

Teach your dog to heel next to you.

He shouldn't cut in front of you or lag behind. If your dog can't keep up with you, running may not be the sport for him, or he may have an injury that isn't obvious. Don't allow your dog to sniff at intriguing scents, other dogs, or passing people. If he thinks that this is the norm, he'll stop short in mid-run every time he sees a potential playmate or catches a whiff of something smelly. This is not only irritating but can also be dangerous.

Respect other runners.

They may not like dogs, may be afraid of dogs, or may be very focused on their run. Do not let your dog sniff them, jump on them, or otherwise impede their run. If they stop and initiate interaction with your dog, by all means let him stop for a quick scratch behind the ears (or if you don't want to stop, it's acceptable to shout out a quick apology as you run by).

Try to avoid other dogs.

Encountering dogs on the road can be problematic. They may not be friendly, even if your dog is, or the handler may not want to stop. Proper etiquette when two runners and their dogs meet on the road is to ask before allowing any interaction. If the other runner looks focused and doesn't slow down, or calls her dog close to her, assume that she isn't interested in doggy playtime. If she does slow to a walk as you pass, and you want to allow your dog a chance to sniff, ask first.

If your dog is aggressive toward other dogs, you may want to plan your run for a path that isn't heavily populated by other dogs and that is wide enough for you to avoid scuffles. (And talk to a trainer about your dog's behavior, as many aggressive behaviors, especially those that happen exclusively on leash, have fairly easy solutions.)

Look for proper footing.

Running on concrete is hard on human knees and doggy joints. If possible, run on grass, running tracks, or trails. For your own health, buy new running shoes every 300 miles. For your dog's health, check his paws after every running session. If there are any cuts or abrasions, you may want to consider using paw wax or outfitting him with protective booties that slip over paws and are tightened with Velcro around the ankles. Many dogs find these uncomfortable or will kick them off as they run, but if pad injuries become an ongoing and serious problem, it's an alternative.

Do not run in very hot weather.

Not only are dogs wearing fur coats, they are not able to regulate their body temperatures as well as humans can. If you are uncomfortable in the heat, you can bet that your dog is miserable. Running in the street exposes your dog to the added discomfort of bare footpads on burning concrete and possibly stepping in hot tar or melted gum. Before setting out, touch the asphalt with your palm — if it's too hot for you to touch, it's too hot for your dog to run on.

Cold weather running has its dangers.

Sidewalks are often treated with salt or de-icing chemicals, which can injure exposed paws, and icy snow can cut paw pads. After running in cold weather, always check your dog's paws for any cuts and rinse them with clean water to make sure that there are no de-icing chemicals on them that he might lick off.

Let's Go!

Running with your dog will be more pleasant if you teach him to relieve himself on command, rather than going mid-run. It's both safer and less irritating than having a dog who stops abruptly to urinate or defecate. A good way to do this is with clicker training. During his regular routine, catch him in mid-poop or pee, say "Good potty!" then click and treat. During your run, don't let him stop to dally around, which signals that it's okay to mark. Of course, you should always give him ample time to relieve himself before and after your run.

Some shorthaired dogs may need a doggy coat in particularly frigid weather or if you alternate running with walking or other exercise in the same outing.

Wear reflective clothing after twilight.

Many running shoes and other running gear have reflective strips, but add to your visibility by wearing anklets and bracelets that flash or by donning a reflective construction-worker type vest. These are all sold at sports stores. Your dog will be safer and more visible with a flashing collar or clip-on light and a leash made of reflective material.

Respect traffic rules.

It's tempting to cross against lights or dash across the street during a break in traffic to avoid breaking up your run, but this can be extremely dangerous. Dogs are unpredictable, and even if you get across the street, he may turn back to see what that squirrel is doing and end up being hit. If possible, avoid running on city streets; try to find a good trail away from traffic to run on with your dog. It's safer and far more relaxing.

Keep your dog hydrated.

As mentioned earlier, dogs cannot regulate their body temperatures as efficiently as humans can. While you are perspiring through your special sweat-wicking running shirt, your dog can only pant. If it's warm or you're doing an especially long run, dehydration can lead to heat exhaustion. If you are not running close to home — for example, if you begin your run at a trailhead or a school track — always take water and a portable bowl with you. You can carry this in your car, or, if you're walking to your destination, in a runner's pack. Offer your dog a small amount of water before and after running.

Don't forget to warm up and cool down.

While you're stretching your legs and limbering for your run, what is your dog doing? We often forget that our dogs' bodies need the same type of care that ours do. Before setting out on your run, ask your dog to jump up on you for a good stretch. Develop a good cue so that he does this *only* when you ask.

A play bow is another good allover stretch. To teach a cue for a play bow, catch your dog in the act and click and treat, or just give him a treat, saying "Bow!" Try to give the command and treat him every time he does a play bow and he'll be doing it on cue in no time.

Once you've both stretched, take a pre-run walk around the block. Now you're ready to go. When you return from your run, take the time for a post-jog walk around the block. Don't let your dog go right back in the house and hop up on the couch, where his still-warm muscles may stiffen and cramp.

HAVING FUN AT DOG PARKS

Many busy dog owners have embraced the world of off-leash dog parks. Dog parks are usually fenced areas in urban locations where dogs have the opportunity to run and play with other dogs. Although dog parks were very unusual until the mid-1990s, they are now found in almost every city in the United States.

Dog parks allow urban dogs the rare opportunity to play off leash and the chance to act like dogs. They are especially valuable for high-energy dogs who live in homes without large, fenced yards. Dog parks engender their own set of problems, however. They are largely unregulated and, unfortunately, many people take their dogs without ensuring that they are properly socialized with other dogs.

Far too many dog park users see it as a sort of doggy daycare, leaving their dogs to do their thing while they talk on their cell phones or socialize with other dog owners. Big, rough dogs who have not learned proper play etiquette can overwhelm smaller dogs, unsupervised play can easily lead to overstimulation and fights, and many owners don't know how to read the messages that their own dogs are sending them.

It is important to follow proper dog park etiquette. The rules posted at dog parks are there for the safety of both dogs and humans. Too many visitors ignore these rules or think that their dog is never the problem, so it is important to be vigilant and keep a close eye on your dog and the other dogs around him.

- **Don't take a puppy** younger than four months old. In addition to the possibility of contracting diseases from other dogs, there is too much risk of unpleasant or even dangerous encounters with unruly or aggressive dogs.

- **Never take an unaltered male** or a female in heat. Unaltered males are prone to squabbles, and females in heat will only contribute to that. Plus, you don't want any accidental litters.

- **Never take an aggressive dog.** A dog with a history of fighting with other dogs or acting threatening toward humans should not visit the dog park. Owners of certain breeds should carefully consider whether to take their dogs to a dog park. Pit bull and greyhound experts generally advise against these breeds visiting dog parks. Although socialized pit bulls may rarely start a fight, they generally will not back down from one. Greyhounds, especially rescues from racetracks, have strong prey drives and may misinterpret play behavior.

- **Don't take treats to the dog park,** and do leave your dog's favorite toys at home. Take a couple of extra tennis balls with you to help defuse confrontations.

(continued)

(continued)

- **Don't let your dog act like a bully** at the dog park. If your dog humps, barks aggressively, or nips at other dogs, he doesn't belong in a pack situation. You may think that your dog is only playing but not all dogs understand this style of play. In fact, this type of behavior often isn't playful and is correctly interpreted by other canines as dominant or aggressive.

- **Don't take more than two dogs** per person to the dog park. It is impossible for one person to regulate or even monitor the behavior of more than two dogs. Dog walkers and pet sitters too often use the dog park as a place to take their charges. These dogs form packs and can act like bullies toward other dogs. As a result, many dog parks are beginning to restrict the number of dogs one person can take in at one time.

- **Don't take young children with you.** Not all dogs are good with children, and even child-friendly dogs can misinterpret a child who is screaming, crying, running, or jumping. Children have plenty of places to play; dog parks should be left to the dogs.

Most important, keep moving — don't just sit and chat with other people, and don't break out your cell phone! Your dog may not get much exercise if you don't keep him moving. In addition, dogs can become territorial surprisingly quickly. If you sit in one place for too long, he may become protective of your spot. Come on, throw the ball for your dog — that's why you're here, isn't it?

On Wheels with Your Dog

Many people enjoy skating or biking with their dogs alongside them. It's a tremendous way to tire out very high-energy dogs without having to run a marathon. There is a lot of equipment now available to use when engaging in pulling sports with your dog. Items such as bike stringers, which keep your dog's leash from getting tangled in your bike tires, and special belts to attach the leash to can make wheeling along much safer for both of you. (See Daredevil Dryland Pulling, page 224, for more information.)

If you choose to skate or bike with your dog the old-fashioned way (holding on to your dog's leash and hanging on for dear life), here are a few tips.

Start with a well-trained dog.

Your dog should know all of his basic commands (*come, leave it, drop it, sit, down,* and *stay*) before you ever trust him to pull you on a bike, skateboard, or in-line skates. In addition, train your dog on the typical commands used in the pulling sports — *easy* (for slow down), *whoa* (stop), *gee* (right), and *haw* (left). Train your dog on these commands before you begin doing these activities, because it's much harder to train your dog from a bike or skateboard that is speeding 20 miles an hour down a trail.

Don't let your dog chase small animals.

If you let your dog chase squirrels when off leash or on walks, there's no reason he won't do it while pulling you.

Don't let your dog weave on leash.

When walking your dog, teach him to heel at your side or walk directly in front of you. Do not let him weave back and forth in front of you. When you're on a bike or skateboard, a weaving dog can be hit by the bike or skateboard or his leash can get caught in the wheels.

Avoid the street or sidewalk.

Instead, go to a park with wide paved trails away from traffic. Even a well-trained dog can act unpredictably, chasing a squirrel into a neighbor's lawn or across the street or crossing abruptly in front of the bike to investigate a passing dog.

Hiking with Your Dog

Hiking is one of the best ways for dogs and people to spend time together. It's good for both of you — mentally and physically — and gives you the opportunity to explore new areas with your four-legged friend. A dog can be the perfect hiking companion: a buddy to inspire you when you get tired, a protector from strangers, and a silent but trustworthy sidekick. If you love to hike alone but not *completely* alone, there is nothing like having a dog by your side.

For the dog, hiking is an exciting change from the humdrum of daily life. Although your dog cherishes his walks around the neighborhood, a hike is like a special vacation. In addition to the great exercise a long hike provides, there are a million new sights and smells to explore.

Do a little research when planning your hike. Although some trails allow dogs, many do not. Before you head out, make sure that the trail you want to explore allows dogs. Finding out that your best buddy isn't allowed after driving several hours is a big disappointment. There are a number of books published on dog-friendly hikes; if you're lucky there is one for your region. If you can't find a book for a particular area, contact a local mountaineering club. They can give you the scoop on which trails are dog-friendly and which are not. Please respect posted trails, and don't take your dog where he isn't welcome.

Once you've found a few dog-friendly trails, choose one that is within both your and your dog's abilities. If you regularly do 20-mile hikes but your dog isn't used to much more than a stroll around the block, keep your initial treks short. Hiking takes a great deal more mental and physical energy for dogs than walking on a city street. Their ears, noses, and eyes buzz with the breadth of stimuli they are taking in. And uneven terrain, loose dirt trails, and up and down slopes will tire them out far more than an average walk. Once your dog is acclimated to the sport of hiking, you can begin to increase the distance and difficulty of the hikes you take together.

If you have a young, strong dog with sound hips and no arthritis, you can eventually ask him to take some of the stress off your back by carrying some of his own gear. There are special backpacks made just for dogs; they have pockets for carrying a portable bowl, first aid kit, snacks, and extra water.

Tips for the Trail

Hiking, more than almost any other dog activity, has a number of caveats that you should keep in mind in order for both you and your dog to stay safe and be good ambassadors. For many dog lovers, there is nothing better than exploring the world with a dog at your side. Here are some tips on making your experience the best it can be.

Watch the temperature.

Don't hike with your dog during the hottest times of the day during warm months, especially in southern climates. Instead, begin your hike in the cool of morning and either finish up or stop for a long lunch when the sun is really beating down. Take breaks when you feel tired. Try to find a cool, shady area in which to rest.

If you begin to feel disoriented or lightheaded, or notice your dog acting disoriented, end the hike and seek help immediately. Always finish your hike with plenty of time before dark.

Protect yourself from the elements.

You should wear a hat, a long-sleeved sun-protective shirt, and sunscreen. Your dog should also wear sunscreen on any light spots and on his nose. If you are hiking in the rain or cold, stay warm but not sweaty with a light protective jacket or raincoat. If your dog is short-coated, he may appreciate a dog coat, but remember that he will be expending a lot of energy, so check to make sure that he isn't overheating.

Drink plenty of water.

It's easy to become dehydrated when hiking, especially in warm weather. Always take adequate water for both of you. Do not let your dog drink from pools of water or even running rivers. He can contract giardia or leptospirosis. Standing water can contain highly toxic blue-green algae.

Keep your dog on a leash at all times.

It's tempting to let your dog roam free, but this is unsafe for him, you, and the wild fauna and flora. Many parks have restricted access for dogs because off-leash dogs have been so destructive to native plants. To your dog, the grasses and shrubs in nature preserves just seem like great places to romp, but their heavy paws can have serious consequences for the plants and the animals that live within them. Unfortunately, much of the native plant life in the United States is seriously threatened. Some of the patches found in national parks are all that remain and any disruptions to their health can be devastating.

Many dogs have strong instincts to chase small animals and may harass or even kill native wildlife. Dogs can also trigger the chase instincts of larger predators: If your unleashed dog encounters a bear or wildcat who decides to give chase, he's likely to run straight back to you for protection, endangering both of you.

Leave word of your plans.

Let someone know where you will be and when you expect to be back, even if you are only taking a mile hike on a well-marked trail. Many hikers have ended up stranded in the woods for the night because they made a wrong turn on what they thought was an easy trail.

If possible, hike with other people.

Do you have a buddy who likes to hike with his or her dogs as much as you do? It's safer and sometimes more fun to hike with a group.

Be prepared for any emergency.

Take an extra layer of clothing (light enough to stuff into your backpack or wrap around your waist but warm enough to keep you safe through a night outside), plenty of water for you and your dog, a small protein snack for you both (jerky and dog-safe trail mix are good), waterproof matches, a flashlight, a compass (and learn how to use it!), and definitely a charged cell phone.

Keep tabs on your dog.

During your hike, look your dog over and check for cuts on his paw pads and burrs caught between his paw pads or on his ears or other sensitive spots.

After your hike, do a tick check (on both of you). If you find one, do not burn it off. Instead pull the tick out with tweezers and drown it in a glass of water. Swab the spot where it was attached to the skin with alcohol and an antibiotic cream.

If you are hiking long distances and your dog's footpads are often beat up after your hike, consider using musher's wax or outfitting him with protective booties.

WATCH OUT FOR SNAKES!

For the most part, snakes leave people and dogs alone. They are secretive creatures whose first instinct is to hide, but a wandering dog who steps on a snake or roots into a den may well be bitten. There are a number of venomous snakes in the United States, and treatment for snakebites is spotty, expensive, and not always successful. Although there is a rattlesnake bite vaccine on the market, it's largely unproven and seems to have minimal effect on many animals.

If your dog is bitten, do not try to suck the venom out or apply a tourniquet. Instead, keep him as still as possible because movement increases the circulation of the venom in the bloodstream. Take him to a qualified veterinarian immediately. Call ahead if possible to be sure that an antivenom is available.

If you are in a backwoods area where you will not be able to reach a veterinarian within several hours, you may have no choice but to try to treat the snakebite yourself. The use of a snakebite kit or tourniquet, however, may only exacerbate the wound if done improperly. Before engaging in backwoods hiking, take a first-aid class with a local outdoors organization to learn the proper methods. In areas with large populations of venomous snakes, parks departments occasionally offer dog snake-proofing classes, which are designed to keep dogs from being bitten in the first place.

Enjoying Winter Sports with Your Dog

In addition to skijoring (see page 216) and sledding (see page 208), there are several other fun winter activities that you can do with your dog. Many people like to have their dogs accompany them while cross-country skiing or snowshoeing. Most dogs love the snow and find it invigorating to spend the day catapulting themselves through the white stuff. This is fun for you both but takes a bit of planning in order to participate safely. Here are a few basics.

Be prepared.

Wear a backpack and carry in it extra water, snacks for dog and human, waterproof matches, an insulated blanket, a compass, and a cell phone. Consider taking a mountaineering class to ensure that you know what to do if you get lost while out walking.

Always let someone know where you are going and when you will be back. While a night outside in the summer can be uncomfortable, a night out in the snow can be tragic. Give your itinerary to a friend or family member before setting out.

Keep hydrated.

Yes, snow is wet and will satiate your dog's thirst. Unfortunately, it will also lower your dog's body temperature dangerously. Take water for both you and your dog, and do not let your dog eat significant quantities of snow.

Stay on the trail.

Not only is it easy to become disoriented and lost when trekking in the snow, it's also very difficult for your dog to navigate in soft snow. Although you are wearing skis or snowshoes, he isn't.

Keep your dog on a leash.

A dog who chases wildlife, wanders off, and crosses the path of other skiers and walkers is a danger to himself and others and should be left in the car or at home for an après-ski walk. Also, your dog can wander off and become lost or can fall into a crevice or pond that is hidden by the snow. If you are skiing and can't keep your dog on a leash, be entirely confident that your dog has an excellent recall before you take him along.

Keep warm.

Not all dogs come equipped with thick fur coats; some snow-loving dogs aren't suited for very cold weather. If your dog has a smooth coat and you are out for a long excursion, take his dog coat along.

NO DOGS ALLOWED

Unfortunately, dogs' access to outdoor areas is being restricted throughout the United States. This is due in large part to the actions of irresponsible dog guardians in the past. Uncontrolled dogs can destroy native flora, harass wildlife, intimidate other hikers and park users, and mar trails when their people don't pick up their dogs' waste. The best way to combat this trend is to demonstrate that dog owners are good stewards of the environment and that dogs and their people can use outdoor areas safely and responsibly.

You can do this not only by following the etiquette and safety rules above but also by looking out for the actions of other dog owners. Pick up waste (and encourage other owners to) when you see it, and remind fellow dog-owning outdoor enthusiasts that we are ambassadors when we are out in public.

Another great way to promote the idea of dogs and people as stewards of the environment is to get involved in dog-friendly mountaineering groups or even to work with local wildlife groups that sometimes use dogs to help humanely control wildlife, such as Canada goose control (dogs are used to gently "harass" or herd the geese in order to keep them away from beach areas). Dog owners and other outdoor users and environmentalists are on the same side; the more we can work together, the better off we will all be.

Becoming a Canine Good Citizen

The Canine Good Citizen (CGC) test was developed by the American Kennel Club (AKC) in 1989 to certify that a dog is properly trained and can remain calm and well behaved at home and out in the community. Although the AKC continues to oversee the Canine Good Citizen program, dogs of any breed or breed mix may participate. Tests are held throughout North America on a regular basis. For information on testing and on training classes near you, visit the AKC Web site.

Even if you're not interested in pursuing formal obedience, training for the CGC test can be lots of fun and extremely satisfying. It can also open up the world for your dog, in that any dog who trains and passes the CGC is easier to handle and will be a good companion for your treks into the world.

Passing the CGC is also a prerequisite for some activities, such as therapy work, and is a good way for organizations to gauge a dog's level of training. Some landlords even require CGCs for the dogs of their tenants.

Before testing, handlers are asked to sign a pledge of responsibility, promising that they will care for their dogs properly and act responsibly with their dogs in public. Handlers must also pay a small fee. Once your dog passes his test, you can proudly add *CGC* after his name!

The CGC tests dogs on the following 10 points.

1. **Accepting a friendly stranger.** An evaluator approaches the handler and dog, talks to the handler and shakes her hand. The dog should not jump on or go to the evaluator, nor act shy or aggressive.

2. **Sitting politely for petting.** The dog sits at the handler's side. An evaluator approaches the dog and pets the dog on the head and body. The dog should stay in place and should not show any shyness or discomfort.

3. **Appearance and grooming.** The dog is examined to ensure that he is the proper weight and is properly groomed. The evaluator then brushes or combs the dog lightly, lifts his paws, and checks his ears. The dog does not need to stay in one place but should not exhibit any shyness or aggression.

4. **Walking on a loose lead.** The dog walks at the handler's side on a loose leash. He should respond to her movements and stop when she stops, although he does not have to heel or sit when she stops.

5. **Walking through a crowd.** The handler walks through a group of at least three people with the dog at her side. The dog can show interest in the people but should not act overly exuberant, shy, or aggressive. He should not jump on the people or lunge toward them.

6. **Sit and down while staying in place.**
   On a 20-foot line the dog must sit and
   lie down at the handler's command.
   Then, depending on the handler's
   choice, the dog must do a sit-stay or
   down-stay while the handler walks
   20 feet away, turns around, and comes
   back at a normal pace. The dog must
   not move from where he was left until
   the handler releases him, although he
   can change position.

7. **Come when called.** The handler walks
   10 feet away from the dog, turns
   around, and calls the dog. The dog
   must come to the handler.

8. **Reaction to another dog.** In this test,
   two handlers and their dogs walk
   toward one another from 20 feet. They
   stop, shake hands, and talk briefly, and
   then walk 10 feet past one another.
   The dogs must show no more than
   cursory interest in one another. They
   should not exhibit aggression or shyness, or go to the other dog or handler.

9. **Reaction to distraction.** The evaluator
   provides two distractions during this
   test, which may include a person running by, or a chair or other loud item
   dropping near the dog. The dog can act
   curious but should not act aggressive
   or fearful.

10. **Supervised separation.** In the final
    test, the handler leaves the dog with
    the evaluator for three minutes.
    During this time, the dog should not
    show extreme nervousness, including
    excessive pacing, whining, or barking.

Training a Therapy Dog

Once a dog has passed his CGC test, many handlers find themselves interested in doing more with their well-behaved dog. If a dog is not able to participate in sports, a logical extension is pet therapy, although lots of canine athletes do both. Pet therapy is used in a number of settings, both professionally and on a hobby level. Therapy dogs visit hospitals or nursing homes, day cares, and schools. They may be used for a short duration of time following a disaster or other emergency, or they may be used on an ongoing basis — for example, by a sex abuse counselor or by a prosecution office specializing in crimes against children.

Most organizations that work with therapy dogs require they be certified by a group such as the Delta Society or Therapy Dog International. Both of these groups offer training sessions and tests that will certify you and your dog as a therapy dog team. Once you are certified, you can join a therapy dog group, which may require additional training and testing.

Therapy is perhaps something of a misnomer because there are two types of work: *animal-assisted therapy* and *animal-assisted activities*. Although these distinctions can be blurry and often overlap one another, animal-assisted therapy means the dog has been specially trained to assist in goal-directed therapy in a formal setting with a trained physical therapist, social worker, teacher, occupational therapist, or other professional. An example would be a physical therapist who encourages a patient to practice manual dexterity by brushing a dog, or a literacy program that uses dogs as passive listeners for children to practice their reading skills.

SEE SPOT READ

Reading with Rover is a literacy program developed to give children who are struggling with reading a safe way to practice their skills. Many children who have difficulty reading avoid the activity because they are mocked by peers or pressured by teachers or parents. Because a dog's presence doesn't have that sort of social pressure, he or she can play the role of an unbiased listener.

At a typical session, a number of dogs and their handlers visit a school library or local bookstore. Children pick out a book to read and then snuggle in for the story. While the child reads, the handler prompts the child to answer questions for the dog or to work through difficult words. The handler may, for example, say, "Daisy didn't understand what that word meant; could you explain it to her?" If the child can't define the word, they may consult a dictionary together.

Dogs who excel in literacy programs may be retired athletes who still love having a job to do, mellow dogs who enjoy just hanging out in the company of people, or very social dogs who adore children. There are definitely Brownie points for a dog who rests his head in the lap of a reading child.

"Dogs need to do something," says Becky Bishop, founder of the program. She adds that although just laying there for an hour listening to a child read seems like nothing, the dogs are exhausted after doing therapy work. Bishop laughs that of her three dogs, Harry Plotter the Plott hound is a perfect fit for this program. "He's a wonderful dog, but if he was a man you'd date him once. He's so boring. But with kids his whole body changes." When serving as a literacy dog, Harry is interested, engaged, and always willing to lend an ear.

In animal-assisted activities, dogs and handlers interact with people without directed goals. For example, a therapy dog group may visit a nursing home on a regular schedule, giving residents the opportunity to pet and interact with the dogs. A handler and dog team may regularly visit one person to cheer her up or to check on her progress. An obedience club or other canine sport club may visit hospitals, nursing homes, and schools to entertain an audience.

Think It Through

As in any dog activity, dog therapy should be the right fit for both the dog and the handler. Part of the certification program includes an eight-hour training session that helps handlers determine the best setting for their dogs. Some dogs excel in nursing homes, while others love nothing more than visiting children at schools or hospitals. Some dogs enjoy showing off their tricks but don't like to be approached by groups of kids, while others are happy to lounge in a lap or cuddle up next to a wheelchair-bound patient for a visit.

It's important for handlers to consider the setting they are best suited to work in and what kind of commitment they can give. Being part of an obedience club that occasionally gives trick demonstrations at nursing homes or hospitals may not require an ongoing and regular commitment, whereas a relationship with one patient or child definitely does. Most organizations ask that teams commit to at least once or twice a month for one year. Many volunteers do pet therapy once a week or even more often.

Handlers also need to consider the kind of emotional toll therapy work can have. Therapy dogs have been used in the aftermath of many tragedies, including the September 11 attacks on the World Trade Center, where they comforted the families of victims who visited the Family Assistance Center of Pier 94. If you regularly visit hospitals and nursing homes, there is a high likelihood that some of the people you visit will become too ill to interact or will even die. This is difficult with adults, but especially hard when the patient is a child.

Regardless of what type of therapy you and your dog opt to do, there's no doubt about the payoff. For people who want to be with their dogs but also help others, the rewards can be enormous.

CHAPTER 3

Before the Games Begin

IT'S EXCITING TO WELCOME A NEW PUPPY OR ADULT DOG into your family, and you are probably eager to start activities right away. But you have plenty of time, and in the beginning the important thing is to make your new dog feel secure, comfortable, and confident. Then, when you do venture out into the world of canine games, you will both be ready to have the best experience possible.

In general, dogs should not begin participating in any serious activity before the age of one. There are exceptions, especially for sports in which it's believed that the dog benefits from early exposure and there's no risk of physical harm to the dog. Puppies, however, should not be doing any jumping or pulling for their first year, which means Frisbee, agility, weight pulling, skijoring, and flyball are all taboo.

Conformation, obedience (without jumps), earthdog, and tracking are sports that dogs can start at any age; other sports fall somewhere in between. For example, dogs are allowed to compete in dock jumping at six months, although many participants and veterinarians believe that this is too early and could lead to long-term injuries.

Do not fear that your pup will fall behind — there is still plenty you can do and should be doing to prepare a young dog for his future as a sports star. In fact, this applies to any dog who is new to your life. The two-year-old rescue Aussie you just found at the local shelter may be physically ready to begin herding, but it's a good idea to get him mentally ready as well.

Proper Socializing Is Key

Before you can even think of involving your dog in a sport, he must be well socialized, meaning that he is comfortable with people and other dogs, that he isn't overly fearful of new situations, and that he trusts you to be a capable leader. The best way to socialize a dog is to take him everywhere with you and expose him to all kinds of new places, situations, and sensory stimuli.

Unsocialized dogs do not fare well at organized sports because they are too distracted, fearful, and defensive to focus on the job at hand. A well-socialized dog is calm and confident in new situations; an unsocialized dog is frightened and nervous. Conversely, participation in canine sports is an excellent way to continue socializing your dog as he ages. It provides the opportunity to meet lots of new dogs and people and to learn and play in new and distracting environments, which will give him loads of self-confidence.

Socializing your puppy or dog is a process that goes on throughout his life. It is important that new experiences are presented in a calm and positive way. Sometimes that means setting up new situations, such as asking visitors to your home to give your pup a tasty treat or inviting well-behaved children over to meet your new addition. It also means including your dog in as many aspects of your life as possible, from running errands with you to politely greeting visitors to perhaps even going to work with you.

Ways to Socialize Your Puppy

Start by making sure your dog will be comfortable being handled by making it a habit to gently touch sensitive areas, such as the feet, the mouth and lips, the belly, and between the legs. Even if your pup doesn't require regular grooming, accustom him at an early age to being brushed, having his ears cleaned, and having his toenails trimmed. Not only will you be helping your puppy to learn about behaving at the vet, you will be building up his trust and confidence in your leadership as well.

Inside your house, there are plenty of things to introduce your pup to, such as vacuum cleaners and other noisy appliances, brooms and mops, rolling furniture and anything that might be scary to a youngster. He should be comfortable with other household animals. Outside there are even more opportunities to expand his experience. Take your dog with you to the store, to outdoor festivals, to downtown streets where there are lots of crowds.

Take him to dog events as a spectator. A dog who will be competing in Frisbee or dock jumping will have to learn to tolerate, or ideally to enjoy, the sound of large crowds, blaring music, and an announcer over a loudspeaker. Agility, conformation, and canine freestyle routinely take place in front of audiences that may be quite vocal in their support of a dog. A dog who is afraid of crowds will not have a chance of being successful when his turn comes in a big canine sports event.

In addition to crowds, it's important for your dog to be exposed at an early age to many different people, helping him to accept a variety of people and to see humans as friendly rather than frightening. Introduce him to men with mustaches and hats, women with long hair and short hair, children, teenagers, and people who use wheelchairs, walkers, or crutches. Ask strangers to give him treats so that he sees new people as welcoming, not threatening.

BUYING A PUPPY

The first step in having a well-socialized adult dog is making sure that your puppy is en route to being well socialized before you even lay eyes on him. That means buying puppies only from ethical breeders who make it a point to socialize their puppies. A visit to the breeder's home will give you a lot of insight into how she raises her litters. Never buy a puppy from a breeder without visiting the puppy in the breeder's home.

At the breeder's home, insist on meeting the puppies' mother, or dam, before even considering buying a pup. If the father, or sire, is on the premises, ask to meet him as well. If a breeder won't let you meet the dam, there is something wrong. When you meet the mother, observe her behavior with you and with other dogs. Many personality traits are inherited, and a puppy with an irritable, skittish mama will often have these tendencies as well. Look for a dam or sire who is friendly, greets you politely, and shows interest, but not aggression, toward other dogs and people.

You'll also want to see how the puppy has been living since he was born. Do the puppies live in the house with lots of regular interaction with the breeder's family? This is ideal. By the time you buy your pup at eight weeks old, the breeder should have introduced him to some friendly people, including children, held and petted him regularly, and provided him some exposure to the world outside his whelping box. A properly socialized pup will not be shy, but rather will greet you enthusiastically and without fear.

If you adopt a puppy or adult dog from a shelter or rescue, ask about their socialization process and what steps they've taken to ensure that the dog is socialized and well adjusted. Many shelters, for example, place litters with foster families to give the puppies and mama dog a safe, quiet place to bond. Foster homes should also provide the puppies with lots of friendly, comfortable exposure to humans, as well as to the sights and sounds of a normal household. Ask the shelter for help in picking out the right dog for your family.

When choosing a dog, whether a puppy or an adult, you can tell a lot by how he greets you. Is he eager to meet you, approaching without shyness or hesitation? Does he lean into you when you pet him or does he pull away or stiffen? Dogs who are too shy to approach you or averse to humans are probably not appropriate as family dogs. If you are experienced with dogs and want the challenge of helping a shelter dog with special needs, discuss the benefits and disadvantages of such a dog with a shelter adoption counselor.

Depending on the sport you're interested in, you might find that one of the young, active dogs often found in animal shelters will be a perfect companion for you. Many a successful disc or flyball dog has been the bane of a suburban family. The same qualities that make them so difficult for a busy family to cope with — high energy, size, strength, and exuberance — make them perfect sports dogs. Again, consult with an adoption counselor about the type of dog that will fit well into your lifestyle.

Never, ever buy a dog over the Internet or from a pet store. In addition to the fact that you will not have the chance to see these dogs with their parents and, possibly, siblings, they may have been bred by a large-scale and/or unethical breeder. Puppy mill dogs often have a host of medical and behavioral problems. In addition, you'll be supporting the ongoing success of these cruel industries.

Socializing your dog with other dogs is also necessary, not only for joining in canine sports but also so that you can take your dog everywhere you want without worrying about his behaving aggressively. To participate in most games, a dog must be tolerant of other dogs.

In flyball, for example, the two dogs crossing paths come very close to one another while both are in an extremely agitated and excited state. Dogs with even a hint of dog aggression or lack of tolerance can easily become aroused and switch from play mode to fight mode.

Even in sports where dogs don't have much interaction with one another, they are usually in close proximity, so an unsocialized dog will find lots of reasons to be irritated or frightened. Make it easier on you both — and the dogs around you — by providing your dog with lots of positive interactions with friendly, calm dogs at an early age.

The more happy, positive experiences your dog has in his young life, the better adjusted he will be as an adult. While you are socializing your dog, be sure to offer him lots of tasty treats and generous praise.

Basic Training: Boot Camp for Bowser

Before you begin training your dog to jump through tires and catch tennis balls from a flyball box, you must teach him his basic manners. The best way to do this is to enroll in a puppy kindergarten class or a beginners' training class if you have adopted an adult dog. In puppy kindergarten you will learn how to teach your dog the fundamental commands such as *sit*, *down*, *stay*, and *come*.

Of course, it is possible to train your dog yourself at home (see page 66 for more on training), but even if your dog is a super student at home, do attend at least one basic obedience class or session of puppy kindergarten. It gives both you and your pup a taste of training in a group setting, provides you with an opportunity to discuss any issues you may be having with the trainer, and allows you to learn from other new owners. Plus it's fun!

Training Methods

Correction-based training was the standard until the mid- to late part of the twentieth century. This method of training punishes unwanted behavior rather than rewarding wanted behavior. For example, in teaching the command *sit*, the trainer forces the dog into a sit position and gives a leash correction using a prong collar if he moves out of the sit. Eventually the dog learns that the desired behavior is sitting and that if he doesn't comply, he is punished. Correction-based training can be very harsh, including hitting with the hands or instruments (remember the rolled up newspaper?) and kicking or kneeing dogs if they jump up. More recently, trainers using this method have advocated limiting corrections to a quick jerk on the leash or using an electronic collar.

The drawback of correction-based training is that it can take some time to take effect. The dog must figure out through trial and error which behavior is the one that avoids punishment. While plenty of people, including professional trainers, still practice this method, many animal behaviorists and trainers now believe that rewarding correct behavior is not only more humane but also more effective, producing happier, more confident dogs and longer lasting results.

Modern dog training began at the end of the nineteenth century with a man and his dogs. Dr. Ivan Pavlov used laboratory dogs to research the digestive system. He also had an interest in what came to be called behavioral science. He noticed that the dogs drooled when scientists with white coats entered the room; he believed that they'd come to associate the coats with feeding time. To test (and ultimately prove) his theory, he rang a bell immediately before feeding the dogs to see if the dogs would asso-

Principles of Operant Conditioning

Positive reinforcement: Dog receives a reward (treat) to increase behavior (sitting)

Positive punishment: Dog receives a punishment (jerk on collar) to decrease a behavior (moving out of position)

Negative reinforcement: Dog receives a punishment (mild shock) that ends when he performs the correct behavior (sits down)

Negative punishment: Dog has a reward (attention from owner) taken away when he performs unwanted behavior (jumping up)

ciate the sound with feeding time and would begin drooling when they heard it. They did.

Some years later, psychologist B. F. Skinner added reinforcers to Pavlov's theory. He believed that if you used a trigger (the bell) associated with a reward (food), you could train an animal to perform a desired behavior. Skinner put rats in a box that had a lever that they could push. When the rats accidentally triggered the lever, a piece of food would drop into the box. True to Skinner's supposition, the rats quickly learned that pushing the lever provided a reward. He called this process operant conditioning.

This idea, or at least the principle of positive reinforcement, forms the basis of modern marker training. The trainer uses a reward (food, praise, a toy) to shape a desired behavior (sit, stay, come) by introducing a trigger (voice command, hand signal, clicker sound). Then the trigger is associated with the desired behavior until the dog learns that the action of sitting in response to the trigger produces a reward.

Correction-Based Training

Interestingly, correction-based punishment also works on the theory of operant conditioning. The dog comes to associate a specific behavior (moving out of a sit) with something negative (unpleasant physical sensation). Using a metal chain or choke collar (also called a training or slip collar) that tightens when pressure is applied is one example of this.

The idea is that a quick correction is administered and then the pressure is relieved when the leash is released. Some trainers advocate the use of prong collars, which have dull spikes that dig into the dog's neck when pressure is applied.

A milder alternative is the martingale collar, which is part chain and part cloth, allowing the handler to correct a behavior without overdoing it. This type of collar is not as prone to misuse as chain and prong collars can be.

Electronic, or shock, collars are used to quell undesirable behavior such as barking. When the dog barks, it receives a low-level shock. They can also be used

to train dogs positively, in a manner of speaking. For example, the collar is set on a very low shock level until the dog performs the desired behavior and then the shock ends. Because the shock ends when the dog performs the desired task, the reward is the ending of the negative sensation. An example of this might be a dog who refuses to perform a command, for example, sit. As long as the dog does not perform the requested command, the electronic collar provides a shock, but as soon as he sits, the shock ends.

It's increasingly rare to find a trainer who uses only correction-based training, as positive reinforcement techniques have been shown to be far easier and quicker. Most trainers who use correction-based training combine it with positive methods, using corrections only to reinforce positive training, or for working on recalcitrant training challenges. For example, a dog is trained to walk nicely on a leash with treats but is given a leash correction with a chain collar when he pulls.

In most canine sports training, the goal is for the dog to have fun, and handlers may rely solely on positive reinforcement. Many handlers feel that a dog who is corrected when learning agility or flyball, for example, will perceive that the sport itself is undesirable and will not perform well. Others believe that a combination of reward and correction can be effective without discouraging the dog.

CORRECTIONS USED IN SOME SPORTS

Some canine sports mix correction-based training with positive reinforcement; this is particularly the case in Schutzhund, herding, and hunting. Schutzhund handlers argue that the use of some corrections is essential for a sport in which dogs are encouraged to work in an intense state (particularly the case in bite work) and must be taught to stop the instant the command is given.

One example of a correction sometimes used in Schutzhund is called "flanking," in which the trainer squeezes or pinches the loose skin of the chest if the dog does not immediately perform a command. It is most commonly used when the dog doesn't release the sleeve immediately when practicing bite work.

Correction-based training is used in herding as well: Dogs have to curtail their high prey drive to interact effectively with vulnerable livestock. If they do not learn to stop the moment the handler asks them to, the stock may be at risk from a dog who becomes overzealous or loses control. In herding, dogs are rarely offered positive rewards other than verbal praise, because the dogs are highly motivated to work the livestock — this is the positive reward. Corrections are usually given verbally and through the use of a shepherd's crook (which may be a rake or a length of PVC pipe), which may be used to guide the dog but is also used to tap or nudge the dog if he becomes too aggressive with the stock.

In hunting, electronic collars are often used when the dog is working far from the handler. This way the trainer can correct a dog even when she cannot physically reach him. Many trainers also value the electronic collar in high-intensity training because the dog doesn't see it as coming from the trainer but as a general consequence (e.g., "If I flush the birds too quickly it hurts" rather than "If I flush the birds too quickly my handler gets mad").

Positive Reinforcement

Positive reinforcement is used to introduce commands by luring the dog into a behavior, and then giving the lure as the reward. For example, holding a treat over a dog's head usually induces him to sit as his nose follows the scent upward and his bottom correspondingly drops to the floor; when he does so, he receives the reward. Rather than correcting unwanted behavior, the handler withholds the toy, treat, or praise when the dog doesn't behave as commanded.

Treats and toys can be used not only as rewards but also as motivation. In flyball, most dogs quickly figure out that the fun ends when their turn is over; thus, many dogs are allowed a quick play session with a tug toy at the end of their leg of the relay, which encourages them to finish the race enthusiastically.

USING CLICKER TRAINING

One drawback to positive reinforcement is that it can be imprecise and time-consuming, because by the time you deliver the reward, the dog may have moved on to a different behavior. For example, the dog sits and you say, "Good sit!" and give him a treat, but by the time he swallows it he's already standing up. This becomes even more problematic as you train your dog in the more complicated and more refined commands necessary in canine sports and when you are training your dog at a distance.

Clicker training is a precise way of providing positive reinforcement that has been widely embraced in canine sports training. The method was developed in the 1960s by trainer Karen Pryor who first used it in her work with dolphins. The use of a metal clicker allows the trainer to more precisely shape the desired behavior and more clearly communicate to the dog just what is expected. The click is delivered at exactly the moment your dog performs the correct behavior. You ask your dog to sit and either lure him using a treat or wait for him to sit on his own. At the exact moment his bottom touches the ground, you click and give a treat. Handlers who use clickers estimate that dogs learn commands, especially complicated ones, in half the time that they would with traditional methods.

To use a clicker you first need to teach your dog that the click means something good. To do this, sit with your dog with a clicker in one hand and about 20 tasty treats in another. Click, give a treat, click, give a treat. Do this several times a day for a few days until he comes to view the click itself as very desirable. After he reaches that point, you can begin to space out the treats so that not every click is rewarded. Intermittent reinforcement has been shown to be more effective in shaping behavior, as the dog doesn't take the reward for granted but instead stays focused on the task in the hope of receiving the treat.

Once your dog has come to realize that the sound of the click is a reward in itself, don't forget to continue to occasionally give treats along with the click during training. At first, give a treat every time you click. Later you can treat every four or five clicks or so. If you never treat when you click, your dog will quickly lose interest in the clicker, as it has no intrinsic value to him; the good thing about it is that it is occasionally followed by a meaningful reward.

Clicker training has become ubiquitous in canine sports — it is used extensively in all types of training and is especially useful in sports with a steep learning curve where there isn't a clear reward for the dog, such as agility or canine freestyle (unlike flyball, where the reward is racing to get the ball, or herding, where the dog sees the livestock as the reward).

Agility is one sport in which clicker training has become the norm. Because so much of agility training is based on shaping the dog's behavior and target training, the clicker comes in to even greater use. It is an excellent tool for coaxing a reluctant dog onto the teeter, teaching a dog to work away from you, and training to touch contacts.

As you and your dog become used to the clicker, you'll find it is useful in many parts of your dog's life — training new commands, ending negative behaviors, and learning increasingly difficult sport moves.

Working on the Fundamentals

Dogs need to know what is expected of them. Just like children, they must be taught the basics of good manners in order to be welcome in society. Before you take up any canine sport, your dog must understand several important commands and must respond reliably to them. Basic obedience work is the cornerstone of nearly every game that we play with our dogs. The main commands are: *come, sit, down,* and *stay.* After your dog learns these commands, you can branch out to the obedience commands, such as heel and long stays, and to other, more fun tricks, such as spin, play dead, and bow.

More advanced tricks are a fun way for you and your dog to train during downtime. Teaching tricks is also an excellent way to strengthen the bond between you and your dog and to enhance your training skills. If you can teach your dog to bow, wave, or spin, you can teach him to climb a teeter or catch a Frisbee.

Below are the recognized basic techniques for training your dog on the foundation commands and tricks. Before you begin, here are some things to remember about training.

- Keep sessions brief — most dogs can't concentrate for more than 10 or 15 minutes at a time.

- Schedule training sessions for times when your dog is a little hungry, not right after a meal when a handful of treats might not be as appealing.

- Make sure that your dog has had some exercise before a training session; you can't expect him to focus if he's brimming with unexpended energy.

- Don't train if you are feeling tired, cranky, or stressed.

- Do not yell at your dog or discipline him while teaching new tricks or commands. If he is too excited to concentrate, end the training session.

- Do not harshly correct your dog when he makes a mistake. Simply repeat the command, or say "whoops" or "nope" in a matter-of-fact tone before repeating the command.

- End each session on a positive note; if your dog is stuck on a new command, go back to one that he has down pat.

- Break complicated tricks into steps, and be sure your dog has a firm grasp on each step before moving on to the next one.

- Reinforce new tricks often; most dogs will need constant refreshers at first.

- Always offset the treats you give during training with less food at mealtime.

Come

A good recall is truly the most important command that you will ever teach your dog. Without it, there are few sports you can train for, as so many canine sports are done off leash. More important, there are few dogs who won't escape from a fenced yard or slip out of a collar at some point. If your dog strays toward a busy street, a good recall may mean the difference between life and death.

1. To teach your dog to come, attach a long line, at least 20 feet in length, to his collar and be prepared with lots of treats.

2. Let your pup wander off and then call "Come!" as you clap your hands and run in the opposite direction.

3. If he follows, let him catch you and then turn around and squat to his level, saying "Good come!" Click. Give him a treat and lots of enthusiastic praise.

4. If he does not come, pull gently on his leash until he reaches you and then praise him lavishly and give a treat, saying "Good come!"

5. Practice the recall on the long line until your dog does it consistently every time you say "come" to him.

Once your dog is reliable with the recall on a long line, you can drop the line and practice from farther away. Until the command is very well established, keep the long line on him so that you can quickly grab it if he becomes distracted or refuses to come.

One key to establishing an absolute, no-hesitation recall is not to let your dog develop the bad habit of running away in the first place. To ensure this, never chase your dog or let anyone else chase your dog. This teaches him that running away from you is a fun game. He won't understand the difference between a romp and a situation in which it truly is important that he come to you.

To help your dog see coming to you as a positive, don't just call him to end the fun. Instead, call him regularly, just to give him a quick treat or ear scratch.

Sit

Sit is one of the easiest commands to teach and to learn, and it is also one of the most valuable behaviors in your dog's repertoire. A dog with an excellent sit can calmly greet guests, wait politely for meals, treats, or toys, and be more easily redirected when overexcited. In addition, many canine sports require that the dog sit. In agility, for example, dogs must sit or lie down in the pause box as part of the course.

1. Stand about a foot in front of your dog with him facing you.

2. Hold a tasty treat to his nose and then raise the treat slowly upward in a straight line, saying "Sit!" Your dog's nose will follow the treat, bringing his bottom to the ground. (If your dog tries to jump and grab the treat, hold it inside your closed hand until he sits. Never allow him to grab the treat until he sits.)

3. As soon as he sits, say, "Good sit!" and give him the treat.

4. Repeat this 10 times daily with small treats until he grasps the concept.

5. Gradually extend the amount of time between his sit and the treat, so that he begins to understand that he can't just leap up immediately.

6. Once he is fairly solid, practice daily, only giving the treat every four or five times he sits.

Some dogs will continue to jump off the ground to get the treat, so if your dog does this despite your efforts, ask a friend for help. She should hold his front paws on the ground while you pull the treat upward. Your dog's bottom will go down but his paws will stay in place, and he'll quickly understand that he gets the treat only when he stays on the ground.

Down

Once your dog knows *sit*, you can teach him *down*. Down is a very useful tool for keeping your dog settled when necessary. You can teach your dog to lie down while you are eating meals or performing chores and you don't want him underfoot. A dog with a solid down can be a true "Starbucks dog," as one trainer puts it — a dog who can calmly lie at your feet at an outdoor café while you sip coffee and talk to your friends. Down is also used in some canine sports.

1. Stand a couple of feet in front of your dog and ask him to sit. Once he is sitting, hold a treat to his nose.

2. Draw the treat down and out in a vertical line toward your shoes, saying "Down!" As his nose goes down with the treat, the rest of his body will follow.

3. As soon as he is down, say "Good down!" and give him the treat. Do not give him the treat unless he actually lies down.

4. At first he will jump right back up, so as he begins to grasp the concept of down, hold the treat longer and longer before giving it to him.

5. Practice 10 times daily, giving a treat each time until your dog reacts immediately when you say "Down!"

6. Then practice daily, giving a treat for a down only every four or five times.

Often, dogs will simply walk forward when you pull the treat downward. To teach him to keep his bottom on the ground, ask a friend to gently hold his rear end in place while you draw the treat to the ground. After enough repetitions, your dog will understand that if his bottom leaves the ground, he loses the treat.

Click Away

For all of these commands, using a clicker will increase retention and shorten training time. See pages 64–65.

Stay

Stay is an important command to know as you learn canine sports because you will often need your dog to stay in one place while you look over a course or while you wait for other competitors. A good stay will ensure your dog is viewed as a polite competitor, with a smart handler to boot. Teach your dog to do a stay first in a sit, then a down, then, if you choose, in a stand.

1. Have your dog sit/down. You should stand about a foot in front of your dog, facing him.

2. Hold up one hand, palm out, and say "Stay!"; pause for one or two seconds, and then give him a treat, saying "Good stay!"

3. Gradually increase the amount of time between the command and giving the treat.

4. If your dog moves during this time, stop and begin again with a shorter pause between the stay and the treat.

5. Once your dog will stay reliably for 10 seconds, take one step back from him. Pause for one or two seconds and then treat and praise.

6. Increase the time until you can be one step back from him for 10 seconds, and then increase your distance. Do this gradually until he will stay for 10 seconds while you stand five feet away.

7. Then increase the time he stays until he can stay for as long as one minute. You can also begin increasing the complexity of the command by turning your back to him, walking a circle around him, and walking longer distances away from him. Finally, leave the room while he is in a down stay. If at any time during the process he moves, end the exercise and decrease the time and distance when you begin again.

Heel

It is no fun to walk a dog who yanks constantly on the leash. More important, a dog who is heeling politely is paying attention to you; he is under control and ready for your next command. You can quickly teach your dog to walk on a loose leash or even heel right next to you as long as you are consistent. Dogs are traditionally taught to heel on the handler's left as described here.

1. Attach a treat bag to the left side of your belt and fill it with super tasty treats, keeping a couple in your left hand.

2. Put your dog on a non-retractable six-foot leather or soft nylon leash.

3. Your dog should be at your left side. With your left hand, hold the leash close to your left thigh, leaving some slack. Hold the rest of the leash looped in your right hand.

4. Say "Heel!" and with your left hand hold a treat next to your left leg, offering it to your dog. When he takes the treat say "Good heel!" Take a step and repeat. Repeat this process with each step. This will show the dog what you want him to do.

5. Once the dog is focusing on you, begin walking at a normal pace. If your dog's attention wavers or he pulls ahead, call his attention back to you with a treat.

6. If your dog continues to pull, stop and do not walk forward until he returns and stands next to your left thigh.

Teaching your dog to heel can be a painstaking and, frankly, boring process, which is exactly the reason so few dogs ever learn to do it properly. Train the heel from the start and be consistent (meaning that even when you're not in the mood to enforce it, you do), and your dog will be walking pretty in no time.

Once your dog is reliably walking by your side, you can complicate things by making turns, walking in a figure eight (you'll need to be able to do this for obedience and rally!), and varying your pace.

On to Fancier Moves

When your dog has a good grasp of the basics of canine commands, you'll be able to teach him all sorts of tricks. This is not only fun, it's a great way to encourage your dog to pay attention to you and to develop the bond that you share. And don't believe the old adage — you *can* teach an old dog new tricks!

Shake

Shake is the standard when it comes to dog tricks, though some people choose not to teach it because you can create a monster — a dog who is constantly pawing at you for attention or for that coveted treat. However, by teaching your dog to shake only on command, and by ignoring him when he paws at you, you can keep the pawing in check.

1. Ask your dog to sit.

2. Pick up his paw (use your right hand to lift up his right paw), say "Shake!" and give him a treat.

3. Ten or twenty times of this and he'll know it forever.

Spin

Spin is an easy but flashy trick with the fringe benefit of providing your dog with a great stretch. For the full benefits, train a spin to either side.

1. Stand in front of your dog.

2. Put a treat to his nose and then while saying "Spin!" gradually move the treat in a small circle around the back of his head. As you move the treat, you want him to follow the treat with his whole body.

3. If he gets confused or loses the treat, simply move it back to his nose and begin to move it again.

4. When your dog is back into his original position, say "Good spin!" and give him the treat.

5. Gradually move your hand farther from his nose until he is following the motion of your hand and doesn't have his nose glued to the treat. Eventually you can stop using your hand altogether, so your dog spins on your verbal cue rather than by following the lure.

Sit Pretty (Beg)

Sit pretty is a trick that is impressive to see while providing your dog with excellent strength conditioning, as it works muscles in the belly and back that are often underused. Some owners find this easier to train if the dog is sitting in a corner.

1. Ask your dog to sit.

2. Hold a treat in one hand and place it next to his nose.

3. Put your other arm under your dog's front legs.

4. Say "Sit pretty!" or "Beg!" and move the treat straight up toward the ceiling with one hand while pressing gently on the insides of his forelimbs with your other arm. He will automatically lift up to get the treat and the pressure on his front legs will give him the support he needs to balance on his haunches.

5. Once he is sitting on his haunches, give him the treat and say "Good sit pretty!"

6. Do this several times until your dog understands what you are asking. Then gradually remove your arm from under his legs while you give the treat.

Sit Up and Wave

Sit up and wave adds a little panache to sit pretty and provides additional strength conditioning.

1. Once your dog is comfortable with sitting pretty and shake, show him a treat while he is sitting on his haunches.

2. Put your hand out as though you are going to shake with him but instead of taking his paw, say "Wave!" and move the treat up and down or side to side. His head and paw will follow the treat, making it look as though he is waving.

3. When he does, say "Good wave!" and give him the treat.

This trick is complicated, so expect it to take a while to perfect. Waving is considerably easier to teach with clicker training and in increments.

Take a Bow

As you may have noticed, dogs often bow when they are very excited and ready to play. Watch your dog when he is about to play with another dog or when you pull out the ball or Frisbee. When his forelimbs fold to the ground and his butt goes up in the air with a vigorous wag, he's play bowing! Teaching your dog to bow is more about conditioning a behavior than actually teaching him a trick. If you use a clicker, it's much easier and quicker to train your dog to do a bow on command.

1. The second you see a play bow, click and say "Bow!"

2. Then give him a treat.

3. Do this every time you catch him play bowing and he'll soon be doing it on command.

Play Dead

Play dead is the quintessential American dog trick. What kid doesn't want a dog who will flop to the ground with a click of the trigger finger?

1. Ask your dog to lie down. You will notice that he leans to one side or another.

2. Push him gently onto the side where he naturally leans, saying "Play dead!"

3. Once he is lying down, say "Good play dead!" and give him a treat.

4. To make it more difficult — and more realistic! — do not give him a treat until he lays his head on the ground. (This is a good "clicker" trick.)

Roll Over

Roll over takes up where *play dead* leaves off — and is an excellent stretch and strengthening exercise for your pooch.

1. Have your dog play dead.

2. Say "Roll over!" and gently push him onto his back and onto his other side. Most dogs will roll back onto their stomachs or spring to their feet.

3. When he is upright, say "Good roll over!" and give him a treat.

4. Once your dog is reliably doing the roll over from the play dead position, ask him to roll over from a down.

Following His Nose

You can also try teaching *roll over* by asking your dog to play dead and then holding a treat for him to follow with his nose; where the nose goes, the rest of the dog usually follows, and he may flop right over, staying on the ground. Some dogs won't do it this way and need a little nudging.

Crawl

Crawl is a fun activity to teach and it's good exercise for your dog.

1. Put your dog in a down-stay.

2. Hold a treat in front of his nose.

3. Slowly move the treat away from his nose, as though a line is attached from the treat to his nose. Say "Crawl!"

4. When your dog inches forward, give him a treat, saying "Good crawl!"

Some dogs find it difficult to stay on the ground, so you may need to use one hand to gently hold him on the ground, while you hold the treat in front of his nose with the other.

5. Gradually increase the distance of the crawl, giving treats every few movements. Do not give your dog a treat if he breaks the down. Instead, put him back in position and give him a treat only when he performs the crawl.

Some dogs will try to crawl out of a down position. To avoid this, never give him a treat for crawl unless you explicitly ask him to perform this command.

Training tricks and commands is a fun bonding exercise for you and your dog, and the rapport you build will be useful when you begin doing canine sports. Some sports, however, train tricks and commands differently from the norm. In competitive obedience, for example, dogs are trained to do a heel without being a centimeter out of place.

Be prepared to tweak your training for the sport that you pursue. If you are already involved in a canine sport, consult a trainer for methods specific to your sport. If your dog simply isn't getting the above tricks using these methods, you may want to consult a trainer for other approaches.

Kids and Dogs: A Natural Combination

If you have a kid and you have a dog, getting them involved in an activity together can be one of the best things you ever do for either of them. The relationship can start early — my three-year-old son, Jack, walks our gentle, disabled corgi/shepherd mix, Muddy, on a leash. With Nelly, our much more active dog, Jack throws balls, sticks, or toys and always seems mystified and pleased to have the item returned. At this age, of course, Jack is never left alone with either dog. But he is making those first vital steps to establishing a bond built on more than just cuddles and stolen food (although those things are important, too).

In playing even these small games with the dogs, Jack is learning that his dogs are sentient creatures who deserve his respect, and the dogs accept that Jack is one of the "bosses" — but a benevolent one. Empathy may not be an aptitude that is fully established until a child is much older, but working with dogs certainly seems to give it a boost.

First Things First

Before you think about involving your dog and kid in a specific canine sport, they both need some fundamentals. Your dog needs to know all the basic commands and be well socialized. A dog who is handled by a child has a few other requirements. He must be easily controlled with voice commands, not strength, and he must be extremely confident under any situation. These are all skills you should develop with your dog before expecting your child to work with the dog.

When attending puppy kindergarten or beginning obedience classes, let the trainer know that your child will be handling the dog on occasion. Take your child with you to all training classes (along with another parent if your child is younger than 12). Depending on the trainer, your child may have the opportunity to handle the dog in class herself. This will not only help your child learn how to train her dog but will also get them both used to training in a group setting.

Many kids make wonderful trainers, but before undertaking any real training, your child needs to be sufficiently mature to understand that dogs think and behave differently than people do. She needs to be patient and able to control her temper when she's frustrated.

Proper Precautions

As much fun as it is to watch your kids working with your dogs, it should never be forgotten that caring for a dog is a significant responsibility and that dogs are capable of seriously injuring or even killing children, and vice versa. If you have children in your home and multiple dogs, neuter your dogs, especially male ones. Two intact males have the highest likelihood for fights and misplaced aggression. And intact males can become aggressive if there is a female in heat in the area.

Children under the age of 12 should never be left alone with dogs. Properly training and socializing your dogs and teaching your children how to behave appropriately with dogs will go a long way toward avoiding bites, but even gentle, well-trained dogs may bite if threatened or hurt. Even gentle, caring kids who are comfortable around dogs can misread a dog's intentions or mistakenly fall on a dog or touch a sensitive spot, causing the dog to react. When supervising your children with your dog(s), watch for the following situations:

- **Are they playing a high-energy game?** Sometimes dogs can become too excited and can nip or misdirect their excitement into aggression. Be prepared to tone down the play when it seems too rowdy.

- **Is your child playing with more than one dog at a time?** Sometimes dog-fights can start over toys or when play strays into aggression. You don't want your child to be in the middle of a dog-fight, so let the dogs play together and then let your child play with each dog one on one.

- **Is your dog yawning, stiffening, or showing the whites of his eyes?** If you notice these behaviors when he is interacting with your child, separate them. These can be signs that your dog is uncomfortable and can lead to a snap or even a full-blown bite.

Fun Things for Kids to Do with Dogs

There are some activities that are great for dogs and kids to play together, others that definitely are not. As far as the unorganized sports go, walking, hiking, and running with your dog are fun for all ages, provided that kids are supervised and practice safe behavior. Some activities that aren't safe for kids to do with dogs are biking, in-line skating, swimming, and boating, all of which take a level of skill that most children don't possess. More important, all of these activities require a high level of control over the dog's behavior.

For many children, the first dog sport they participate in is conformation, or dog showing. The American Kennel Club's Junior Showmanship program is open to children between the ages of 9 and 18. For rural children, 4-H can be an excellent way to enter into dog sports, including dog showing. The United Kennel Club is another dog registry that offers junior handling conformation. If you have a mixed breed that your child wants to show, she can join the Mixed Breed Dog Clubs of America (MBDCA).

Many other sports offer junior divisions for young handlers. Kids who are attracted to obedience, rally, agility, flyball, disc dog, skijoring, sledding, or canine freestyle, for instance, will find opportunities to compete with their dogs. Some sports attract the whole family: dock jumping, weight pulling, hunt tests and field trials, and earthdog competitions often feel like family reunions, and children are more than welcome to attend and work with their dogs. Therapy work is another option for a child. Children as young as 10 years old can work with therapy dogs, although they need to have a guardian with them until they are at least 16 years old.

No matter what sport you and your child decide on, remember that it should be fun for all participants — child and dog and parent. Let them try out a few sports before settling on one or two. A good experience with a dog now will help your child embark on a lifetime of wonderful canine adventures.

CHAPTER 4

Keeping Your Canine Athlete Fit & Healthy

As your dog's guardian, the most important thing that you will do for him is to help him remain healthy. Dogs, like people, with active lifestyles stay healthier longer than do sedentary dogs. Regular exercise, excellent nutrition, and the opportunity to do something they love on a regular basis contribute immeasurably to a long, full life. At the same time, participating in sports with your dog increases his likelihood of being injured. It is up to you to be a strong advocate for your dog — being aware of what he is doing, when he is doing it, and never pushing him beyond his capabilities.

The Importance of Proper Nutrition

Canine nutrition is an area of growing concern for dog owners in general, and canine athlete handlers in particular. Although the vast majority of dogs do quite well on a good commercial diet, a number of canine sports enthusiasts have opted to offer their dogs a homemade diet, or a commercial diet made specifically for high-energy dogs, or to supplement their dogs' commercial diet with vitamins or herbs.

Dr. Eric Hartmann, DVM, a canine acupuncturist and herbalist, recommends that canine athletes exerting a high level of energy should be fed a homemade diet. In his opinion, there simply isn't a commercial alternative that provides the type of nutrition that will make canine athletes thrive.

Dr. Tia Greenberg, a veterinarian with a number of agility and flyball dogs among her clientele, disagrees. She and many other veterinarians feel that a good commercial food can supply everything that a dog of any given age and energy level needs to maintain a healthy lifestyle. You can choose a food made specifically for young, active dogs, often called performance diets, or pay attention to the label. Always buy a dog food that lists a whole source of meat (not byproducts) as its first ingredient.

If you decide to feed your dog a homemade diet, seek the guidance of a holistic veterinarian who has experience in creating diets for canine athletes. Depending on your dog's size and weight, age, and training regimen, his diet will differ greatly from other dogs'. Some handlers who like the idea of a homemade diet but don't have the time or inclination to provide all of the necessary ingredients choose to supplement a high-quality commercial kibble with steamed veggies and cooked lean meats such as chicken and lamb. You can also purchase frozen homemade diets from some specialty pet supply stores.

Some dogs, such as sled dogs who may be running for multiple hours in freezing cold temperatures, may need additional nutrition. Mushers will often feed their dogs a meat broth consisting of high-protein wet food and fresh meat mixed with warm water. To supply additional protein, they may offer their dogs meaty chicken broth rather than water.

HEALTH PRECAUTIONS

Any competition with large numbers of dogs poses the risk of exposure to disease, so all dogs should be vaccinated. Many competitions will require proof of rabies, at least, so it's a good idea to keep a sturdy envelope with copies of all of your dog's health certificates to take along to any events that you attend.

Any sport involving jumping or pulling should wait until your dog is done growing — for most breeds, that is around one year of age. While obedience, rally, herding, earthdog, and water tests are fine for older puppies, agility, flyball, dryland pulling, skijoring, sledding, and weight pulling can cause serious and long-term injuries to developing bodies. Even though some of these sport organizations permit a dog to participate before he hits his first birthday, don't take the chance. Instead, sign up for a pre-sports class or obedience class to prepare your pup to join the fun once he's cleared to play with the big boys.

Developing a Fitness Program

As you begin working with your dog in any sport, you may notice that he occasionally experiences small aches and pains just as a human athlete does. Perhaps after a hard day of fun in the sun, he seems especially tired or stiff the next day. Or maybe when scootering you find yourself on an especially rough surface and your pooch ends up with cuts on his paw pads. Your dog will work tirelessly for you, but in exchange you must protect him — sometimes from himself. There are many dogs who will simply work themselves into the ground for their love of the sport and their loyalty to you.

Dr. Carol Helfer is a veterinarian who specializes in sports medicine. She also competes in sports with her three dogs, each of whom has taught her something about the physical capabilities of dogs involved in sports. In her experience, the number one cause of injuries in canine athletes is out-of-shape dogs exceeding their capabilities. Dogs who are overweight or have previously been sedentary need a gradual training program — taking an obese dog on a 10-mile run is no different from an obese human suddenly jumping into a half-marathon, except that dogs often don't have an off switch. Many dogs will keep going until they drop.

Just as human athletes need to stay in excellent condition, so do canine athletes. A dog who is sedentary all week and then engages in intense exercise like flyball practice on weekends is susceptible to myriad injuries.

"If I were going to design my ideal conditioning schedule for a dog," says Helfer, "I would alternate endurance days and strength-training days for six days a week and then I'd take a day off. Intensity can be variable. Give them two or four weeks off every year to just be dogs."

To participate safely in a sport, dogs should be within a normal weight range and regularly engage in exercise. In addition to daily walks, a canine athlete should participate in higher intensity training at least three times per week. Running and swimming are both excellent ways to increase general fitness. Canine athletes should also do high-intensity strength training several times a week.

Dr. Helfer believes that increasing the core body strength is a facet of canine athletics that handlers don't pay enough attention to. "I think that could be a significant contributor to decreasing injuries." For endurance training, she recommends a 20-minute jog or swim. For strength training, she recommends high-intensity exercise of short duration, such as retrieving a ball up a hill.

Warming Up

When we go running or compete in a sport, we wouldn't consider setting out without properly warming up. We stretch our legs, windmill our arms, and walk briskly around the block before we begin our run. But with our dogs, we often pull them off of the couch or out of the car or crate with little or no preparation and expect them to break into stride without hesitation. Before doing any sport, do at least a five-minute walk to increase your dog's circulation and pulmonary functions.

Another culprit is the downtime that you will experience at a typical sports class. Your dog may be expected to sprint a course or go all out in a herding exercise, then wait for 10 minutes or even an hour for his next turn. In the downtime, keep your dog warmed up by doing tricks in place, spins, play bows, and other good stretching exercises. If your dog waits for his next turn for more than 20 minutes, a quick walk around the block or around the course perimeter can get him moving again.

Trials and tournaments are particularly difficult for trying to keep your dog warmed up, as dogs may need to wait in a crate for several hours between heats. This is especially the case if the handler is running more than one dog. Handlers who have multiple dogs in back-to-back races are often forced to keep one dog in

Work Those Abs!

Although dogs are often in great shape when it comes to endurance or overall conditioning, many could benefit from stronger core muscles. As with people, canines with stronger abdominal and back muscles are less prone to injury and fatigue. A fun way to increase core strength is to teach your dog a variety of tricks that work different muscles. In Dr. Carol Helfer's dog exercise classes, she teaches the following core-building moves:

Sit up and beg: increase difficulty by having the dog sit on uneven ground or follow a treat back and forth with his nose

Roll over: teach from both directions and ask for several repetitions

Spin: again, both directions and several repetitions

Crawl: increase length as dog becomes more proficient

a crate while handling another dog, then pulling the first dog out of the crate and onto the course without adequate time for warming up.

Cooling Down

Dr. Helfer likens warming up and cooling down to taking a rubber band out of a freezer. Intense warm-up stretching can overtax muscles and ligaments that are not properly warmed up. Handlers should stretch their dogs after a workout rather than before, and they should always provide a cooldown walk. This can be around the block or for much longer. Cooling down can actually be more important than warming the dog up, and safer as well.

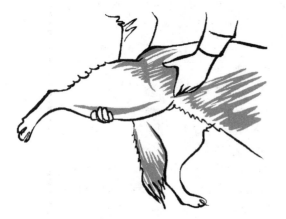

Stretching the rear legs

Stretching the front legs

Dr. Helfer explains that there is some controversy around the concept of stretching canine athletes: although all dogs need some stretching, the degree of stretching differs among individual dogs and the sports that they are involved in. A disc dog or agility dog, for example, needs more flexibility than a sled dog.

There are several stretches that you can introduce to your canine athlete. One is the cookie stretch, in which you hold a treat to your dog's nose and then move it to his tail. If he's at all food motivated, his nose will follow the treat and give him a good side stretch. Perform this to either side. If your dog tries to follow the treat by turning his entire body, instead of bending to reach it, hold him in position or do this trick against a wall. There is also the play bow (see how to train this in On to Fancier Moves, page 72), in which the dog bends his elbows but leaves his behind in the air.

There are also manual stretches you can do on your dog, such as what Helfer calls the "boy-dog pee position." In this stretch, fold the back leg and hold it out to the side. Do this on both sides. For another good rear stretch, stretch the back legs straight out behind, one at a time. You can also stretch the front limbs by pushing the elbow up and slightly forward.

Once the stretches are done, take a nice 5- or 10-minute stroll outside and enjoy your time with your pooch.

Knowing When to Stop

Many canine injuries could be avoided if owners knew when to stop. Energetic and highly motivated dogs often will not stop running, jumping, retrieving, or swimming on their own — they need their handler to make the decision for them. Fatigue and overexertion factor prominently in sports injuries for both humans and dogs. "These dogs will give us their heart and soul but sometimes they just need a break," says Helfer. "The fact that they will do it for you doesn't mean it's the best possible thing for them to be doing."

Some dog breeds are more prone to this go-all-out-until-they-flop behavior than others. Diane Jessup is a pit bull expert and dog trainer who participates in multiple dog sports. Jessup believes that the pit bulls' do-it-or-die attitude toward life in general, and sports in particular, is both their best asset and greatest detriment. In weight pulling, they have outdone the sled dogs that the sport was developed for. But their drive to keep going despite pain or exhaustion can be dangerous for them in the wrong hands. "These dogs will literally self-destruct to do their masters' bidding," says Jessup.

Handlers should always end a training session before their dogs want to end it. This is good for training because it ensures your dog always stops on a high note, and it also prevents him from being injured as he begins to tire. This is especially the case with high-drive dogs like Aussies, Border collies, and pit bull types. If they actually want to stop, it usually means the session has gone on too long.

Dealing with Injuries

The most common sports injuries seen by veterinarians are soft-tissue injuries, ranging from cruciate ligament ruptures to strained muscles to ligament and tendon strains and sprains. They also see a number of spinal issues, including ruptured discs. Ex-racing greyhounds may present with left-side neck and shoulder injuries related to the way the dogs lean into the oval track as they run.

Different sports have the potential for different injuries, and some sports are harder on dogs than are others. While tracking, obedience, and rally are physically low-key and rarely the source of injuries, agility, flyball, and Frisbee are physically much harder on dogs and, unless handlers are careful not to overwork their dogs, can be the source of repetitive-use injuries.

In agility, the most common injuries involve soft tissue, usually of the front limbs, particularly the shoulders. The contact obstacles, including the A-frame, dogwalk, and teeter, are the biggest culprits, which is why trainers and trial organizations are such sticklers on hitting

KEEPING COOL

One of the great dangers when exercising your dog is that he can over-heat. Dogs are not able to regulate their temperatures as easily as humans are, so if you're feeling uncomfortable on your jog or when training your dog outdoors on a hot day, you can bet your dog feels worse. Never exercise your dog during the hottest times of the day. If you train your dog through summer, limit hard exercise to dawn and dusk.

Make sure your dog has access to a nice shady area to rest; if he enjoys water, consider buying a child's pool and filling it with cool water so your dog can take a quick dip when he feels like it.

Keeping your dog hydrated is likely the number one most important safety tip when doing canine sports. Always take a supply of water with you; if you're engaging in winter sports, don't let your dog eat the snow for hydration. It may quench his thirst, but it will also lower his body temperature dangerously.

Handlers are sometimes afraid of offering water to their dogs during workouts for fear of bloat, but this fear is exaggerated. Heat exhaustion is far more likely, so offer your dog water before, after, and during workouts.

And just because your dog doesn't indicate that he wants a drink doesn't mean he doesn't need it. Often dogs are too excited to drink. If your dog refuses to drink water, tempt him by offering a bowl of salt-free chicken broth.

the contact zones, which minimizes the chance of injury. Both the design of the course and the manner in which the dog is handled during a run can have a serious impact on the incidence of injuries. At very high levels of agility, courses may not be both challenging and safe for all sizes of dogs. The courses are designed for the average dog — generally a 35- to 40-pound Border collie and not necessarily an 80-pound Rottweiler.

In flyball, the injuries are often related to the spine because of the angle in which the dog hits the flyball box and the timing of the ball's release. For very fast dogs, the release of the ball may be too slow. For this reason, a number of flyballers have worked to redesign the flyball box and to teach their dogs to do safer turns that cause less stress on their spines. Injuries can also occur as a result of handlers using tug toys as a lure for the dog to come back to. While the handler stays immobile, the dog latches on to the tug toy at top speeds, potentially leading to strained muscles or torn ligaments.

Disc dogs probably have the most dramatic potential for injury, particularly soft tissue injuries that are the result of bad landings. If a dog gets big air and then comes down awkwardly on just two legs, he can be seriously injured. Despite this potential for injury, disc dogs are typically among the best-conditioned dogs in canine sports — a well-conditioned dog cuts down the potential for injury dramatically.

Weight-pulling dogs can suffer muscle strains because the transition from muscle to tendon is the weakest spot in a dog's structure, and determined dogs can overcome the strength of that weakest part. Although weight pulling has yet to reach the popularity and competitive level of agility, flyball, or Frisbee, there is great potential for injury in this sport when handlers push dogs beyond their limits or engage in some of the new innovations in the sport, which range from extreme weight pulling to sled pulls in which weight is added suddenly to make the dog work harder.

Is My Dog Hurt?

When participating in sports, watch for signs of injury or illness. If you observe any of these symptoms, stop immediately. If symptoms continue, take your dog to the veterinarian.

- Limping
- Restlessness
- Panting
- Vomiting
- Diarrhea
- Lethargy
- Reluctance to interact
- Lack of interest in surroundings
- Very pale gums
- Licking at a particular part of the body

The most common injuries in sledding and skijoring, as well as dryland pulling, are paw pad injuries. Although it's difficult to get a dog to keep booties on, handlers should be aware of the potential of pad injuries and make an effort to have dogs wear booties on very icy snow, on concrete or asphalt, or when running very long distances. If possible, mushers should work slowly to condition dogs' pads to the surfaces they will be running on, and if possible, dryland pullers should run on grass or at least dirt.

Prevention Is the Key

If dogs are well conditioned, well hydrated, and properly warmed up and cooled down, and if you keep your dog's workout within his limitations, your chance of avoiding injuries is high. That said, injuries do happen, sometimes unavoidably. If an injury is sustained, remember that your dog needs time to heal, and he is probably not the best judge of how much time he needs. He will want to get back on the course before he's ready. Don't let him. If you give him the time he needs for his body to repair itself, the chances are that you'll have years back in the game together.

An important part of preventing serious injuries is responding appropriately to minor aches and pains that your dog suffers. Don't assume that a limp will just work itself out. Instead, stop the workout and observe your dog closely over the next few days. If it isn't serious, he'll be back up and around in days; if it is, the worst thing you can do is keep working him.

"A human being as a general rule does a lousy job of adequately assessing her dog's level of discomfort," says Dr. Helfer. "One, know your dog. Know how your dog reacts; know how your dog responds. Put your hands on your dog so you know what he normally feels like. Two, observe your dog. Sometimes injuries can be quite subtle. Sometimes it can be a matter of how he holds his body. Watch him standing. Maybe he is consistently taking weight off that one leg. Sometimes it's a small thing like the way he holds his tail. If there is lameness in the rear leg, he'll hold his tail away from the leg. In a front leg injury, watch for a head bob."

An injured dog may hold his body stiffly or keep his weight off of a particular leg.

Handling Your Senior Dog

The key to participating in a canine sport with your senior dog is listening to him and correctly interpreting what he's telling you. This isn't always an easy task, because most dogs are not inclined to tell you their problems. To a dog in the wild, showing weakness is a death sentence, so most dogs will make great efforts to hide pain and illness.

It's always important that you know your dog's body well, but this is especially true once he becomes a senior dog (see Dog Age chart on page 92). Look for new bumps and lumps, limping, and other signs of injury or disease. Back injuries often show up as a dragging back leg or the tail carried differently than usual. A twice-weekly massage is a great way to keep your old dog's muscles feeling good, and it provides an opportunity for you to see if anything has changed. As you gently work along his body, watch for signs of pain. This can be wincing, moving away, or stiffening. If he shows any signs of discomfort, stop immediately.

Begin at his head with soft broad strokes, checking in his ears and stroking under his jaw. Look in his mouth to see if there are any cracked teeth or red and inflamed gums. Also notice whether he winces or pulls away when you touch certain areas of his mouth, indicating soreness. Move down his neck, gently kneading the muscles along his spine. Stroke each forelimb and bend each joint. Look at his footpads to see if there are any broken nails or cuts. Continue down his sides with soft strokes, ending with the area above his tail. Carefully extend his tail. Stroke down both back legs and check his back feet. End the massage with a nice chest scratch and belly rub, while you check for fatty lumps or other changes. If you notice anything unusual, it's time for a trip to the vet.

Dealing with Arthritis

Many dogs who have been active for their whole lives develop arthritis as they age. This is especially true for canine athletes in sports that involve a lot of jumping and hard running. Arthritis can cause a dog to slow down and stiffen up, yet arthritic dogs can — and should — continue to be active. Many dog owners assume the dog needs to rest on the couch once he's been diagnosed with arthritis, but this couldn't be further from the truth. In fact, moderate exercise can actually be good for a dog with arthritis. What isn't good is intense exercise followed by no exercise. A regimen of moderate daily exercise will keep an older dog feeling well both physically and mentally.

The prevalence of arthritis in older canine athletes, especially those who jump a great deal, such as Frisbee dogs and agility dogs, has led many veterinarians to recommend that canine athletes begin taking a daily dose of glucosamine/chondroitin as a prophylactic supplement even before the signs of arthritis show up. These supplements have been shown to have some effect on the severity of arthritis and may delay the onset and severity of arthritis in active dogs. Work with your veterinarian to figure out the correct dosage for your dog.

There are also alternative treatments for arthritis. Gentle massage and the application of warm towels or a heating pad can help ease stiffness. Acupuncture provides amazing ongoing results for many dogs who suffer from arthritis. Treatments typically start out weekly but are reduced gradually to monthly treatments. Most dogs seem to enjoy acupuncture, or at least tolerate it. A needle placed slightly above and between the eyes makes them sleepy and relaxed, and some dogs even fall asleep with the needles in.

Finally, as older dogs become more sedentary, they often gain weight, which exacerbates their arthritis symptoms. The best way to keep an arthritic dog active is to keep excess weight off of him, and the best way to do that is to monitor his calorie intake to reflect his activity level. Make sure that your canine athlete continues to burn the same number of calories as he takes in.

Keep on Keeping On

Many age-related ailments, from poor eyesight to deafness to dementia, can have an impact on a dog's ability or desire to participate. Handlers should keep a close eye on their dogs and be prepared to intercede if necessary. Some ailments and certain sports do not mix. It may be unsafe for a dog with very limited eyesight to herd, for example.

That said, if your dog seems eager to participate as usual and doesn't have an injury that can be exacerbated by continuing to train, there's no reason why he shouldn't keep doing what he enjoys. In fact, many dogs are active until 15 or 16 years of age. Handlers with senior athletes say their dogs are happier and healthier when they continue to engage in their sports on at least some level. But it's important to remember that sports vary widely, and "old" in one sport can be quite different from "old" in another. Skijoring and sledding dogs may run well into their teens, whereas weight-pulling dogs usually retire by about seven or eight.

Some handlers point out that their older dogs are their best dogs in many ways. After years together, human and dog are an experienced team and are so in tune with one another that they barely need direction. Many handlers will continue to do a sport with a dog just for fun as he ages. Most sports have veterans' divisions, which give the older dogs

OLD DOG, NEW TRICK[S]

When my dog Desi was nine years old, we discovered agility. For the next three years we spent every Tuesday night jumping hurdles, climbing A-frames, and balancing on teeters. Although Desi had been my daily running and walking partner and an unofficial therapy dog throughout her life, agility brought out her true nature like nothing before. Her muzzle was gray and her eyes were rheumy, but she bounced with excitement when we arrived at the practice field.

Desi wasn't the fastest dog in her class, but she was one of the smartest. She had the confidence of her years and an understanding of what I expected from her. She had a casual indifference to the things that scared many of the younger dogs, like the teeter. I never had to teach her how to do a rear cross; she was just so in tune to me that she got it immediately.

One evening, Desi approached a hurdle and sat down. I called her, tried to tempt her over it with a treat, and finally set the hurdle pole on the ground. She wouldn't budge. Her teacher, Terry Long, looked at me and shrugged, "I think she's done." And she was.

...ce to play but without the intense ...petition.

Ultimately, it's the job of the handler to decide how much is too much. Sometimes the dog wants to do more than he should; sometimes the handler wants him to do more than he can. A good handler knows when the time has come to back off on a sport or even end it. In the best-case scenario, a canine athlete doesn't really have to retire but can slowly cut down on the intensity of the work he does.

Leo is a seven-year-old Frisbee dog who has placed several times in the world disc championships. In 2007, he qualified to go to the worlds again but handler Aaron Abrahamson decided not to go, pointing to the 100-plus temperatures in Atlanta at that time of year and the intensity of the competition.

Abrahamson has also changed the way he and Leo play, so that instead of encouraging vaults and high jumps, he now throws the Frisbee low so Leo can continue to compete without accelerating the minor arthritis in his knees. He shrugs when asked if it's difficult to curtail Leo's stellar Frisbee career, saying simply, "We've got to take care of him. He's taken us all over the country."

There is no reason senior dogs shouldn't engage in sports, as long as their handlers are conscientious and realistic about their dogs' abilities. If the dog stops wanting to perform, it's time to stop the activity. Until then, enjoy!

A DOG'S AGE IN HUMAN YEARS

The old saying that one year in a dog's life equals seven human years is roughly true, but the following chart gives a more accurate comparison based on the dog's weight.

AGE	WEIGHT			
	0–20 lbs	21–50 lbs	51–90 lbs	>90 lbs
5	36	37	40	42
6	40	42	45	49
7	44	47	50	56
8	48	51	55	64
9	52	56	61	71
10	56	60	66	78
11	60	65	72	86
12	64	69	77	93
13	68	74	82	101
14	72	78	88	108
15	76	83	93	115
16	80	87	99	123
17	84	92	104	
18	88	96	109	
19	92	101	115	

= adult   = senior   = geriatric

Created by Dr. Fred Metzner, DVM, State College, PA

CHAPTER 5

It's Only a Game:
Keeping It All in Perspective

IN CHILDREN'S SPORTS, THE PHRASE "SOCCER MOM" or "hockey dad" can have multiple meanings. It may be a jokey way to describe a parent who spends hours shuttling a child to and from after-school and weekend activities, or it may imply something darker — a parent who pushes and pushes a child in sports to a level that is unhealthy, both physically and emotionally.

In this age of organized activities, the world of dog sports — in which many handlers consider themselves more parents than owners — has become surprisingly similar to the extracurricular world of children. Those who become completely engulfed by the world of dog sports say that it is enriching, fulfilling, and exciting. Many dog sports fanciers say without hesitation that club members are like family and are their closest friends. They may practice together several times a week and travel to competitions together on weekends. They share dog-sitting duties and may even have keys to one another's homes. For many dog owners, the world of canine competition has replaced small-town community, PTA, and church. If it's an obsession, say handlers, it's a healthy one.

And many handlers are able to find a balance in canine sports. Flyball is a good example of a sport that can be as lighthearted or as intense as you want it to be. Flyball participants often choose their teams based on how much time and energy they are willing to commit and the level of competitiveness found on one team or another. Joy Adiletta, a flyball handler from the Pacific Northwest, points out that her area isn't the most serious region in flyball. "If you want to see really serious flyball you should go to Michigan where they're chasing the new world record," she says.

Going Too Far

While many canine sports enthusiasts participate in their chosen sport once or twice a week, there are others for whom their dogs' activities take up every night of the week, as well as all weekend. The majority of the people I met in the course of writing this book participated in at least two sports. One woman, for example, does four sports with her dog: dock jumping, herding, agility, and flyball. She also does work in search and rescue. On its own, each of these sports (excluding dock jumping) requires weekly practice and monthly competition — in combination, that's at least four nights or weekend days per week. And she's not alone. Although there are still a fair number of dog sports handlers who focus on just one sport, participation in multiple sports is fast becoming the norm.

A handler and dog try one, like it, meet people and dogs who do other sports, try those, like them, and suddenly they're booked every night of the week. For many handlers, the world of dog sports becomes the most important part of their lives. Handlers with young children at home or a number of other nonwork commitments seem to limit their sports to one or two; individuals and couples without children may devote far more time to their dog sports hobby. Anecdotally, I was stunned by how often I'd meet a handler at a flyball or agility

THE MUSHER'S COMMITMENT

Dina McClure is a skijorer and sled dog musher who has alternated between the sports depending on the circumstances in her life. She explains that while skijoring is a hobby, dogsledding is truly a way of life, 365 days a year. When you adopt the lifestyle of a musher, you take on the care of at least four dogs, and usually more. That means that your day revolves around your sled dogs: feeding and watering them, exercising them, and caring for them. And that's all in addition to cleaning up after them, maintaining equipment, and actually sledding with them, which mushers may do three or four times a week (or more!).

"It's definitely a big commitment," says McClure. "That's why skijoring and scootering are more popular."

Mushers may turn to skijoring or scootering when mushing becomes untenable because of family commitments, expense, or a move away from a snowy or rural area, just as competitive agility dogs and handlers may enter veteran class divisions for less intense competition as the dog ages, or they may turn to another, less physically demanding and competitive sport, such as rally or tracking.

class and the next week encounter the same person and dog at a herding class or dock-jumping event.

There are people who participate in upwards of six or seven sports, handlers who keep up to a dozen dogs in order to engage in their activities of choice, and handlers who make major lifestyle changes to do sports with their dogs. It's not unheard of, for example, for an urban herder to decide to fully embrace her dog's rural roots and buy a farm and a flock of sheep. Sled dog mushers regularly adjust their entire lifestyles to meet the needs of their dogs and the demands of their sport, commuting long distances to paid employment to be able to live on enough acreage to house 12, 16, or even 24 dogs. Their gear costs thousands of dollars and their dogs' training, exercise, and care takes up almost all of their free time.

Dogs Aren't People

Many of these handlers want only the best for their dogs, but perhaps go too far in that quest. And then there are the handlers who go too far in a way that is decidedly unhealthy, who push their dogs to extremes and see their animals as extensions of ego rather than as individual animals.

Jon Katz, a well-known author on dogs who himself moved to the country at least in part to allow his dogs a chance to herd their own sheep, commented on the negative side of dog sports in the online magazine *Slate* (March 5, 2004), "[What about] the pet owners who make their dogs hyper by believing they need to 'play' continuously, like overprogrammed boomer children? They drag them to unruly play groups, toss Frisbees and balls night and day, haul them to an endless round of organized activities — but fail to teach them how to be calm."

Katz had also discussed this topic in an earlier *Slate* article (August 8, 2003) in

which he comments, "A dog that chases balls, sticks, and Frisbees and races around all day is sometimes an obnoxious, aroused, or hyper dog, not necessarily a fulfilled one." Katz brings up a fair point and one that is sometimes overlooked in our endless quest to find the perfect sports for our dogs. Dogs do not need to be champions, they don't need to be entertained day and night, and they don't need to be with us every second of the day.

Canine sports are fun for dogs and handlers, create community for many people, and are an excellent source of exercise for both the humans and the dogs involved; however, there is such a thing as too much of a good thing.

Even a seemingly tireless dog who loves to do several different sports needs to kick back and relax. Don't overschedule your dog with too many outings and activities — he doesn't need to be busy all the time!

Caught Up in Competition

Not only can our quest for constant mental and physical stimulus at some point become detrimental for our dogs, but there is also a point at which the handler's desire for the dog's success overrides the dog's ability or desire. Although almost everyone starts out in canine sports for the fun of it, the increasing attention and rising competition in many of the sports can lead to handlers pushing their dogs too far. Practicing every single day and attending three or four tournaments a month is too much for most dogs. They need time off and the chance to relax and just be dogs.

Even in Frisbee, a sport that is often seen as immune to the competitive nature of other canine sports because of its free-spirited reputation, handlers can begin to make choices less on the basis of what's good for the dog and more on their success in competition or their success on the professional circuit. Whenever the question of money is brought into a canine sport, the focus can easily skew away from fun to success. There are Frisbee dog handlers who re-home dogs who don't do well in disc competition. Even if the dogs go to good homes, the idea of not keeping a dog simply because he doesn't excel in a sport is troubling to many people.

One of the most disturbing tendencies seen in canine sports is the same one that is seen in children's sports — the point at which competition becomes so intense for the parent or handler that the child or animal suffers for it. Most organizations monitor closely for this behavior and sanction handlers who appear to push their dogs too hard, who swear or yell at their dogs out of frustration, or who physically reprimand their dogs.

"If we see someone who is a little too aggressive, we talk about it," says flyball handler Barbara Reisinger. "We've had people thinking punishment is slamming the dog on the ground. That's not what we do in this sport. There are punishments — if dogs misbehave, they don't run that day. That's what we encourage."

As a sport becomes more competitive and a handler commits increased amounts of time and expense in training a dog, disappointments and setbacks can be difficult to accept. I've seen handlers in tears after a dog has balked or performed poorly.

In some instances, failing to perform or pass a test can feel like a year's training has been wasted. Tracking tests, for example, are notoriously difficult to schedule and a dog who bombs may not have the opportunity to take the test again for another year.

Putting Things in Perspective

Agility trainer and handler Michael Bruce tries to teach his students that being too competitive is counterproductive. Not only is it bad for the dog, it's bad for the handler–dog bond. Teams that aren't bonded tend to be less successful than teams in which handlers have great relationships with their dogs.

"People who don't know how to train or haven't done it properly aren't going to win. It's sort of self-regulating," says Bruce. "I see people yelling at their dogs, and I want to tell them, 'You know what, if you do this differently, you'd be more successful.'"

Some sports have a reputation for handlers who are overly competitive or who push their dogs too hard. This is something responsible handlers try very hard to counteract. Dan Riddle competes in weight pulling with his four American pit bull terriers, Flex, Mecca, Jade, and Rage.

"Most of the people I've met really love their dogs," says Riddle, "but there is a fine line and some people lose sight and become too competitive. To me it's always about the dog. Each dog's potential is only so much and if they are trying as hard as they can, how can they do more? My dogs are my team. They're not only my friends but they're my kids. I don't put them in situations where they can't succeed.

"Your dog has to have ample amounts of respect for you," he continues. "I always work on obedience first. Some people say that weight-pull dogs should be outside dogs and if you oversocialize them and let them sleep in the house, you soften them. I feel exactly the opposite. If my dogs will do anything for me, then they're going to do better for me. To me, weight pulling is secondary, the dog is first."

There is no doubt that canine sports can be beneficial for everyone involved. Dogs receive exercise and stimulus that can be hard to come by in an urban or suburban environment. Humans develop friendships with like-minded people and find a fun avenue for exercise. Human–dog teams can develop surprising bonds, leading to a better relationship in and out of the home.

At the same time, dog sports can bring out the worst in human handlers, some of whom push their dogs way beyond their capabilities as they become increasingly focused on winning. And in the quest for the perfect sport for their dogs, some handlers can become almost obsessive in their pursuit. Yes, it's a thrill to see your dog leap over a hurdle or snatch a Frisbee out of the sky, but it's just as important to remember that your dog doesn't share your drive for the gold.

Dogs participate in dog sports because they like to run and play and, more important, because they like to be with their people. It is easy to be swept up in the idea that one or another particular sport will finally fulfill your dog, but the fact is, dogs don't need to be fulfilled in the same way humans do. If you want them to play Frisbee, sure, they'll play Frisbee. But they are also happy to loll on the couch next to you, fetch a ball in the backyard, or just be invited in the car when you run to the store.

The Darker Side of Canine Sports

Not all canine sports have a sunny side. In fact, there are dog sports that are only about the pain and suffering of the animals and the profits and questionable status it brings to the human participants. Even calling these activities "sports" is a stretch. There are also sports that have invited bristling controversies for many years. While some sports aren't essentially bad for dogs, the industries under which they are done are inhumane. Other times, the sport is bad for other animals. And sometimes there is simply a lot of gray area — according to one person it's the ultimate expression of a dog's athleticism and will, but to another it is simply cruel.

Dogfighting

Dogfighting is one of the oldest dog sports, if you can call it that, and is also the cruelest. Bulldogs were developed in the United Kingdom as butchers' dogs. They were used to control animals in the slaughterhouse and to hold bulls in place. They were later crossed with terriers; these mixes were called bull and terriers. In the 1800s, the breed immigrated to America with working-class English and Irish immigrants. Their skill with bulls segued into the blood sport of bullbaiting, in which bulldogs teased and attacked chained bulls. Later, the dogs were used to fight one another: they were placed in an enclosed area and encouraged to fight to the death. The dog with the greatest tenacity won, and often the loser — sometimes the victor as well — ended up dead.

Although today dogfighting is illegal throughout the United States (and a felony in 48 states), it continues seemingly unabated. And if there was ever some kind of a code of honor among dogmen, it seems to have largely disappeared.

Dogfighting is a catastrophe for pit bull type dogs for myriad reasons. The obvious reason is their brutal deaths in the pit. Dogs kept for fighting are almost uniformly mistreated on a general level as well. They are cruelly culled for not being "game" enough — a dog who will not or cannot fight is killed, often by inhumane methods such as shooting, beating, drowning, or electrocution. Dogs who will fight are not only subjected to tortuous pain in the pit but are usually kept in substandard living conditions — tied out on short, heavy chains with only a plastic or metal barrel to protect them from the elements.

Beyond that, there is the societal level of mistreatment that has befallen the breeds associated with dogfighting. Wide-scale breed-specific legislation (called BSL) has banned pit bull types, and even dogs that simply resemble pit bull types, from many municipalities and counties, and even entire countries. BSL may require dogs that resemble pit bull types to be spayed or neutered, or even to be rounded up and euthanized.

Blame can be widely spread— politicians seeking easy answers to dog-bite problems, media looking for a way to sell newspapers in an increasingly difficult business climate, residents subject to hysterical fads. But the ultimate blame lies with the cruel and unethical practice of dogfighting that has no place in civilized life.

Greyhound Racing

Another sport with a dark side is greyhound racing, which fortunately is quickly becoming an anachronism. No one argues that greyhounds don't love to run. For thousands of years, sight hounds have been bred to exert short, intense spurts of energy in pursuit of prey animals. The arguments against greyhound racing pertain to the life that goes along with it. Proponents of greyhound racing argue that not all racetracks keep dogs in inhumane living conditions, cruelly cull poor runners, or uniformly euthanize dogs once their careers are over — but the fact is that many do.

Large numbers of greyhounds are bred for racing, with only a percentage of these dogs ever making it to the racetrack. The rest are either culled or sold to research laboratories. When a puppy is culled

The Dog Sports Dilemma

As much joy as dogs and humans derive from participating in canine sports, there is always the opportunity for abuse. In every sport, there are instances of a handler punishing her dog harshly when he doesn't perform to her standards, dogs being kept in less-than-ideal living conditions, or dogs being pushed to do too much too fast.

In the vast majority of these cases, handlers need to be educated on better ways to conduct themselves. In other cases, canine sport organizations must be accountable for the behavior of those testing or trialing in a sport. Most organizations severely sanction instances of verbal or physical abuse of competing animals; however, some organizations do this better than others.

because he does not show exemplary racing ability, he is euthanized, sometimes by the cheapest method possible, which may be gunshot or even bludgeoning or electrocution. Other kennels cull puppies with standard euthanization methods, overdosing the dogs with an injectible anesthetic. Only a small percentage of these dogs are placed for adoption.

A dog who does make it to the racetrack has a career that will last only a few years; because the sport depends on greyhounds going faster and faster, a dog who does not routinely race in the top percentage is retired. Retired dogs may be used for breeding, euthanized, sold to research laboratories, or released to adoption agencies. Although there are a large number of greyhound rescue groups, according to the Humane Society of the United States, about 25 percent of retired greyhounds are still euthanized each year.

During the 1990s a number of states passed laws banning greyhound racing, fortunately, and the sport overall has seen a tremendous decline. Many believe that greyhound racing may soon be a thing of the past.

Dogsled Racing

Whatever the fate of greyhound racing, highly competitive dogsledding is firmly entrenched in many parts of the country. The ultimate test of a musher, in the minds of many people, is the Iditarod, a 1,151-mile race held annually in Alaska. Those who promote the contest say that it is the ultimate test of a dogsled team's endurance, skill, and athleticism. Opponents say that it is a cruel exercise in which dogs are pushed past their limits. According to many animal welfare groups, there have been more than 100 canine deaths in the course of the race's 35-year history — and that's just the deaths during the race. The bigger cause of death linked to the Iditarod is the culling of puppies by breeders who are seeking the next great sled dog.

Another concern surrounding the Iditarod is that the competitiveness of the race has led to the introduction of non-Nordic breeds into Alaskan husky stock. These dogs tend to be faster but are poorly suited for the rigors of the sled-dog life. Whereas huskies are genetically adapted for life in the Arctic, short-coated hounds and pointers, which are some of the common breeds now bred into sled-dog lines, are not.

Conversely, dogsledding as a recreational hobby or for subsistence is largely accepted, even encouraged, by animal welfare groups such as the Humane Society of the United States and the American Society for the Prevention of Cruelty to Animals (ASPCA). Both groups point out that sled dogs who are housed humanely often receive better care and certainly more exercise and stimulus than the average house dog.

All the
SPORTS
That Are Fit to Print

CHAPTER 6

High-Energy Games for High-Flying Dogs

Agility / Flyball / Disc Dog / Dock Jumping

FOR ENTHUSIASTIC, ATHLETIC DOGS, such as Border collies, Labrador retrievers, and pit bull types, there is nothing like the excitement of a high-intensity canine sport to focus their enthusiasm. Agility, flyball, disc dog, and dock jumping give these super athletes the platform to truly show their stuff—and ample opportunity to burn off all that excess energy that sometimes makes them difficult to live with. There is nothing like watching your dog leaping into the air after a disc or flying over a hurdle to make you appreciate his athletic prowess.

AMAZING AGILITY

On a rainy day in early fall, a bright green swatch of grass is covered with agility equipment and surrounded by colorful tents. People and dogs mingle under the tents, waiting for their chance to walk the course. When the judge gives the signal, a hundred or so handlers put their dogs in crates and head out onto the field to begin walking the course, their arms gesticulating as they memorize the course and mentally rehearse the best way to move their dogs quickly and accurately through the obstacles.

In the first class, Xena, a Border collie, is a blur of black and white fur as she whips through the weaves, races over the dogwalk, and tips the teeter with a crash. The slender dog is the quintessential agility dog — smart, fast, and lithe — while her handler, Michael Bruce, is the quintessential agility handler as he directs Xena through the course with his own grace. As Bruce explains, agility is as much about the movement of the handler as it is about the dog's athleticism and speed.

Good agility handlers will tell you that the best thing about agility is the bond it creates between a person and a dog. "It's all about attention, it's about playing with the dog, it's about spending time together," says Bruce. "You have to have a dog that's paying attention to you in order to become successful in agility."

The Basics of Agility

Agility consists of a course of 10 different obstacles that the dog navigates with his owner running beside him. The goal is to run the course in the shortest length of time with the least number of faults. The course layout changes for every competition; some agility courses combine jumps and weaves but leave out the other obstacles. A standard course has all three — jumps, weaves, and obstacles — but can be arranged in a way that changes the level of difficulty.

Each obstacle is numbered and must be run in order. Practice runs are not permitted, but handlers are given the chance to walk the course and strategize the best method to direct their dogs through the course quickly and accurately. Faults include skipping an obstacle, taking an obstacle from the wrong direction, knocking a bar, and missing a contact zone.

Agility had its start in 1978 in England at the Crufts Dog Show. According to legend, a Crufts committee member, John Varley, and a dog trainer, Peter Meanwell, put together a canine obstacle course for entertainment at the show. The course was a very rudimentary version of the modern agility course and was perhaps based on certain equestrian events, as well as canine demonstrations given at agricultural shows.

There's no question, however, about how the audience responded to the impromptu Crufts demo — enthusiastically! Within a year, agility was a full-fledged canine sport, with clubs offering classes and an agility competition held at the 1979 Olympia, the London International Horse Show, where it continues to be a popular annual event. Two years later, England's Kennel Club sanctioned the sport and it returned to Crufts, this time as a bona fide canine competition.

Agility first crossed the pond in the early 1980s. Charles (Bud) Kramer (who later went on to largely invent the sport of rally) established the National Committee for Dog Agility (NCDA) in

Some Words to Know

Away work: When the dog is following commands at a distance from the handler

Contact zone: A painted section on certain obstacles; the dog must touch it with at least one paw upon both entering and leaving

Crossing: When the dog moves in front of or behind the handler to approach an obstacle

1984 and several years later published *Agility Dog Training for All Breeds*. At the same time, the United States Dog Agility Association (USDAA) was started by Kenneth Tatsch and quickly became the gold standard for agility in North America. The sport has developed rapidly, and at the national level there are now three main agility organizations: the USDAA, the North American Dog Agility Council (NADAC), and the American Kennel Club (AKC). Trials are also run by the United Kennel Club (UKC), whose agility division merged with Kramer's NCDA, and by the Australian Shepherd Club of America (ASCA).

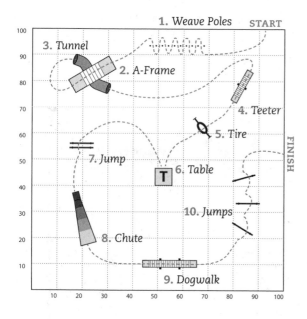

A typical agility course: the obstacles are numbered in the order of approach.

Who Does Agility?

Agility is the fastest-growing dog sport in the world. The number of participants has increased exponentially in the United States, Canada, and Western Europe, but it's also taking off in Russia, Japan, Mexico, South Africa, and Costa Rica. In 2007, there were more than 800,000 entries for AKC agility events — a staggering number given that AKC dogs make up only a small percentage of the dogs who participate in this sport.

Agility is found in every state in the union and there are literally thousands of agility events — large and small — held each year. With the coasts continuing to lead the rest of the country in agility enthusiasm, this sport has increased dramatically in popularity and registered numbers since its inception.

Agility is a fast-paced, challenging sport, but it can accommodate almost anyone, human or canine, who is interested and enthusiastic. All kinds of people participate in agility: male and female, young and old, occasional and obsessed. The top agility contenders do tend to be athletic people in good shape; however, there are plenty of handlers who aren't in peak form. Even handlers with limited mobility can still navigate an agility course alongside their dogs.

The dogs, too, vary greatly in their physical characteristics. Focused, athletic breeds such as Australian shepherds and

SAFETY FIRST

As with all dog sports, the safety of the dog should be paramount when participating in agility training or competition. That means never pushing your dog beyond his capabilities, always making sure your dog gets enough rest and is hydrated, and not working your dog during the hottest times of the day. Be conscious of his behavior at all times. If he shows signs of heat exhaustion — panting excessively, lethargy, or acting disoriented— it's far past time to stop the game.

Always check the equipment to make sure that it's safe and in good working condition. Obstacles with splintered wood or worn and slippery contacts are not safe and should be fixed or replaced. Most courses are designed for 35- to 45-pound Border collies, not 100-pound Rottweilers, so if you are running a large dog, talk to your trainer about her equipment. If you are buying your own equipment, ask how it's made and about weight limits.

In general, agility obstacles aren't made with big dogs in mind; an overly flexible dogwalk, for example, can bounce a large energetic dog right off. The more advanced an agility dog course becomes, the more dangerous it can be for large dogs because the turns become tighter and the pace quickens. It is difficult to design a highly advanced course for dogs of every size, so if you are going to do agility with your large dog, you may need to accept that you will be doing it just for fun. Before competing in advanced-level courses with a large dog, make sure the equipment is safe. Keep the speeds low and keep the work light.

Border collies tend to excel, but dogs of all sizes and shapes take part, and accommodations are made for older dogs, large dogs, and dogs with physical limitations.

Talking about Training and Time

Agility trainers can be broken down into two groups. Some are trainers who believe that the fundamentals are everything; that is, the slower you go, the more correctly the dog learns, and the more correctly the dog learns, the more successful he ultimately becomes. And then other trainers believe that dogs learn more quickly, and have more fun, jumping right into the game.

Michael Bruce, for one, is clearly in the fundamentals camp. He believes that novice dogs should not even touch the agility equipment until they have gone through at least one session of agility, and perhaps two or three. So Bruce's students spend at least the first eight weeks of their agility training on the ground with no agility equipment in sight. Students begin by doing a lot of running with and without their dogs, practicing serpentines and crosses — learning where to put their own bodies in relation to the dogs'.

The goal is to teach the dog first to pay attention to the handler, second to be interested in the toy or treat reward the handler is offering, and third to follow the handler's body movements. Ideally, the dog becomes so attuned to the handler that he will follow even the slightest indication, and the handler becomes so streamlined that there is no body movement that is not intentional. Bruce's vision makes sense — he teaches his students to see the invisible path that leads from start to finish and presents the obstacles as challenges to completing the path, rather than the goal itself — but it can be hard to garner a lot of enthusiasm for a class that consists mostly of running back and forth on bare ground with your dog tied up at the fence.

To embrace Bruce's philosophy, your goal must be the finish line instead of the fun you having getting there. It's no surprise that the lion's share of his students are experienced agility dog handlers looking to hone their skills and handlers who have become frustrated about remaining at a plateau in their pursuit of perfection. But not every agility instructor is as esoteric as this. There are plenty of more traditional agility instructors out there, and at least at the start, their classes are, frankly, a bit more fun.

THE MORE TRADITIONAL APPROACH

A more traditional class includes lots of obstacles. Even beginning dogs work on the A-frame, dogwalk, and teeter. With the obstacles set at low heights, the dogs are led over the obstacles on a leash, with lots of treats and praise as they go. From the very first class, dogs are becoming familiar with the equipment, doing weaves, learning about target touching, running through tunnels, getting lots of treats, and enjoying the activities.

Typically, agility novices encounter classes like the latter, where handlers and dogs have lots of fun and get hooked on the sport. For many people this kind of course is all that is needed, but as you become more competitive, you may find that after three or four trials your dog is not progressing. He knows how to navigate the obstacles, but he doesn't really know why he's doing it — he doesn't see the finish line at the other side. When people start to compete seriously or decide to get a second, more focused agility dog, they will often turn to a more experienced instructor with the fundamental approach. As long as the instructor keeps things safe, either method is fine.

When looking for a training class, visit both types of class and think about what it is you want to achieve. If you're just looking for a bit of fun and don't plan to compete at very high levels, the "jump right in" philosophy is perfectly adequate. If your goal is to compete at very high levels, it may be worth taking the slow route. In either case, positive reinforcement training is by far the most common means of training agility. Many handlers use clicker training, which can dramatically reduce the learning curve.

Whatever class you choose, you'll want to be sure that the trainer's primary goals are to keep the dogs safe and the learning pleasurable. Training should start with the obstacles and the hurdles set low, and emphasis should be placed on accuracy before speed. A trainer who pushes a dog beyond his limitations or comfort is never correct. If you get a bad feeling from a class or a trainer, you're probably right to trust that warning; turn around and find another class where you and your dog are comfortable.

Most agility handlers attend weekly classes and follow up with training at home. While few handlers keep their own agility obstacles at home, training in crosses, away work, and those sticky weaves is common. You could easily find an agility trial every weekend in spring and summer if desired, but most dogs compete about once a month.

Evaluating Equipment and Expense

The expense incurred from training in agility is minimal unless you become very competitive. Most people and their dogs attend a weekly group training session, which may cost between $10 and $20. During competition season there are trial entrance fees, which vary according to the organization and the number of events entered.

While training fees are reasonable, agility is an equipment-heavy sport. Fortunately, you don't need to buy competition-quality obstacles unless you become obsessed, which certainly happens, and feel that you need your own agility course in your backyard. Many obstacles can be made fairly simply with inexpensive material from the hardware store, so it is also possible to build your own course over time. A broomstick on two bricks, for example, makes a good first hurdle.

You will, however, need the following equipment to get started:

- A 6- to 8-foot leash made of leather or soft nylon with a handle

- A quick-release or flat buckle collar

- A "grab tab" (a 4-inch handle that allows you to control your dog)

- A treat bag that attaches to your belt

- A supply of treats that your dog loves

- Many trainers also recommend a clicker and some sort of target to facilitate target training.

These illustrations show the basic equipment used in agility.

JUMPS (HURDLES)

The jump setup involves two upright supports that are a minimum of 32 inches high with one 4- to 5-foot horizontal bar that is adjustable between 4 and 30 inches off the ground. The crossbars must be lightweight so they move if the dog hits them; they can be made of PVC, wood, or plastic; some have side wings on the supports. Jumps can be set up as a single obstacle or in a series.

Long Jump
(spread or broad jump)

The long jump is a set of 6- or 8-inch-wide steps that ascend upward and outward, creating a horizontal jump that is set from 16 inches to 52 inches, depending on the height of the dog.

Tire Jump

This circle is made of PVC pipe or foam with a diameter of 20 to 22 inches. The form for the dog to jump through hangs in a frame and is adjusted between 4 and 30 inches from the ground. The tire is fastened at the top and sides of the frame but swings free at the bottom.

Tunnel

This flexible tube is made of heavy nylon with an inside diameter of 24 inches. It can be 10 feet to 20 feet long. It may be set up as a straight tunnel or in a curve. The tunnel kept in place with 20-pound bags of sand or 3-gallon bags of water.

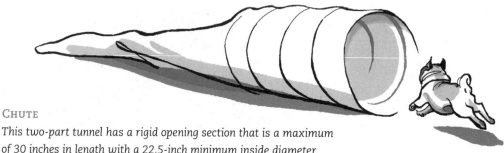

CHUTE

This two-part tunnel has a rigid opening section that is a maximum of 30 inches in length with a 22.5-inch minimum inside diameter, and an attached tube that is made of lightweight fabric and is a maximum of 8 feet long. The circumference flares to 96 inches at the chute opening. The dog enters at the opening and must push through the fabric sleeve, or tube, to exit.

WEAVE POLES

A succession of upright plastic or PVC poles form one of the more challenging obstacles. The poles are between 36 inches and 48 inches in height and between 20 inches and 21 inches in distance from one another (the middle of one pole to the middle of the next pole). Depending on the level of competition, there will be 6 to 12 weave poles in a set. The object is for the dog to run through the poles (entering between the first and second pole going from the right to the left), alternating from one side to the other without missing any.

PAUSE TABLE (BOX)

Depending on the organization, this will be either a raised table or an outlined box on the ground. The dog must stay in either a sit or a down for a specified length of time before the handler releases him to finish the course.

A-FRAME

This obstacle consists of two ramps joined at the top to make an A shape. The ramps are 8 or 9 feet in length and 3 to 4 feet wide. The total height ranges from 5 feet to 5 feet, 11 inches, depending on the venue. The dog must climb up one side of the A-frame and down the other.

TEETER

Similar to a child's teeter-totter, the teeter is 12 feet long, 12 inches wide, and 24 inches high at its tipping point. The dog must walk up one side of the teeter, tip it, and then walk down the other.

Contact Zone

The A-frame, the teeter, and the dog walk are contact obstacles — that is, each has a 42-inch yellow contact zone at the beginning and end of the apparatus. The dog must touch the yellow part with at least one paw as he enters and leaves the obstacle or he will be penalized.

DOGWALK

Requiring careful maneuvering, the dogwalk consists of two sloped ramps with a 6- to 12-foot-long board in between. The center board is 46 to 50 inches high. The ramps and center board are usually 12 inches wide. The dog must ascend one ramp, cross the center board, and descend the other ramp.

Canine Competition

Agility offers a huge array of competition opportunities — from very small local trials to very large televised national and international trials. Not everyone who does agility competes. Many handlers prefer to simply participate in weekly classes as a way to have fun with their dogs and enhance their bond. Other handlers become very competitive. Most trainers recommend entering a trial at least once, if only to figure out whether you and your dog enjoy it or not. You might be surprised by how much your dog likes the action and the attention!

At an agility trial, the standard, or regular, agility courses consist of a numbered course with the teeter, A-frame, and dog walk, as well as tunnels and weaves. The course has 15 to 22 obstacles depending on the level of competition. Everyone at the same level runs the same course; dogs at higher levels run more complicated, difficult layouts. The goal is to complete the course in the shortest time with the fewest faults. Agility dogs are vying to complete enough points to title, but in some organizations they also place against the other competitors on a particular day.

Many organizations also offer games that are played just for fun. A few of the most common are described here.

- **Jumpers and Jumpers with Weaves.** These courses have just jumps or a combination of jumps and weaves.

- **Snooker.** Teams complete a sequence of obstacles, then accumulate points by choosing obstacles with point values based on difficulty, and then complete a final sequence of obstacles.

- **Gambler's Choice.** Obstacles are given points and handlers have to strategize and choose which obstacles to try to complete for the most points possible.

- **Team Relay.** Two teams complete a course together.

- **Defined Gambler's.** The handler directs the dog from behind a line to perform the obstacles at a distance.

ORGANIZATIONS

American Kennel Club (AKC) AKC events are open only to purebred dogs.

North American Dog Agility Council, Inc. (NADAC) NADAC attracts both serious competitors as well as those who are in it just for the fun of the game. Some participants feel that NADAC is not as competitive as USDAA; however, NADAC places more emphasis on speed.

United Kennel Club (UKC) Although the UKC is a purebred organization, its performance events are open to dogs of all breeds, including mixes. The UKC promotes the "Total Dog" and the idea that working ability outweighs looks.

United States Dog Agility Association (USDAA) Serious competitors often prefer USDAA to the other organizations, saying that the courses are more difficult and the competition level is higher.

QUALIFYING FOR AGILITY TITLES

Each agility organization has its own titles and requirements.

LEVEL	QUALIFICATION REQUIREMENTS
AKC	
Novice Agility Dog	Obtain 3 qualifying scores in Novice Class
Open Agility Dog	Obtain 3 qualifying scores in Open Class
Agility Dog Excellent	Obtain 3 qualifying scores in Excellent Class
NADAC	
Novice Agility	Earn 30 points in Novice Agility Class
Open Agility	Earn 30 points in Open Agility Class
Elite Agility	Earn 30 points in Elite Agility Class
UKC	
United Agility Dog I	Obtain 3 qualifying scores, 3 different events
United Agility Dog II	Obtain 3 qualifying scores, 3 different events
United Agility Champion	Earn 100 points in qualifying classes
USDAA	
Agility Dog	Obtain 3 qualifying scores in Starters Standard Class
Advanced Agility Dog	Obtain 3 qualifying scores in Advanced Standard Class
Master Agility Dog	Obtain 3 qualifying scores in Masters Standard Class and 1 qualifying score in each game (Pairs, Gambler's, Snooker, and Jumpers)

FABULOUS FLYBALL

Holding a flyball dog who is waiting for his turn is pure adrenaline — especially if that dog is a large, young, and muscular black Lab named Taz. As I hold on to his leather collar I need to brace myself against the wall to keep from being knocked off my feet. As the third dog in the relay comes barreling over the final hurdle and seemingly straight at us, Taz strains and fights, barking madly.

When I release him, he immediately goes silent and leaps away from my hands. For a moment it looks as if he will collide with the incoming dog but they pass one another with just inches separating them. Taz bounds over the hurdles, slams all four paws into the flyball box, catches the ball, and hurdles back toward me.

As his reward, I offer him a rope toy that seems disconcertingly short to me.

When he leaps over the last hurdle and straight at the rope, it takes all of my strength to keep him from ripping it out of my hand. We play tug-of-war for a minute until his owner relieves me. I look down at my hands, which are wet with saliva, and realize that my thumb is bleeding where Taz bit into me instead of the rope. My hands are shaking, my arms are like wet noodles, and I feel like I just rode a roller coaster. I totally get this sport.

The first thing handlers point out about flyball is that you have to have the right sort of dog. A flyball competition is chaotic, noisy (the dogs rarely stop barking), and intense. But amazingly, the adrenaline that is so clearly surging through the dogs as they play and wait their turns is rarely misdirected toward other dogs. Flyball dogs must be extremely focused and motivated. They have to summon a high pitch of excitement for the game, but need to be able to keep the excitement directed toward the game and only the game. "We love this sport; it's a lot of fun," says Barbara Reisinger, who competes with her 11-year-old papillon, Tiffany. "It's beneficial to any dog — the socialization and the ability to maintain a focus in absolutely chaotic surroundings."

The second thing about flyball is that it is a team sport in the true sense of the phrase and, as such, completely unlike any other canine sport. Each handler–dog team is part of a relay team made up of four dogs and four handlers (plus a handler–dog team alternate and a flyball box loader), none of whom can compete without the others. Then there is the club team, usually made up of a number of relay teams (and some handler–dog teams switch between relay teams, depending on where they are needed most). All of the teams depend on one another and often become quite close in the process.

The Basics of Flyball

Flyball reportedly got started in the early 1970s when a group of dog trainers added tennis balls into an obedience hurdle and scent-discrimination exercise. The sport came to national attention when one of those dog trainers was invited to give a flyball demonstration on the *Johnny Carson Show*. Some 30 years later, the North American Flyball Association (NAFA) registers over 16,000 members.

Flyball is a relay race among dogs. Each team has a minimum of five people and a maximum of six dogs. Only four dogs run each relay. Each dog needs a handler and each team has a box loader, who loads a new tennis ball for each dog. Because the dogs are spaced just seconds apart, this seemingly minor job can have great importance. A fumbled ball by the box loader can lead to a loss.

Some Words to Know

Height dog: The smallest dog on the team, whose size determines the height of the hurdles for the whole team

Standard dog: Larger dogs who can run faster than the height dog

There are four 51-foot tracks laid out at least 10 feet apart and lined with long mats. Along the track are four hurdles with 10 feet between each and a flyball box at one end. The height of the hurdles depends on the height of the smallest dog, so most teams have at least one "height dog," often a fleet-footed Jack Russell terrier. The hurdles measure four inches higher than the height of the shortest dogs, so generally range from 8 inches to 16 inches.

In the game, each canine team member jumps over each of the four hurdles, hits the flyball box with all four paws, releasing a spring-loaded tennis ball that the dog must catch in his mouth. In this same movement, the dog pushes off the flyball box and starts back over the hurdles. As the dog crosses the finish line, the next dog is released. Teams of experienced flyball dogs seem almost to cross on top of one another.

The first team to complete the run wins, and points earned toward titles are based on the times in which the teams complete the relay. In this way, each team competes against the other teams, as well as their own time.

Who Does Flyball?

If your dog is fast, ball-crazy, and very tolerant of other dogs, flyball might be just the sport for him. As papillon Tiffany shows, the size of the dog doesn't matter in flyball, though there are two sizes of dogs that appear most often in flyball. Speedy medium-sized dogs such as Aussies, Border collies, and American Staffordshire terriers excel at this sport.

And then there are the smaller height dogs, whose size determines the height of the jumps. Lower jumps mean faster times for the larger dogs, but that must be balanced with the speed of the height

dog. While some teams are happy to use almost any small but spirited dog, such as a rat terrier or bichon frise, other teams exclusively run Jack Russell terriers as height dogs because of their tremendous speed and drive. Though flyball is a sport for the speed demons of the canine world, sight hounds such as greyhounds and whippets aren't often seen because these dogs tend to be less ball-motivated than a flyball dog needs to be.

RESCUE DOGS ROCK

Many outstanding flyball dogs are rescues, who often have the perfect disposition for a fast-paced, high-energy sport. Often the same dogs who are too energetic for a working family are heaven-sent flyball dogs.

"Most of our dogs are rescues," says Joy Adiletta of the Jet City Jumpers team of Seattle. "They are all personal pets and none have been bred specifically for flyball. We have goldens, many Labs, a fox terrier, a rat terrier, a shepherd, a Jack Russell terrier, a papillon, a flat-coated retriever, and a beagle. In the past we've had a Sheltie. We're open to just about anybody as long as the dog has play drive and is not aggressive."

Flyball is, however, one of the few canine sports other than sledding where you still see active breed development to meet the standards of the sport. Carol Hefler, a sports medicine veterinarian and longtime flyball handler, for example, bought a Border collie/Staffordshire terrier cross who was bred specifically for flyball. Hot Shot is already living up to his name. A number of other handlers now run Border collie/Jack Russell terrier crosses, looking for height dogs who don't sacrifice speed.

THE PEOPLE PLAYERS

As for the people who do the sport, they are split about evenly between the genders, with perhaps a small percentage more women than men. "There are a lot of couples in flyball," says Adiletta. "Our club is almost all couples. Because it's more of a team sport, you have the opportunity to work with your spouse or partner."

If you don't want to do a sport in which three other dogs and their handlers depend on you, flyball isn't for you. It's not uncommon for flyball team members to become so close that they celebrate one another's birthdays, babysit each other's dogs (and children), and travel together. Married couples may run two dogs, each handling one dog, or if they have a singleton dog, one person might handle the dog while the other works as the ball loader or helps out in other ways.

Flyball teams range from the very casual to the very serious. Many dog athlete handlers point to flyball as the most competitive of the modern dog sports, but it definitely depends on the club. It's

FLYBALL SAFETY

Unfortunately, flyball is one sport that gives some veterinarians cause for concern. Although competitors are working hard to develop a more orthopedically friendly flyball box, the speeds and quick turns necessary for success in flyball have led to back problems for many dogs. Individual dogs with spinal problems or breeds disposed to spinal problems, such as dachshunds, should not do flyball. For this reason, many competitors are now training their dogs to do turns that have less impact on their spines.

"We try to teach the dogs to hit the flyball box with all four legs, in what we call a swimmer's turn," says Joy Adiletta of the Jet City Jumpers team. "This mitigates the potential for injury. I'm sure there will be other improvements over time, but training is a big part of it." Adiletta adds that there have been several safety improvements in just the past six years.

Another important safety requirement in flyball is that dogs be very tolerant of other dogs. Because flyball involves dogs hurtling toward each other at very high speeds, a flyball dog must be confident and nonreactive toward other dogs.

Handlers also caution against overtraining dogs and pushing them too hard. An aggressive training regimen may work for a year or two, but eventually the dogs burn out. Weekly flyball training coupled with cross-training in other dog sports or daily runs or walks is just about right for most flyball dogs.

important to consider what you want before you join one. If you just want to do something fun and stress-free with your dog once a week, a casual club is your calling. If you want to make it to national competition, however, look for a club that has the same goals and level of dedication.

Talking about Training and Time

Training for flyball begins with exposure to playing ball, basic obedience, and great socialization. Because of the high intensity of flyball, it's very important that a flyball dog be well-trained and responsive to commands. He should also have had a lot of early socialization with loud noises, other dogs, new people, and unfamiliar places.

Although some dogs take to flyball with little incremental training, most dogs must be introduced to the sport slowly. Nearly all trainers recommend that dogs learn first the hurdles and then the flyball box before putting it all together.

BEGINNING TRAINING

To begin training the hurdles, two handlers are required. First, the dog is placed at the finish line, facing away from the box. The helper holds the dog while the handler runs away from the dog, calling to him. The helper releases the dog, and the dog runs to the handler. Next the helper holds the dog immediately behind the first hurdle, and the handler runs away. Each time the dog reaches the handler, he receives lots of praise and a tug game or other reward. After each training jump is trained reliably, the next hurdle is added, until the dog is racing over all four hurdles after the handler.

Then the direction of the training is reversed, aimed toward the flyball box, one hurdle at a time. Once the dog is reliably doing all the hurdles each way, the ball is added. At first it is placed on the

ground. Once the dog is grabbing the ball from the ground after the four hurdles, the flyball box is introduced. To introduce the flyball box, the helper loads the box while you hold your dog about a foot away. Letting your dog see you do it, you throw the ball to the box loader, who immediately places it into the box. When the dog moves forward to get the ball, he triggers the flyball box, which is spring loaded to release the ball when the dog puts two paws on it.

A dog can become hung up at any point in the training process, so it's best to work closely with a team to get your dog over the humps. And there are always new techniques that are being invented by motivated flyballers.

Although some dogs learn more quickly, it takes most dogs about six to nine months to really understand the game. Handlers recommend that the dog be encouraged to watch other dogs doing flyball while learning the game, because they often catch on more quickly after watching the other dogs play.

Evaluating Equipment and Expense

The necessary equipment for flyball include a flyball box, hurdles, mats, and a ball. The balls come in different sizes (3, 2, and 1½ inches), and there is no rule about what size ball must be used. The flyball box is a wooden or molded plastic box with a slanted front; a spring system shoots the ball into the air when the dog hits the front panel. Although flyball boxes can be bought, many teams and individuals build their own according to the regulations laid out by NAFA. Teams need boxes for practice and must supply

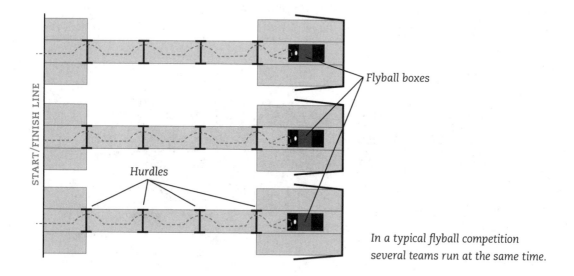

START/FINISH LINE

Flyball boxes

Hurdles

In a typical flyball competition several teams run at the same time.

their own boxes for competition. They also provide their own balls. The host team provides the mats and hurdles for competition.

Part of the reason that individual teams work as part of a larger club group is to help defray training and equipment costs. Most clubs share several flyball boxes and sets of mats. They must also rent indoor arena time for practice. (Although tournaments are sometimes held on grass, it's considered harder on the dogs and is rarely used as a regular practice surface.)

With costs shared by all of the club members, practice fees are usually reasonable — perhaps $5 or $10 per dog per practice. Tournament fees can run between $80 and $100 per team per day, which adds up if you run more than one dog. There are also travel fees to consider.

Canine Competition

In competition, the goal of the game is to beat the other teams and to beat your own time. Teams place according to which team finishes the race first, but they title based on their own speed regardless of the other teams.

Points are based on the team's time, regardless of how they place against other competitors. Times under 32 seconds earns each team member 1 point; times under 28 seconds earns each team member 5 points; and times under 24 seconds earns each team member 25 points. Points are accumulated toward titles.

At a competition there are three to five heats per race and four to six races per day. Although only four dogs race in each heat, each team can have six dogs, allowing two to be switched out if one dog is racing better than another.

ORGANIZATIONS

North American Flyball Association (NAFA) NAFA is the predominate flyball club in the United States.

TITLES	POINTS
Flyball Dog	20 points
Flyball Dog Excellent	100 points
Flyball Dog Champion	500 points
Flyball Dog Champion-Silver	1,000 points
Flyball Dog Champion-Gold	2,500 points
Flyball Master	5,000 points
Flyball Master Excellent	10,000 points
Flyball Master Champion	15,000 points
Onyx Award	20,000 points
Flyball Grand Champion	30,000 points
Hobbes	100,000 points

AUDACIOUS DISC DOG

"Nice!" The announcer sounds more like a teenage surfer than a sports announcer as a Border collie named Zephyr leaps into the air and catches the disc thrown to him by handler Robert Gutierrez. A few minutes later Aaron Abrahamson and his seven-year-old blue merle Aussie, Leo, take to the field. This is a team that consistently makes it to the World Championships. As the music begins, Abrahamson kneels on the grass and lightly tosses several discs in a row to Leo, who catches them easily.

As the routine progresses the moves become increasingly difficult, with Leo vaulting off of Abrahamson's thigh, rolling on the ground and leaping up to catch a disc, weaving through Abrahamson's legs, and finally vaulting off of his back. The routine ends with Leo jumping into Abrahamson's arms while catching one final disc.

It's the Expert division at the Sky-houndz Northwest Regional Canine Disc Championship. Held at a local golf course, it's canine disc in high style — rock music blaring as dogs flip and spin while catching discs in midair; a crowd of onlookers, many with their own dogs; and lots of young guys in bare feet and tie-dyed shirts playing with their dogs and occasionally grabbing a beer from a cooler.

This is the essence of canine disc — athletic but laid-back, fun but competitive. Disc dogs and their handlers train hard, compete hard, and play hard — they are the extreme athletes of the dog sports world. A combination of edginess, irreverence, and sheer athleticism differentiates disc dog from other canine sports.

Millions of dogs and their people play with flying discs every day, but only a few take it to the high art of competition and demonstration. Canine disc began in the early 1970s with a high-flying publicity stunt by Alex Stein, a Los Angeles college student with a Frisbee-loving whippet named Ashley. During a 1974 baseball game between the Kansas City Reds and the L.A. Dodgers, Stein and Ashley snuck onto the field and stopped the game by doing the first televised canine disc demo. The crowd was wowed by the stunt, and soon Stein and Ashley were doing demos all over the country. In 1975, Stein started the Frisbee Dog World Championships.

The Basics of Disc Dog

There are several organizations that oversee disc dog competitions, including Skyhoundz, Ashley Whippet, and International Disc Dog Handlers' Association. They each have nuanced differences in the way they judge and divide competitions. Each organization has two main divisions: Freestyle or Freeflight, and Distance and Accuracy, which is also called Catch and Retrieve, Toss and Fetch, or Mini-Distance.

Distance and Accuracy consists of the handler throwing as many discs as possible as far as possible in a limited amount of time. The dog is judged on how many discs he catches, how long the throw is, and whether he catches the disc with all four feet in the air.

Disc-o Dancing?

In spite of the casual approach, disc dog uses the same skills — in both handler and dog — as those found in obedience, agility, and even canine freestyle. Although the latter may seem diametrically opposed to disc dog, the two sports are surprisingly similar. Except for the discs, the costumes, and the choice of music, the routines consist of athletic tricks performed by handler and dog in time to music.

In Freestyle, the team does a routine that is set to music and involves complicated tricks as well as disc catching. The tricks include vaults, jumps, and flips.

Disc dog isn't all about competition, though. There are a number of very talented disc teams for whom competition isn't the end-all and be-all. Rather, they are among the rare few that actually make a living pursuing their sport, mostly by charging to perform demos and occasionally by sponsorships. There are also a number of teams who do occasional demos for local TV shows, other dog events and charities.

Who Does Disc Dog?

Disc dog depends on the skill of both members of the team more than almost any other canine sport. If the handler throws the disc poorly, the dog won't be able to catch it well. This may explain why disc dog is one of the oddball canine sports whose humans are almost all male and younger than 50. In most canine sports, older women far outnumber men, but in disc dog the ratio is about 80 percent men to 20 percent women.

It may be that the abundance of males in canine disc has more to do with their confidence in throwing a disc than anything else. Many boys grow up playing Frisbee, so the skill translates easily into canine disc. Some of the top canine disc handlers have experience in Frisbee golf or Ultimate Frisbee, giving them a real edge on the competition. Women tend not to have this Frisbee background and some people may find learning a new skill in front of an audience disconcerting.

OPEN TO ALL DOGS

Most dogs can play disc as long as they are sound. Tiny Yorkies play (with specially made smaller discs) and American Staffordshire terriers play. The exceptions are larger dogs for whom jumping takes a toll on hips and joints. However, as in many canine sports, it's the Aussies and Border collies who excel. At most

DISC SAFETY

With so much jumping, disc has the potential to be one of the most dangerous canine sports. Dogs are not allowed to compete until they are 14 months old because jumping on young legs can lead to serious arthritis as the dog ages. Jumping and landing on just two feet puts a great deal of pressure on the knees and spine, so dogs are taught to always land on four paws, though this isn't always realistic.

Overworking happens easily with highly driven animals who will not stop when they're exhausted or even in pain. Keep a close eye on your dog when training and performing. If he indicates any reluctance to jump or run, it's time for a break. Watch for limping or tenderness of any sort.

Although disc seems like the perfect summer-day sport, good handlers avoid playing during the hottest times of the day. Dogs exert a huge amount of energy doing canine disc and can quickly become dehydrated or even suffer from heat stroke if not well monitored. The dogs should be offered water before, during, and after a disc session. Many dog handlers keep a filled children's wading pool available for their dogs to jump into for a cooling break.

Bloat is also an issue for this high-intensity activity. Dogs shouldn't be fed during the half hour to two hours before or after playing disc depending on the breed.

events, fully 75 percent of the participants are Aussies or Aussie mixes.

Even dogs with disabilities can compete in canine disc. Troy Kerstetter and Lynne Ouchida's Aussie, Maty, has only three legs, but that didn't stop her from placing seventh at the 2007 Hyperflite Skyhoundz World Championship.

The dogs who do best in canine disc aren't simply the fastest or the most agile. "In disc, your dog has to have creativity, really," says Jenny Abrahamson, who competes with her husband, Aaron, and their dogs, Leo and Elsa. "Your dog has to have a feel for it. He needs to know where your body is."

Dogs less than 14 months of age are not allowed to compete. Dogs who are overweight or have joint problems or arthritis should not participate. As disc dogs age, their handlers may begin to throw the disc closer to the ground so the dog doesn't need to jump in order to catch it. Because dogs are off leash when competing, aggressive or easily distracted dogs should not compete in canine disc.

The Right Stuff

Always use a disc made for dogs. Standard Frisbees will quickly break and cut the dog's mouth or be ingested. The sharp edges of a Frisbee shard can perforate the dog's intestines, in addition to causing impactions. Because discs can be hard on dogs' teeth and gums, handlers should regularly check them for snags or bits of broken plastic and smooth rough spots with sandpaper.

There is some concern that the spinning of the disc can wear down dogs' teeth. Handlers say that tennis balls are actually harder on dogs' teeth and that proper discs made for dogs should not cause problems; however, some handlers prefer to use softer discs when practicing.

Talking about Training and Time

The basic training for disc dog is getting your dog used to and interested in the disc. Some dogs are naturally interested; others aren't. If possible, begin exposing your dog to the disc when he's still a puppy. To prevent him from jumping, roll the disc on the ground for him to chase. Leave it out where he can sniff it and play with it. Most dogs with the disc gene will show an interest right away. Gradually begin throwing the disc to him and slowly increase the distances as he makes more frequent catches.

To ensure that he will bring the disc back to you, never throw another disc for him until he's brought the first one back (you may need to attach a long line to his collar to reel him in if he is more inter-

ested in the catch than the retrieve part of the exercise). In addition, teach him a reliable command to release the disc. "Leave it!" or "Drop!" work well.

Finding a spot to play disc can be difficult as you need a wide open area, and you can't keep your dog on leash to participate in this sport. (For this reason, your dog must have a rock-solid recall before you take him out in public to train.) Be aware that this can put you at risk for fines and can cause negative interactions with other residents where you live. Also, always be aware of what other off-leash dogs in the area are doing. Your dog may be way too focused on his disc to start a fight, but his running can lead to a chase instinct among other dogs, which can possibly end in a scuffle.

CHECK IT OUT

A good way to get started is to check out some demos or competitions. Go to one of the recognized disc organizations' Web sites and see what is going on in your region. Watch the competitors, ask lots of questions, and see if it looks like something you would be interested in doing. Take your dog along, too. Canine disc competitions are almost always open to canine spectators (unlike many other canine sports), and you may even get a chance to try your dog out.

Try to meet up with a friendly competitor who will be willing to practice with you. Almost all competitors get their start in disc by being adopted by a veteran who is willing to share his or her experience.

Evaluating Equipment and Expense

Of course, the only vital equipment for a canine disc dog is a disc! But participants warn emphatically against using a standard Frisbee with your dog, even when just messing around at home. Pet supply stores carry a number of floppy or rubber discs that are appropriate for practicing with. Handlers who plan to compete should use discs that are made of soft PVC and are no heavier than 110 grams. Competition discs are available over the Internet from canine disc organizations and can also be bought at competitions.

Buying discs can get expensive, but canine disc veterans shrug it off. Before long you won't be buying discs as you'll get so many free ones as prizes and giveaways at canine disc events. A regular competitor may gather 100 free discs a year!

For teams who do Freestyle, the handler will need some protective gear. Most handlers wear a neoprene vest or thick hunting vest for protection from sharp doggy nails when doing back vaults. For thigh vaults, a wraparound, reusable stretch bandage works well. To avoid eye injuries, handlers can wear protective goggles if they choose.

Canine Competition

There are several different organizations under which dogs compete. Each has different rules but there are set divisions that are common to all.

DIVISIONS

Distance Accuracy (Catch and Retrieve, Toss and Fetch, Mini-Distance) The dog has 60 seconds to catch and retrieve as many discs as possible. The dog is scored by the distance of the catch and how many catches he makes.

Freestyle (Freeflight) The dog and handler have 90 seconds (120 at the World Championships) to complete their routine. They are scored on presentation, athleticism, "wow" factor, and success (number of discs actually caught).

In freestyle, handlers pick the music and, although the routine isn't synced to music the way it is in canine freestyle, a good choice of music that highlights the dog's skills is appreciated. Although flashy moves such as vaults are awarded points for their athleticism and difficulty, safety is paramount and points are deducted if a dog lands awkwardly or jumps too high for safety.

Pairs Freestyle Two handlers and one dog perform a freestyle routine.

ORGANIZATIONS

International Disc Dog Handlers'
Association
This is an international disc dog organization that serves as a sanctioning body for many of the regional disc dog clubs.

Skyhoundz
This disc dog organization sponsors a series of qualifiers and local and regional championships, culminating in the World Championship.

Unified Frisbeedog Operations (UFO)
Founded in 2000, the UFO organizes an international World Cup series showcasing the world's best disc dogs.

U.S. Disc Dog National
An international organization, USDDN hosts several disc championship series, including the U.S. Disc Dog International Finals.

TITLES

Each organization divides handlers and dogs by factors including handler and dog's experience, handler's gender, and dog's size. For example, in Skyhoundz, dogs and handlers compete in distance accuracy and freestyle in the following divisions:

Expert

Masters (for dogs over 9 years of age)

Novice

Youth

Micro (for dogs under 25 pounds)

Women

DIVING INTO DOCK JUMPING

On a cool early-summer day in Kirkland, Washington, a crowd of onlookers fills a parking lot. Although my mental image of a dock-jumping contest involved a long dock on a mountain lake, these onlookers are, in fact, filling bleachers that surround a large portable pool with about four feet of water.

At one end of the clear blue pool is a wooden dock covered with indoor/outdoor carpeting. Loud rock music pumps through speakers, punctuated by an announcer's voice and nearly drowned out by the barking of excited dogs. The area behind the pool is swarming with at least 30 handler–dog teams waiting their turns. The dogs — large, small, hairy, and nearly hairless — are all sopping wet and grinning big doggy grins.

A woman parked in a folding camping chair cheers loudly as a big black flat-coated retriever takes to the dock. His handler tosses a rubber bumper into the air, and the dog runs down the dock and launches off the end of the dock into the air after it. His body arcs as he reaches for the bumper, and for a moment he seems suspended above the clear blue water. As the dog leaps, the woman rises from her chair and when he hits the water with a loud splash, she pumps her fists into the air. With a huge grin on her face she turns toward me and says as excitedly as the proud parent of the game-winning football kicker, "That's my dog!"

Kristi Baird is a dock-jumping handler and trainer who says that the joy of dock jumping is watching how much the dogs love to jump and how much their owners love to watch them. "With dogs, toys, and water, you just can't go wrong!" The older of Baird's two chocolate labs, five-year-old Henna, is a Master Jumper, meaning she jumps over 20 feet. Baird, her husband, Chris, and daughter, Elizabeth, are all active in dock jumping. Like many of the sport's enthusiasts, Baird first learned about dock jumping on ESPN and knew that it was the perfect sport for Henna. "Henna is just a natural jumper," she says. "She loves jumping off docks and bulkheads, and she even leaps from the edge of the beach into the water."

At her first competition, Henna took second place with a jump of 15 feet. "We were hooked!" says Baird. "It was cold and wet, but we were having a blast. We've gone to nearly every competition up and down the West Coast since."

For those who love dock jumping, much of the attraction is seeing their dogs' intrinsic skill and athleticism. Dock jumping celebrates a specialized hunting skill bred into many hunting dogs — the water entry — and many of the best dock-jumping dogs are retrievers, spaniels, and setters. Although most hunters who work waterfowl discourage big, splashy water entries when actually hunting, some dock jumpers are also active hunting dogs, such as Baird's chocolate Labs who hunt upland fowl. Most of the dogs who participate, however, just plain love to jump into water and retrieve a toy.

The Basics of Dock Jumping

"It's dock *jumping,* not diving," Dave Garland corrects me with a little irritation. Garland is the president of the Puget Sound Dock Dogs club and the handler of five-year-old Daniel, an English springer spaniel whose best jump is 18 feet. Garland fields a lot of questions about this newly minted sport — clearly, some of them more often than others.

Dock jumping has received a lot of press and has grown in leaps and bounds since its debut in 2000 on the ESPN show

"Great Outdoor Games." The show promoted outdoor sports such as archery and bass fishing and also included canine hunting tests and dock jumping, under the name of Big Air Dogs. Though expected to be a novelty demonstration with a small draw, the Big Air demo proved more popular than many of the Games' competitive events. Thousands of people showed up and even more watched on TV. Although water entries are an intrinsic part of waterfowl hunting, and dock jumping had long been a hobby enjoyed by privileged dogs with access to a dock, dock jumping as a sport had never been seen before.

The interest was immediate. DockDogs was established in 2002 as a sanctioning organization to field competitive events and establish rules and regulations. In their first year the group sanctioned six events. In 2006 it sanctioned 65 events and the organization continues to grow.

COMPETITION STANDARDS

In competition, dogs jump from a dock that is exactly 40 feet long and 24 inches above the pool. Dogs take a running start or jump from the end of the dock. The distances are measured from the edge of the dock to the point where the base of the dog's tail lands in the water. There are two judges on either side of the pool and a steward on the dock, who signals the teams when they are on deck and when it's clear for them to begin.

At national DockDogs events, the jumps are measured using video cameras equipped with digital measurement software that was developed by ESPN for the Olympics. At local club events, the jumps are measured by sight by two certified judges, who estimate to the nearest inch.

In addition to the Big Air distance events, there is the Extreme Vertical event, in which dogs try to grab or knock off a bumper that hangs in the air from an extender at least eight feet from the dock. There are two divisions: one for novices with the bumper starting at five feet above the water and an advanced one with the bumper starting at six feet.

Who Does Dock Jumping?

The number-one prerequisite in this sport is a dog who loves water. There are no breed restrictions or limitations, though the bird dogs that were bred to hunt waterfowl, such as Labs, Chesapeake Bay retrievers, and flat-coated retrievers, are among the most common and often most proficient in the sport. Mixed breeds of all shapes and sizes compete, however, as do a surprising number of American pit bull terriers, who thrive in many dog sports. According to Dave

Garland, a 130-pound Leonberger in the Puget Sound Dock Dog club consistently places among the finalists. The 2008 world record holder, at 28 feet 10 inches, is a greyhound mix.

Dogs must be at least six months old to compete. They should be very toy-motivated (no treats are allowed in competition) and confident — jumping off of a two-foot dock into clear blue water with rock music blaring and hundreds of onlookers shouting is intimidating.

Many of the people who participate in dock jumping are off-season hunters or former hunters. Like those handlers involved in hunt tests and field trials, they love to show off their gun dogs' instinctive skills and passion. Unlike in most dog sports, there appear to be more men involved in dock jumping than women. This may well stem from the fact that hunting attracts more men than women.

Competitors can vary as much as their dogs, however. A burly guy in a camouflage hunting cap holding the leash of a field-bred pointer may be waiting for his turn behind a young woman with a pierced eyebrow and a pit bull/Aussie mix. Many families and couples are also involved in this sport. Children who are seven years old and older are invited to participate, and many do. While Mom or Dad jumps one dog, the child may jump another. In some multi-dog families, every member of the family jumps a dog.

The friendly atmosphere attracts many to the sport. "We have traveled around this country and met wonderful families and individuals who become like a giant extended family," says Baird. "There are folks from all different walks of life who come out to play on the dock. The thing we all have in common is that we like to take our dogs out to play."

Talking about Training and Time

Basic preparation for dock jumping, in pups and adults, comes down to lots of water time and lots of toy time. A dog who loves water and loves toys will enjoy the sport, regardless of breed or background. If possible, owners interested in getting their dog into dock jumping should try to find a public dock, bank, or really nice friend with a pool to do some confidence building.

Experienced dock jumpers recommend that dogs be comfortable in the water, interested in toys, and confident with noise and crowds. A Big Air competition can be intimidating for a first-timer, so dogs shouldn't be pushed or bullied in any way. Rather, keep it upbeat and fun. If the dog is too nervous to jump, there's always next time.

Safety Considerations

The beauty of dock jumping is that dogs jump into water, making the impact much less severe. As they become more competitive, however, many handlers will train their dogs on land in the off-season or when they don't have access to water by doing hurdle jumps and high jumps.

As in all sports that involve jumping, handlers must take care not to stress their dogs' joints and muscles. Repetitive jumping can lead to serious joint disorders, including osteoarthritis, as the dog ages. To prevent injury, dry-land training should be moderate and dock jumping should not be overdone.

Dogs less than one year of age, whose bodies are still developing, should not engage in any jumping activities, including dock jumping.

And, as is the case with many modern dog sports, the circumstances of a large number of very excited dogs in a small locale can lead to fights among aggressive dogs. Dogs who show aggression toward other participants — dog or human — are disqualified from the event.

THROWING TECHNIQUE

For those who are really serious about dock jumping, there is some ongoing training for both dog and handler. A good throwing technique can make the difference between an Elite and a Super Elite jumper. Although many handlers just throw the toy and encourage the dog to jump into the water after it, the 40-foot dock provides room for some technique as well.

Handlers generally choose either the chase technique or the place technique. With the chase technique, the handler places her dog toward the middle of the dock and gives the command to stay, releasing the dog as she throws the bumper right ahead of the dog's nose. In the place technique, the handler takes the dog to the front of the dock and throws the bumper into the water, making sure the dog sees it. Then the handler takes the dog to the back of the dock before giving the command to fetch the bumper.

A good throw also depends on what a particular dog needs — some dogs respond best to a long, arcing toss, others to a canine fastball. You can have the best pitcher's arm in the world, but if your style doesn't excite your dog, it won't do you much good in dock jumping. The best handler–dog teams work hard to perfect the best technique for their particular team.

THE PEOPLE PLAYERS

The people who participate in dock jumping are highly motivated to attract new teams, so they make it easy to participate. Every DockDogs competition offers newcomers a chance to try it out for a few dollars. If the dog enjoys it, the handler can then pay the standard fee to enter the competition. Most competitions cover two days and offer at least two noncompetitive jumps per day. These events offer a great opportunity to learn as there is always a trainer on hand, and most handlers are happy to share their experience.

Evaluating Equipment and Expense

All you need is a fun toy, some water, and a dock. Most people use tennis balls, floating toys, or the bumpers used for training hunting dogs. The toy should be something the dog becomes very excited about. Although a standard length dock or pool setup is required for competition, the dock height really doesn't matter in training. A bank into a lake or river also does fine. When possible, handlers try to find public docks where dogs are allowed to emulate more closely a competition scenario. Unfortunately, these are few and far between, although some dock-jumping clubs are able to make arrangements to use private docks or to obtain occasional permits to use public docks for practice.

In competition, the equipment requirements are more stringent. The dock is 40 feet long and 24 inches off the water and covered with rubber matting or indoor/outdoor carpet to prevent slipping. If a portable pool is used, there is a ramp leading out of the water onto an exit ramp. Dock-jumping organizations also use public lake ramps for competition. Although the dock must always be 40 feet or be marked at 40 feet, the 24-inch height requirement is sometimes waived.

Dock jumping is among the sports that require the least amount of expense and time commitment. This sport is really just for the fun of it. Practice is done individually and occasionally with a club. Members are expected to pay a small fee to help offset costs. To compete, handlers usually pay $20 per heat or wave (consisting of two jumps).

The greatest expense incurred is in traveling to and from competitions. Because of the newness of the sport, there isn't yet the opportunity to compete as compared with other sports. Many competitors travel several hundred miles to compete. But this can also be part of the fun.

Canine Competition

At sanctioned DockDogs events, dogs are split into several divisions that compete in waves or heats. At their first Big Air competition, the dogs do a qualifying jump and then compete at that distance until they make at least five jumps at their division level. Once they complete five jumps, they earn a title in that division and are allowed to move on to the next division if they wish. They are also invited to the National Championships.

ORGANIZATIONS

DockDogs is the largest and best established of the dock-jumping organizations. It was begun in conjunction with the Big Air Dog events held at the ESPN Great Outdoor Games and has the official license with ESPN.

Splash Dogs is an unaffiliated national dock-jumping club that for now operates only in the western United States. Their rules and divisions are slightly different from DockDogs.

TITLES	QUALIFICATIONS
Novice Jumper (NJ)	Five jumps, or legs, within Novice division in a one-year period
Junior Jumper (JJ)	Five jumps within Junior division in a one-year period
Senior Jumper (SJ)	Five legs within Senior division in a one-year period
Master Jumper (MJ)	Five legs within Master division in a one-year period
Elite Jumper (EJ)	Five legs in Elite and/or Super Elite division in a one-year period

DOCKDOGS DIVISIONS	
Novice	1 inch to 9 feet 11 inches
Junior	10 feet to 14 feet 11 inches
Senior	15 feet to 19 feet 11 inches
Master	20 feet to 22 feet 11 inches
Elite	23 feet to 24 feet,11 inches
Super Elite	25 feet and above
Veterans	Dogs 8 years of age and older
Lap Dog	For dogs 17 inches or shorter at the shoulder
Junior Handlers	For handlers between the ages of 7 and 15
In the Extreme Vertical event, there are 2 divisions:	
Cadet	Dogs who have not previously competed nationally in a DockDogs Extreme Vertical event or have not reached at least 6 feet in height in a DockDogs event. In the Cadet division, the bumper begins at 5 feet.
Top Gun	Dogs who have competed and reached at least 6 feet in height in a DockDogs Extreme Vertical event. In Top Gun, the bumper begins at 6 feet.

— CHAPTER 7 —

Sit, Stay, Do the Hustle!

Obedience / Rally / Canine Freestyle

THE BEAUTY OF OBEDIENCE, rally, and canine freestyle is how naturally they extend a dog's basic obedience training. From puppy kindergarten to basic training and on to the rigor of competitive obedience, the fun of rally, or the grace of canine freestyle — these sports are natural outlets for an inquisitive and trainable dog's skill and interest. They also complement other canine sports, as well as other aspects of a dog's life. A dog who excels in any of these sports will make a better companion and be able to join in almost any family activity.

THE ELEGANCE OF OBEDIENCE

In a cavernous hall full of rings outlined by white wooden fences, a golden retriever looks up at his handler with what can only be described as adoration. As they wait for the judge's cue, the dog stands so close to his handler that he almost seems attached to her. The judge, an older woman with a serious look on her face, signals the team, and they step forward.

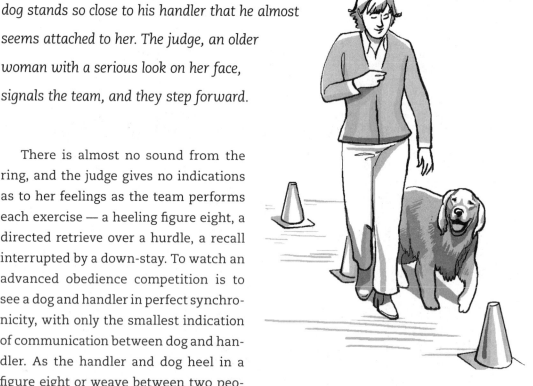

There is almost no sound from the ring, and the judge gives no indications as to her feelings as the team performs each exercise — a heeling figure eight, a directed retrieve over a hurdle, a recall interrupted by a down-stay. To watch an advanced obedience competition is to see a dog and handler in perfect synchronicity, with only the smallest indication of communication between dog and handler. As the handler and dog heel in a figure eight or weave between two people, it almost seems as though the dog knows what the handler is thinking. The golden remains bouncy and eager to please throughout, and after the final exercise the judge allows herself a slight smile and a nod, while the handler's rigid posture relaxes.

The sport of obedience is a natural extension of any dog training. For many handlers, it makes sense to go from puppy kindergarten to beginning dog training and then on to more advanced levels of training. Competitive obedience takes all this obedience training to the highest levels. In competitive obedience, dogs and their handlers train diligently and are scored rigorously. Competitive obedience is also an excellent way to become involved in canine sports — a dog who can succeed in obedience can do almost anything!

Obedience is a particularly precise sport. In competition, teams begin their round with 200 points; points are subtracted each time a command is not completed perfectly. A dog may heel on command but lose points because his body doesn't align precisely with the handler's body. Handlers are not allowed to touch, lure, praise, or encourage their dog. They may give each command only once, and in some exercises the command must be nonverbal.

Although many dog owners are turned off by the precision and formality of competitive obedience, Curt Curtis, assistant vice president of AKC performance events, owes his involvement with dogs to the sport. When he was a child in Portland, Oregon, his black Lab, Prince, was threatened with being destroyed by the city after numerous incidents with aggression. The boy was given a chance to redeem his pet by undertaking an obedience test; if the dog passed he would be given a provisional license and allowed to live. Curtis threw himself into the training, and Prince became the fourth dog in the city's history to receive a provisional license.

Curtis went on to become a professional handler and judge in a number of canine sports but always comes back to what he considers the cornerstone of all dog sports. "No matter what canine sport you do," he says, "there is some element of obedience," going on to add that "obedience is one of the few [AKC] sports in which all registered dogs can participate."

The Basics of Obedience

In obedience trials, dogs and their handlers perform increasingly complicated and difficult exercises with the goal of acute accuracy. Dogs compete at one of three levels: Novice, Open, and Utility. The complexity of exercises and the rigor of judging increase at each level.

Some Words to Know

Directed retrieve: The dog must find an object marked with the handler's scent from among several similar objects.

Down-stay: The dog must remain lying down for an extended period of time, sometimes while the handler is out of sight.

Recall: The dog must come promptly when called.

Among the skills a dog is tested on are recalls; long sits and downs; retrieves, directed retrieves, and retrieves over a hurdle; heeling; and scent discrimination. Dogs are judged individually, but there are also group exercises. For example, a group of dogs from a class are brought into the ring and asked by their handlers to sit or lie down. The handlers then leave the ring. The dogs cannot get up or interact with the other dogs while the handlers are gone.

Dogs are working for their individual titles but also compete against the other dogs within their class, with ribbons awarded for first through fourth place. Ribbons are awarded to all dogs who qualify in a test.

What's an ILP?

Both the AKC and the UKC offer unregistered dogs the option of an Indefinite Listing Privilege (ILP). This designation allows dogs without papers to compete in sanctioned events (everything but conformation).

You obtain an ILP by declaring the breed most dominant in your dog's ancestery — or basically what your dog looks like — and sending a photo to confirm it.

Who Does Obedience?

Dogs of all shapes, sizes, breeds, and mixes excel in obedience. There is no one breed of dog that does better than others (although there always seem to a lot of golden retrievers in the ring!). While the AKC and UKC allow only purebreds and mixes with an Indefinite Listing Privilege (ILP) to compete, the American Mixed Breed Obedience Registry (AMBOR) and the Association of Pet Dog Trainers (APDT) allow all dogs, regardless of parentage, a chance to show off their smarts.

Although obedience was once the most popular canine performance sport, its numbers have slipped over the last 20 years, as less exacting and more exciting sports have arrived on the scene. Handlers tend to be older, longtime participants in the sport, as many younger handlers have moved into other sports, such as rally and agility. A number of junior handlers do compete in obedience, often through 4-H or through the AKC junior handlers program.

Talking about Training and Time

Competitive obedience builds on the basic training that should begin when a dog is just a pup. Many people in obedience become interested at this early stage if their dog shows that he has a biddable and trainable disposition. Once they see their three-month-old chocolate Lab holding a sit-stay while the rest of the class members are chasing imaginary butterflies and begging for treats, they're hooked.

Training a dog for high-level obedience can be time-consuming and patience-trying because the smallest mistakes make a huge difference here. Advanced obedience teams train every day, usually in short stints to avoid burnout. Although some handlers train their competitive obedience dogs on their own, most find far greater success by training with an obedience club.

Safety Considerations

Because obedience is a low-impact sport, there really are no safety considerations besides the one or two hurdles a dog might do in a course. One of the great things about the sport is that handlers and dogs can be very limited physically and still excel.

Evaluating Equipment and Expense

The expense incurred in obedience is limited, unless teams begin traveling often for events. The equipment changes depending upon what class you are participating in. In Novice Class, the only necessary equipment is a flat collar and standard, six-foot-long leash. In Open Class, the leash is gone but a dumbbell and jump are added. In Utility Class, gloves are used for scent discrimination, in addition to the dumbbell and jump.

Canine Competition

An obedience competition is made up of a series of increasingly difficult exercises. Tasks include basic commands such as sit, stand, down, and stay; jumps; retrieves; and scent discrimination.

In a competition the dog and handler start with 200 points. Each exercise has a point value and points are taken away for faults. To pass an exercise, the team must retain at least half of the exercise points. To pass the overall test, the team must score at least 170 of the 200 points.

CLASSES

Novice Class

(most exercises performed on leash)

- Heel on and off leash, sitting when the handler stops

- Recall off leash from 50 feet

- Remain in a stand-stay while the judge touches him

- Sit-stay for one minute

- Down-stay for two minutes

Open Class

(entire test performed off leash)

- Heel

- Recall with a down before reaching handler

- Remain in a stand-stay while the judge touches him

- Sit-stay for three minutes with handler out of sight

- Down-stay for five minutes with handler out of sight

- Complete a directed jump over a hurdle, return back over the hurdle to the handler

- Retrieve a dumbbell on the flat

- Retrieve a dumbbell over a hurdle

Utility Class

(entire test performed off leash with hand signals)

- Must perform heel, down, sit, come, and stay on signals

- Remain in a stand-stay while the judge touches him and handler moves away

- Directed jump over a hurdle

- Directed retrieve

- Scent discrimination — retrieve a dumbbell and glove marked by handler from among several options

ORGANIZATIONS

American Kennel Club (AKC) AKC is the oldest and most popular obedience organization and the one on which most others are based. Classes are open to purebred registered dogs or dogs with ILP numbers.

United Kennel Club (UKC) The UKC is a purebred registry that sanctions performance events such as obedience.

Australian Shepherd Club of America (ASCA) Although this is a breed club, competition is open to other breeds if there is room in the class.

Mixed Breed Dog Club of America (MBDA) MBDA was formed to give any dog the option to title in obedience.

TITLES	QUALIFICATIONS
Companion Dog (CD)	Must complete three "legs" (events) in Novice Class with a qualifying score of 170 under three different judges
Companion Dog Excellent (CDX)	Must complete three legs in Open Class with a qualifying score of 170 under three different judges
Utility Dog (UD)	Must complete three legs in Utility Class with a qualifying score of 170 under three different judges
Utility Dog Excellent (UDX)	Must pass the Open A and Open B divisions of Utility Dog in one day at 10 different trials. (Open A is for dogs trying to earn a CDX; Open B is for dogs trying to earn a UDX. Handlers who are judges, relatives of judges, or have titled an Obedience Trial Champion cannot compete in the Open A class.)
Obedience Trial Championship (OTCh)	Must earn 100 points in competition and win three first-place ribbons under three different judges

ROMPING THROUGH RALLY

Blue the Rottweiler stands in the ring with his giant head erect and straight ahead, except for the occasional loving glances he sneaks at his handler, September Morn. Together, the pair move through a series of stations, stopping at each to perform the command indicated. The big dog heels so closely he almost seems lost in Morn's voluminous skirt. As he moves through the course, his rear end wags eagerly and Morn smiles broadly.

Each time he completes an exercise, she tells him, "Good boy!" and he wags even harder. It's hard not to smile too, watching the pair work together, the 100-pound Rottweiler looking like a giant in the small ring but clearly comfortable in his own skin.

Experienced rally enthusiasts cluster around the ring, waiting for their turns and good-naturedly sizing up the competition. A number of spectators look on, taking in the atmosphere of this fun new sport.

Rally, sometimes called rally-obedience or rally-o, is one of the big new things in the dog sports world. An offshoot of obedience, it was initially dismissed by traditional obedience handlers as "doodling," a term used to describe training tricks and doing other warm-ups for obedience. For "serious" obedience handlers, the implication is that doodling is playing, not working. However, rally is attracting many ex-obedience handlers with its looser format and more playful quality. Compared with obedience, rally is downright jovial.

"Some people in obedience denigrate rally," says Morn. "They don't realize that it's very handler-intensive; you really have that partnership with your dog and it still takes a lot of training." Morn allows, however, that rally is easier than obedience: "You don't have to memorize the course in rally; you don't have to memorize where the turns are and where you have to turn after a jump."

Being allowed to talk to your dog and encourage your dog as you go through the course also makes this sport easier than obedience. In addition, it's scored more leniently than obedience, where the slightest mistake costs points.

Tony Kim has done a variety of sports with his Rottweilers Buddy and Alley. Alley is the AKC's top obedience Rottie, and today she cruises through the rally Advanced class with 99 points out of 100. Kim comments that in rally, camaraderie is the rule rather than the exception. "Rally is very nice . . . people tend to cheer each other on and it's more fun than regular obedience. What I like best is that when there's a mistake, it's the handler's, not the dog's." He encourages newcomers to give the sport a try, adding, "It's fun for the dog; it's fun for the person."

The Basics of Rally

Rally was the brainchild of dog trainer Charles (Bud) Kramer, who was also instrumental in the establishment of agility in the United States. Kramer was looking for a way to make obedience more fun, a way to re-ignite interest in the flagging sport, and came up with the basics for rally. In 2000 he published an article in *Front and Finish,* discussing his idea for the new sport. By 2003, the AKC had adopted the sport.

In rally, there are 10 to 20 stations, each with a number and a command. The dog and handler approach each station in numerical order and perform the commands printed on the placard, which may be quite simple, such as sit or down, or may be more complicated, such as a 270-degree turn to the right while the dog stays in heel position. For example, a sign reading Turn Right One Step — Call to Heel starts with the dog sitting in heel position. The handler tells him to stay, takes one step to the right away from the dog, and the dog moves to the sit heel in the new position.

Rally is similar to obedience in that handlers begin with a certain number of points and may potentially lose points as they proceed through the course. Depending on the organization, dogs may begin with 100 or 200 points. Rally is radically different from obedience, however, in the way teams are judged and how the exercises are performed.

In obedience, the judge tells the handler which exercise to perform, while in rally the handler reads the sign at the station and then instructs the dog. Rally handlers can give commands both verbally and with signals and can give their dogs praise and encouragement throughout the exercise. In rally, teams lose only whole points, not half points, and points are deducted only when exercises are not completed or for clear faults. In obedience, half a point may be deducted when an exercise is not precisely correct. For example, if a dog sits promptly but is a few degrees off the correct angle, the team would have half a point deducted in obedience, but in rally the team would win the full point as long as the dog sat.

Who Does Rally?

A huge range of people has shown interest in this new sport. It is the only canine sport sanctioned by the American Pet Dog Trainers Association (APDT), a large and varied group. One of the beautiful things about rally is that almost any handler and any dog can do it, regardless of size, age, or physical ability.

"Agility is one of our most popular events and rally is rapidly moving in that direction," says Curt Curtis, assistant vice president of AKC performance events. "Rally is a new sport [but] it almost doubled in growth in its first year of existence." There were 74,000 total AKC entries in its first year and over 104,000 AKC entries in its second year. Although AKC rally events are open exclusively to purebreds, the APDT welcomes mixes.

Safety Considerations

Because rally is a low-impact sport, there really are no safety considerations besides the one or two hurdles a dog might do in a course. One of the great things about the sport is that handlers and dogs can be very limited physically and still excel.

Talking about Training and Time

Training rally, as with other dog sports, begins with basic obedience. A puppy kindergarten class is the perfect place to start, followed by at least one additional beginning obedience class.

Once your dog understands the basic commands, you can enroll in a rally class. If there are no classes in your region, shop around for an obedience teacher who is open to rally. You can also train on your own.

As with most sports, limit training to a couple of 10- or 15-minute sessions per day to keep your pooch from getting bored. The great thing about rally is that the exercises vary, so you're not just training one thing over and over, and you're encouraged to praise and talk to your dog while performing an exercise, making it that much more fun for both of you.

Evaluating Equipment and Expense

Other than hurdles, there is no equipment in rally. To train your dog on hurdles at home, use a broomstick over two stacks of bricks. The expense is minimal. Handlers may choose to take weekly or biweekly classes, and there are small entrance fees at rally competitions. If teams become serious, there may be travel expenses.

Canine Competition

Rally competitions are divided into three classes: Novice, Advanced, and Excellent. Each class is split into A and B sections in order to make smaller groups. In Novice, the dog proceeds on leash through 10 to 15 stations. Advanced is done off leash with 15 to 20 stations. The Excellent course is done off leash and includes 15 to 20 stations with two jumps. Teams begin with 100 points in AKC Rally and 200 points in APDT Rally.

ORGANIZATIONS

American Pet Dog Trainers Association The APDT was the first organization to embrace rally, which they call rally-o. Any dog, mixed or purebred, can compete in the APDT's rally-o events.

American Kennel Club (AKC) The AKC allows only registered purebred dogs, or dogs with an Indefinite Listing Privilege (ILP) number, to compete in rally.

TITLES	QUALIFICATIONS
Rally Novice (RN)	Must qualify in Novice at 3 different trials
Rally Advanced (RA)	Must qualify in Advanced at 3 different trials
Rally Excellent (RE)	Must qualify in Excellent at 3 different trials
Rally Advanced Excellent (RAE)	Must qualify in Excellent and Advanced 10 times each

CANINE FREESTYLE, CHA-CHA-CHA!

Canine freestyle gets a bad rap. This is the thought that runs through my head as I watch freestyle trainer Corrine Lawson lead her dogs, Genevieve and Toby, through a Spanish-themed routine that looks and sounds like flamenco. Lawson, a former professional ballet dancer, moves in a contained way that speaks of her years of training. But the amazing thing is that her dogs do, too.

The routine, called a brace because it is done with two dogs, incorporates heeling, spinning, jumping, and weaving, all done in time to music. The moves are as complicated as those in obedience and rally and as athletic as those in agility and Frisbee. It's wonderful to watch.

This sport has something of an image problem, which means that its athleticism and dog control are often overlooked. To many people, the idea of dogs dancing seems silly, but performed at this level, freestyle looks like a beautifully enhanced version of a number of dog sports, including agility, disc, and obedience. Lawson, who teaches classes in canine freestyle, comments that freestyle is something like a football player refining his skills by doing ballet, in that a well-trained canine freestyle dog can do well in almost any other dog sport. It's not unusual for dog trainers like Lawson to be attracted to the sport because it combines so much of what the other canine sports entail, perfecting dog and handler skills that can be used across the board.

You need only to watch the training process to see how difficult this sport is. Lawson's Saturday morning freestyle class comprises six women and six dogs lined up evenly across the room, which looks a lot like the rooms where millions of little girls take their first ballet classes. It's an eclectic group of dogs: two golden retrievers, an Aussie, a Maltese, a Sheltie, and an Aussie mix. The women are white and middle-aged, the typical demographic for canine freestyle.

Using Toby, her nearly 13-year-old miniature Aussie mix, as a demo dog, Lawson shows the class the first exercise of the day. She walks to the end of the room with Toby at her left side, his nose glued to her thigh. She reaches the end of the room and spins, putting Toby on her right. They return with Toby's nose just as glued to her right leg. Easy? Not really. Heeling on the left is one of the basic obedience commands, and most

dogs learn it well. When they're suddenly confronted with heeling to the right, which is called a strut, many balk or become confused. Freestyle depends on a dog's ability to move easily on either side of the handler.

Next comes the weave, as integral a part of freestyle as it is of agility. But in freestyle, the weave poles are the human's legs, and there are different types of weaves. There is the lateral weave, in which the dog starts on the right or left and weaves between the handler's legs, ending on the other side. Then there is the moving weave, in which the handler walks across the room, with the dog continually weaving between her legs.

Lawson and Toby make the moving weave look effortless, but it's immediately clear when the rest of the class tries that it is not. When one handler and her Aussie get tangled in mid-weave, her feet crossed in front of one another and the dog's head poking between her legs, she laughs sheepishly and says, "I think I need the treats, not my dog!"

Basics of Canine Freestyle

Canine freestyle sets advanced obedience work to music, with an emphasis on difficult but artistically presented routines that highlight the working relationship between a dog and a human. A Canadian named Val Culpa is considered the godmother of canine freestyle. She began developing the sport nearly 20 years ago, envisioning a sort of canine dressage. Other dog lovers were attracted to the idea immediately, and soon several teams were training and performing in canine freestyle. The Canadian Musical Canine Sports International (CMCSI) was founded in 1991.

Soon after, there was a split in ideology, with some teams moving toward flamboyant costumes and dramatic routines, and others favoring a more formal interpretation, without costumes and with more emphasis on obedience work and precise timing than on musical interpretation. These differences ultimately led to the formation of several other freestyle organizations, including the World Canine Freestyle Organization (WCFO), the U.S. freestyle organization that is linked to CMCSI. WCFO and CMCSI embrace a looser, more dramatic type of freestyle, with the handler more actively involved in the dance. Canine Freestyle Federation (CFF) is more formal and models routines after equine dressage in that the dog's movements are emphasized over the handler's.

In 1996, Heinz Pup-peroni dog snacks began sponsoring canine freestyle events, dramatically increasing the sport's visibility by hosting large competitions and providing television opportunities. Freestyle events began to be incorporated into existing obedience events and soon longtime obedience handlers were lining up to find out about the new sport.

A SPORT BY ANOTHER NAME

Canine freestyle has been described by a number of names, including heelwork to music, canine dressage, doggy dancing, and canine musical freestyle. On a popular level, the term "doggy dancing" has stuck, but most handlers involved in the sport prefer "canine freestyle." Unfortunately, the cutesy moniker may be one of the reasons the sport has languished while other new canine sports have attracted unprecedented numbers.

In canine freestyle, timed routines are done in a set performance area. The team is expected to use as much of the ring as possible and is judged on technical execution, creativity, and artistic expression.

Performers may be a single human–dog team, a brace (two dogs and one

Safety Considerations

There are few safety concerns with this sport, as the moves are primarily low impact. Dogs aren't allowed to wear costumes that they can trip on or that will block their vision. Dogs cannot be lifted higher than their handler's shoulders. In competition, dangerous moves, such as high vaults, are faulted.

human handler), or a group of handlers and dogs. Depending on the organization and individuals, competitors may wear costumes and focus heavily on the dance choreography, or they may perform without costumes and have more emphasis on the athleticism and skills of the dog, as well as on the human partner's ability to handle the dog.

Who Does Canine Freestyle?

Although the uninformed might assume that a typical canine freestyle dog is a tiny lap dog dressed in a pink tutu, this perception couldn't be further from the truth. In fact, most canine freestyle dogs are the same medium-sized to large athletic dogs who excel in all of the canine sports.

Dogs must be at least six months old to compete, but there are no breed restrictions. There are lots of Aussies, golden retrievers, Shelties, and Labs involved in canine freestyle, as well as many mixed breeds. Dogs who are athletic enough for Frisbee and smart and biddable enough for obedience will thrive.

As for the handlers, there are probably more women involved in freestyle than in other sports. Lawson estimates at least 80 percent of handlers are women, with the other 20 percent made up of children and some men. Lawson, in her early 40s, is decidedly younger than her students. Most are retired or nearing retirement age with teenage or adult children. Curiously, at the very upper end of competitive canine freestyle, there are a number of well-known male handlers.

Talking about Training and Time

Although sometimes derided as just dancing with your dog, there is far more involved than that. To do well in freestyle the handler–dog pair must be highly in tune with one another. It is like very high-level obedience in that the dogs perform extremely complicated commands, but it's much faster-paced than obedience, with dogs and handlers moving fluidly from one move to the next. In addition, handlers must have some ability to choreograph and keep time to music.

Your first step in training a dog for freestyle is a good obedience class. An obedience class will teach your dog basic commands, but more important, will teach him to pay attention to you. After you get the basics down, you can move on to more difficult tricks and commands. Try to find a trainer who offers a canine freestyle class, or look for an obedience instructor with an interest in canine freestyle. Expect to spend some time training your dog every day.

"All of the top dogs have excelled at obedience before they went into freestyle," explains Carolyn Money, an enthusiastic trainer who hosts her own freestyle competitions. "I've done most of the performance sports and this is the hardest one. Not only do you have to teach your dog a number of tricks but you also have to work out the choreography and combine the two to look polished, which isn't easy."

If you can't find a local trainer, order a DVD or videotape to get some training tips. Look out for local events, where you can meet people who are involved in the sport. If you're really serious, try to find a seminar where you can gain a lot of insight into canine freestyle in a short amount of time. You may have to travel outside of your local area to attend a seminar or freestyle event.

Lawson also emphasizes that you train each movement separately, not as part of a dance. Otherwise, dogs learn the chain of movements but not the individual movement. While training, play music, which will help you and your dog to focus and will also get you used to the idea of doing tricks and commands to a beat.

Evaluating Equipment and Expense

Equipment is minimal, consisting of a costume for the handler (or not — many handlers don't wear costumes at all), music, and perhaps a prop or two, such as a scarf or a cane. One important note: If you are using published music for a performance you must use a song in the public domain or pay a royalty fee. You can contact the American Society for Composers, Authors, and Publishers (ASCAP) or Broadcast Music, Inc. (BMI) for information.

Canine Competition

Because there are three major canine freestyle organizations currently in operation, there is a range of competition levels in which teams can earn titles. All divide classes into levels based on how skilled the dog is on and off leash, how well the handler manages and directs the dog, how closely the dog and handler perform in synchronicity, and the degree of difficulty of the routine. There are also divisions for single teams, multiple teams, and brace teams.

ORGANIZATIONS

Canine Freestyle Federation Incorporated (CFF) CFF interprets canine freestyle more closely to canine dressage. It discourages costumes and gratuitous human dancing. Rather, the human's job is to highlight the dog's abilities.

There are four levels of competition and two divisions: individual dog (one dog and one handler) and multiple dogs, which is divided into team (more than one dog and more than one handler) and brace (one handler with two dogs). To achieve a title at any level or division in CFF, the team must receive a score of at least 65 in one competition. Once a title is awarded, the team must move up to the next level, except in the case of Level IV.

CFF CLASSES	REQUIREMENTS
Level I	On leash; must include right or left heel, turns or pivots, pace changes, front work, and either serpentines, circles, or spirals
Level IIA	Off leash utilizing the same movements as Level I
Level IIB	For teams who have titled at Level IIA
Level III	Off leash; must include right and left heelwork, turns or pivots, front work, serpentines, circles, or spirals, turns or pivots, backing, and lateral work to right or left
Level IV	Off leash; must be well-choreographed, complex, fluid, and include right and left heelwork, pivots and turns, front work, backing, right and left lateral work, and distance work

CFF TITLES
CFF I
CFF II
CFF III
CFF IV
CHFF IV (Champion)
For brace or team, a B or T is added at the end of each title (for example, CFF IT).

Musical Dog Sports Association (MDSA) MDSA was formed recently by well-known canine freestyler Carolyn Scott in response to a perceived shift from the traditional canine freestyle focus — teamwork between a human and a dog — to too much flash. Their goal is to promote the "original" canine freestyle. This group offers Novice, Standard, and Premier Classes, as well as Veterans, Rookies, and Fledglings.

World Canine Freestyle Organization (WCFO) WCFO tends toward a more flamboyant form of canine freestyle, with costumes and flashy routines. Their mission is to promote the bond between people and dogs through canine freestyle as both a sport and entertainment.

There are single, brace, and team divisions, as well as doubles (two handlers, two dogs), sassy seniors (for handlers 65 years or older and/or dogs 9 years or older), and handi-dandi (for handler with a mental or physical disability and/or a dog with a mental or physical disability). There is also a junior division.

Teams can work in one of two styles: Musical Freestyle (MF) or Heelwork to Music (HTM). In HTM, dogs and handlers are to work closely together and the moves are more precisely scored. In MF, dogs and handlers may work farther away from one another and any move is allowed.

Dogs are scored on Technical Merit, including Content, Precise Execution, Flow, Difficulty of Routine, and Stepping in Time to Music, and Artistic Impression, including Animation, Attitude, Attention, and Harmonious Interaction (Bonding), Quality and Creativity of Choreography, Use of Ring Space, Coordination of Routine with Music, Musical Interpretation, Costume Coordination with Music and Routine, and Spectator Appeal.

Competition levels are Beginner, Novice, Intermediate, and Advanced. Juniors are scored separately. WCFO also has a video competition, in which competitors compete remotely.

WCFO TITLES
Beginners
W-FD/HTM: Adult singles
W-BFD/MF: Adult brace
W-PFD/MF: Adult pairs
W-TFD/MF: Adult team
W-SSFD/MF: Adult sassy seniors
W-HDFD/MF: Adult handi-dandi
Novice
W-FDX/HTM or W-FDX/MF: Adult singles
W-BFDX/MF: Adult brace
W-PFDX/MF: Adult pairs
W-TFDX/MF: Adult team
W-SSFDX/MF: Adult sassy seniors
W-HDFDX/MF: Adult handi-dandi
Intermediate
W-FDM/HTM or W-FDM/MF: Adult singles
W-BFDM/MF: Adult brace
W-PFDM/MF: Adult pairs
W-TFDM/MF: Adult team
W-SSFDM/MF: Adult sassy seniors
W-HDFDM/MF: Adult handi-dandi
Advanced
W-CH.FD/HTM or W-CH.FD/MF: Adult singles
W-BCH.FD/MF: Adult brace
W-PCH.FD/MF: Adult pairs
W-TCH.FD/MF: Adult team
W-SSCH.FD/MF: Adult sassy seniors
W-HDCH.FD/MF: Adult handi-dandi

— CHAPTER 8 —

It's Instinctive

Herding / Tracking / Field Trials & Hunt Tests
Earthdog / Lure Coursing / Water Rescue / Schutzhund

THERE ARE SOME ACTIVITIES FOR WHICH dogs have been bred for centuries — even millennia. For the most part, these sports are limited to the breeds traditionally bred to them — either by rules or practicality. Other breeds tend not to excel or even to understand what is required of them. Although a dachshund may be free to try herding, he probably won't be very interested. For dog lovers, there's nothing like watching a Border collie stare down a sheep, an Irish setter on point, or a greyhound practically gliding over the ground.

HERDING: IT'S ALL ABOUT THE EYE

The first thing I hear as I approach Jan Wesen's sheep paddock is a woman's voice yelling angrily: "Dakota!" In the paddock, a tricolor Aussie is eying several woolly sheep nuzzled together against the fence. The handler is attempting to send Dakota away from her so the dog will bring the sheep around the large paddock. In one hand she holds a wooden rake handle to guide the dog when he comes too close to the flock. Each time she sends the Aussie out, he loses two of the sheep and then circles back around trying to catch them, which causes the sheep to panic and run in the wrong direction.

After several attempts, the woman throws the rake toward the dog in frustration and he skitters away. Wesen turns to me and says implacably, "It's going to be a hard day. The sheep are wild." When the student picks up the rake and tries to send Dakota out again, the dog just looks at her. "He doesn't trust you because you threw that rake," Wesen says without judgment. The student looks exhausted, her hands on her hips. "I'm done," she says. "I'm tired."

"Do something easy," suggests Wesen. The handler takes a deep breath and asks Dakota to bring the sheep toward her and the gate. The Aussie does this easily, his tail wagging as the sheep bunch up at the gate. "Now pet him," says Wesen. The student does, finally relaxing and giving her dog a good scratch.

Herding evokes the image of bucolic green fields providing the backdrop to a graceful and athletic dog easily herding fluffy white sheep while following his handler's almost imperceptible commands. Reaching that goal, however, involves a fair amount of work, frustration, and, yes, yelling. Herding is something of a contradiction — the people who do it say it brings them closer to their dogs but at the same time it is a frustrating and sometimes harsh sport.

"People forget that herding is modified hunting," says Joe Kapelos, who owns a herd-dog training school with his partner, Linda Leeman. "It looks so beautiful and romantic, but you have to understand the dog is a predator and you have to have control of him. That's why it's so intense."

Herding captures the canine predator drive and redirects it for human purposes. Herding dogs often seem to be almost in a trance when they work livestock, with an uncanny focus and ability to tune into the flock's movements. Unchecked, that drive might lead to an attack, but the beauty of herding is the control of the drive. Kapelos adds that although many handlers prefer not to think of their dog's drive as predatory, instead labeling it "performance drive," a strong prey drive is essential for a successful herding dog. "If he didn't have that motivation," says Kapelos, "he wouldn't do anything."

The Basics of Herding

For thousands of years, humans have used dogs to herd livestock ranging from reindeer to ducks. Herding dogs are found on every continent except for Antarctica. Next to hunting and companionship, it is the most essential use of a dog in human lives.

Many modern herding dogs are still active working dogs, spending their days on midwestern cattle ranches and Irish sheep farms. Dogs who herd for sport, however, now outnumber those who herd for work, and most only venture into farmland for a weekly herding class or trials.

It's not uncommon for urban dog handlers to drive hundreds of miles to work their dogs. The sport of herding has become increasingly popular in North America in the past 20 years. Increased media coverage and a widespread interest in providing dogs with the opportunity to test their natural instincts have led to this rise in interest.

Herding is the use of dogs to move live-stock — it may be moving a flock of sheep from one paddock to another, separating out an animal for shearing or a vet check, or penning animals at night. An old adage says that Australia was built on the back of the Australian kelpie, because the herding dog's assistance was so essential in the country's economic development, but the same could be said for almost any farm-based community, including the American West, where Australian shepherds (which despite their name are an American breed) were once essential farmhands.

The sport of herding reproduces these movements in front of judges; in a typical herding event, the dog will be asked to move ducks, sheep, or cattle through a gate into a paddock, around a fence or two in the paddock, and then back out of the paddock.

Who Does Herding?

Obviously the best herding dogs are the ones who have been bred over centuries for this specific task. Border collies, Australian shepherds, Australian cattle dogs, Australian kelpies, corgis, old English sheepdogs, collies, and Shetland sheepdogs are popular herding dogs. Less commonly seen herding dogs include Belgian sheepdogs, Bouviers, Canaans, German shepherd dogs, and Rottweilers.

That doesn't necessarily mean the sport is restricted to those dogs with an illustrious herding heritage. In fact, American pit bull terriers, rat terriers, and Labs have all taken a stab at this game, with varying degrees of success. Although Leeman and Kapelos won't turn any dog away, they admit that herding with a Lab is a far cry from herding with a cattle dog. As Kapelos puts it, "Other breeds can do it, though their ability is going to be limited. But some can do pretty darn well; some perform better than Border collies we've had out here."

Many organizations that arrange herding trials restrict competition to the herding breeds; however, there are opportunities for non-herding breeds to participate and many people just herd with their dogs for fun, never going to trials at all.

Some Words to Know

Away to me: The dog moves counterclockwise away from handler and behind the animals, driving them to the handler.

Eye: The distinctive gaze used by herding dogs to influence the movement of livestock

Fetch: The dog brings the stock directly to the handler.

Go by: The dog moves clockwise away from the handler and behind the stock, driving them to the handler.

That'll do: Job well done

"If you're just into it for the fun and challenge, herding dogs can come in all shapes and sizes and breeds," says Mary Polikoff, owner of a Canaan dog. "As far as individual dogs go, they should have some ability and they should be in decent shape; otherwise, it probably won't be too enjoyable for you or for them."

THE PEOPLE PLAYERS

Herding attracts people who favor active dogs and an active lifestyle. Many competitors are ranchers and farmers who use herding dogs in their work lives. Junior handlers often become involved through 4-H activities. Although many serious handlers live a rural lifestyle and even purchase sheep for their dogs to train on, a fair number of competitors live cities and become involved in herding as a way to give their high-energy dogs a physical and mental outlet.

Some handlers are drawn to herding because they want to show off their herding dogs' inherited skills, others because they want to preserve and promote the herding instincts of particular breeds. Polikoff herds with her Canaan dog to promote the breed's historical utility. "There aren't many Canaan dogs in the sport even though they're in the herding group," says Polikoff. "It's nice to feel we're promoting that in the breed. The Bedouin have been herding with Canaans for thousands of years."

Successful handlers tend to be people who are driven and want to work — a lot — with their dogs. Leeman points out that people who are very analytical have a hard time with herding because it's not a black-and-white exercise. Every time the dog goes into the pen, it's a different experience, depending on the course, the dog's mood, the sheep, and even the temperature and wind variances.

Talking about Training and Time

Training a dog to work stock is time-consuming and intensive. Although herding dogs are bred to do this job, it is not quite like lure coursing or earthdog in which you can — with some direction — just let the dog do his thing. Most serious handlers have their herding dogs instinct-tested before they are a year old.

HERDING SAFETY

The issue of safety is paramount in herding. First, there is the safety of the livestock. Because dogs herd out of a predatory instinct, there is always the possibility that the dog will try to maim or kill rather than herd.

Second, there is the safety of the handler, who can be rammed or knocked over by sheep or goats and stepped on or kicked while on the ground. The term "sheep surfing" refers to the experience of being crowded and jostled by a group of animals. The possibility of more serious injury exists when working cattle.

Finally, there is the safety of the dogs. Dogs face the same potential for injury as in any rigorous sport — strained muscles and ligaments, torn nails, and cut pads — but they also face danger from the livestock. Ducks, obviously, can't do much harm to a dog, but sheep can cause some damage, and cattle can inflict serious, even life-threatening, injuries.

Cattle herding is more dangerous for several reasons. For one thing, the dogs must actually nip at the cattle to move them — with the sheep and ducks a good stare-down or feint is usually enough. A dog can break a tooth or be stepped on when working so close to livestock. A more serious issue is that cattle are large, strong animals who often don't take kindly to being pushed around. They may turn on a dog and charge him, and a well-placed kick can easily kill a dog. For this reason, many handlers will not work with their dogs on cattle. Besides the physical complications from an injury, a dog who is injured by stock may just shut down and refuse to work.

This usually gives a good indication as to whether a dog has drive and an interest in livestock.

Early training differs depending on a dog's basic herding instinct. Some dogs are very prey-driven and much of their initial training will center on controlling that drive through the use of the crook and voice commands. Other dogs need their prey drive encouraged, so early training is about hyping them up and teaching them to focus on the livestock. Training typically begins in small pens on dog-broke sheep that are not afraid of dogs and are used to being herded by them. Dog-broke sheep help a dog gain confidence as they respond quickly to a dog's pressure, and they usually stay bunched together.

A herding lesson usually lasts about 5 or 10 minutes; if lucky, the dog will get into the pen twice in one day, although usually only once. This may sound like an extremely short session, given the fact that handlers often drive hundreds of miles for one lesson, but herding work is extremely intense, involving not only physical but mental exertion.

LEARNING THE LANGUAGE

Herding training differs quite a bit from that in other canine sports. For example, treats and toys aren't used in herding, because the dog is working at a distance and also because the work itself is suf-

ficient reward for most dogs. Herding handlers use both positive reinforcement and reprimands when training. Corrections are mostly verbal, but in some cases, a physical correction is called for if a dog becomes too excited or aggressive.

Both dog and handler need to learn the traditional commands used in herding, most of which have been used for hundreds, if not thousands, of years. As the dog's training develops, the handler begins to learn how to control the dog verbally and with other sounds, such as a whistle. The tone of voice is especially important when working with a herding dog, as the handler's voice controls the dog's power and energy — if he is too excited, you need to calm him down; if he is acting lethargic, you need to wake him up. In many respects, the training is more for the handler than the dog — this is especially true for dogs bred from established herding lines. For them, herding is largely instinctual, but the handler is truly learning a new language. Both dog and handler must be able to adjust to constantly changing situations and conditions.

Although training never really ends, most dogs require a certain amount of time before they can work reliably and are ready to trial. This may be six months, it may be several years, and it may be never. Leeman admits that some handlers are simply too impatient to ride out the process, but even if it takes several years before a dog is ready to trial, there are big rewards.

Evaluating Equipment and Expense

In addition to the livestock and fencing, the most important piece of equipment in herding is the crook or stock stick. The crook is used both to guide dogs in training and to separate them from the stock. It can be made of wood composite, aluminum, or fiberglass, and may be any length. In training, some handlers will use a common garden rake without tines or a crook made of PVC, which won't hurt the dog if you need to tap him with it to move him away from the stock. Dogs are trialed either collar-less or with a standard flat buckle collar.

The cost of herding can be high. Lessons typically last only 5 or 10 minutes, and most trainers encourage handlers to take one to two lessons per week. Weekend seminars can cost several hundred dollars, and trial entry fees are expensive as well, not to mention the cost of driving hundreds of miles to get to a training facility and trials. For some handlers the ultimate expense is the purchase of a piece of farmland and a flock of sheep.

Canine Competition

Herding trials have a number of levels. AKC trials, for example, have the following divisions:

Herding Instinct Test In this pass/fail test, dogs must show interest in the livestock by attempting to move the animals toward the handler or ahead of the handler. They must stay within the testing boundaries and follow basic commands.

Pre-trial Trial In this pass/fail test, dogs must follow their handler's basic commands to herd the livestock through four gates and pen at least 80 percent of the livestock within 10 minutes. The judge may assist the handler with directions and the team may attempt gates and penning multiple times.

Herding trials have three classes: Started, Intermediate, and Advanced. Within each class, there are two courses, A and B. To advance through each class, Started, Intermediate, and Advanced, the dog must receive at least 60 points under three different judges at three different trials.

Dogs can be worked on ducks, sheep, or cattle. On occasion, turkeys or geese are used in place of ducks, and goats in place of sheep. Dogs are not allowed to attack or abusively bite the livestock, and will be excused from competition for such behavior. After three excusals they are disqualified from competition for six months.

Junior classes are open to handlers up to 17 years old. They are judged for their ability to handle and direct their dog, rather than on their dog's achievements.

ORGANIZATIONS

There are several organizations that sanction herding trials; the following three are the most respected in the U.S. herding world. Each organization scores points differently. To qualify on a course at an AKC trial, for example, the dog must receive at least 60 percent of the available points. At an AHBA or ASCA trial, the bar is higher, with the dog needing at least 70 percent and 75 percent of the available points, respectively.

American Herding Breed Association (AHBA) Widely considered the most serious of the sanctioning organizations. All herding dogs and herding dog mixes are allowed to compete, as well as all-purpose farm dogs; dogs are judged on a combination of style and precision.

American Kennel Club (AKC) Only purebred dogs (of any registered herding or working breed) are allowed to participate; dogs are scored on how precisely they follow the lines of the course.

Australian Shepherd Club of America (ASCA) Purebred and mixed herding breeds can compete; emphasis is placed on a dog's style.

HERDING TITLES
American Herding Breed Association (AHBA)
Herding Trial Dog (HTD)
Started-Herding Trial Dog (HTD I)
Intermediate-Herding Trial Dog (HTD II)
Advanced-Herding Trial Dog (HTD III)
Herding Ranch Dog (HRD (I/II/III))
Herding Trial Arena Dog (HTAD (I/II/III))
Herding Trial Championship (HTCh)
Australian Shepherd Club of America (ASCA)
In ASCA, dogs must work ducks, sheep, and cattle in order to earn titles.
Started Trial Dog (STD)
Open Trial Dog (OTD)
Advanced Trial Dog (ATD)
Post Advanced Trial Dog (PATD)
Ranch Dog (RD)
Ranch Trial Dog (RTD)
Working Trial Champion (WTCh)
American Kennel Club (AKC)
Herding Tested (HD)
Pre-trial Tested (PT)
Herding Started (HS)
Herding Intermediate (HI)
Herding Excellent (HX)
Herding Trial Champion (HCH)

TRACKING: THE NOSE KNOWS

At a defunct military site in Seattle, a young golden retriever is presented with an old glove. He buries his shiny black nose in the material, sniffing deeply, and then looks up at his handler expectantly. He knows it's time to play the game. Dressed in a tracking harness, the young dog puts his nose to the ground while his handler walks behind him. He closely follows the trail that was set an hour before, finding his first article — another glove — quickly.

Several times, he pauses and then sniffs frantically on the ground in various directions before deciding on a path once more. Once around the corner of an old barracks, he finds his second scent article. His pace quickens as he heads toward the end of the trail and his reward, a final glove and a hearty "Woohoo!" from his handler.

To a person, a cinnamon roll smells like cinnamon. To a dog, a cinnamon roll smells like cinnamon and flour and sugar and butter, not to mention the baking pan, the baker, and the server who set it on your plate. In comparison with a human's five to 10 million olfactory receptors, dogs have more than two hundred million. They are able to sniff odors in parts per billion. Tracking takes this skill and turns it into a game.

Craig Green is a tracking judge and trainer with 30 years of experience. For him, one of the main appeals of tracking is that the dog is in charge, something that isn't true in most canine sports. "Some of the most successful obedience trainers cannot let go of the dog," says Green. "In tracking, you follow the dog. In training you try to motivate them so they want to find the glove, but when it comes to the test you're at their mercy. The best advice I can give my students is don't screw up your dog. You have to listen and observe; when you've gone too far, your dog will tell you."

The Basics of Tracking

Tracking dogs have been used to find people for centuries. There is evidence that bloodhounds, for example, tracked escaped prisoners and wanted criminals as far back as the fourteenth century. The use of tracking dogs, also called search-and-rescue dogs, to find lost hikers or victims of crime has greatly expanded in the last century, first in Europe and now in the United States.

Although tracking handlers make a clear distinction between the tracking done in competition and the trailing done by bloodhounds or the air scenting done by search-and-rescue dogs, it was this same skill that prompted the AKC to first begin testing dogs in tracking in 1936 under the Utility Dog title. In 1947, the organization created a separate entry for tracking, and since then thousands of dogs have earned the titles of Tracking Dog (TD), Tracking Dog Excellent (TDX), and — since 1995 — Variable Surface Tracking (VST), awarded in an urban environment over a variety of surfaces.

Ed Presnall, a longtime tracking enthusiast and AKC tracking judge, says that to dogs, all humans resemble the *Peanuts* character Pig Pen, with scents swirling around instead of clouds of dirt. "We see in color," he says, "but our dogs smell in color." Presnall explains that humans shed skin cells constantly and that the sport of tracking is training a dog to follow a particular human smell. What makes it different from search and rescue is that the dog must be as concerned with following the track as with finding the object at the end.

"The dog must follow the track within a few feet, he must find the articles, he must indicate in a way that the handler can recognize," says Presnall. "We care that the dog gets from the start of the track to the end of the track."

Who Does Tracking?

Although hounds or German shepherds are often considered to be the ultimate tracking dogs, Presnall prefers to track with his favorite spaniels. While any dog can participate in tracking, AKC tracking only titles purebred dogs of a breed recognized by the AKC. "I think most dogs can be trained to track," say Presnall. "I've trained over one hundred breeds." "Of course, different breeds have different advantages and disadvantages," says Green. "Little dogs have inherent disadvantages to big dogs on the longer tracks. But I'll tell you, the most heroic performances I've seen have been from little dogs." He describes one woman with papillons who got two TDXs on her dogs. Green has even helped title a bulldog, although he admits that it took seven years and was the most challenging task he's had as a trainer.

Green points out that different breeds have different training needs based on their temperament. For example, many sporting and herding breeds tend to be very biddable and are the highest performers. Irish setters, on the other hand, can be more difficult to train and are rarely seen tracking. About 70 to 80 percent of the people involved in tracking are women, and nearly all trackers enjoy being in the outdoors and love spending time with their dogs.

Talking about Training and Time

The first thing to realize in tracking training is that everyone has a different method, and everyone thinks his method is the best. The granddaddy of tracking trainers was Glen Johnson, who wrote what many consider to be the definitive book on tracking, *Tracking Dog: Theories and Methods* (1975). Most modern training is based on the theories he developed in this book, although every trainer has his or her own spin.

"You can take any dog out there and teach them how to do this," says Presnall. He advises potential handlers to buy a book, a harness, and a lead, and to start out on their own. Although there are tracking clubs, most handlers train their dogs by themselves.

Positive training is the norm; most handlers believe that their dogs simply wouldn't work if they received negative discipline. "This is a game of motivation," says Presnall. "We're not going to use a choke collar, we're not going to use any intimidation. The more fun we have, the better the dog will become at the sport."

BEGINNING TRAINING

You must first expose your dog to the glove, which is used as the scent item in the sport of tracking. Any old leather glove will do. You will need a helper to get started. Holding your dog from behind (don't let him move), have your helper walk one pace from the dog and then put the leather glove on the ground with a treat on top of it. Release your dog to get the glove.

Do this several times at a close distance until your dog relates the glove to the treat. Then, ask your helper to gradually move back, offering the glove and treat at 2 feet, 4 feet, 6 feet, and 10 feet. Some handlers will place barriers of some kind to either side to reinforce that the dog stays on the track.

At this point, your dog is probably not using his nose to find the treat, but locating it visually (although some dogs with a strong tracking instinct will use their noses right away). The idea is that your dog begins to see finding the glove as a fun game that he is motivated to do.

Presnall tweaks the training component a bit by placing a series of gloves along a 20-foot track and giving the dog treats from his hand as the dog reaches each glove. This way, the dog looks to him each time he reaches a glove. Once the dog is consistently finding five or six gloves, Presnall turns the track to make it slightly more difficult.

No book can teach you to train your individual dog, so in addition to books and Web sites, new trackers often look to trackers who are experienced in training a similar breed (a herding dog if you have an Aussie or a gun dog if you have

Safety Considerations

- Make sure your dog is hydrated.
- Do not track in extreme heat.
- If tracking in wilderness areas, be aware of local venomous or predatory animals.
- Do not allow your dog to put his head into burrows or dead logs.
- After tracking, check your dog for any burrs, stickers, and ticks; check his pads for cuts.
- Always tell someone where you are going and when you'll be back.
- Carry a cell phone.

a Lab) to act as mentors. Most tracking clubs have plenty of members who are happy to mentor a newcomer.

Green adds that when he trains dogs, he never pushes them past their comfort level. "We gradually increase the complexity; as soon as they have a problem, we back up." For example, Green never teaches a turn until the dog is good on the straight.

"The overall training regimen is start slow and easy; move forward gradually; when your dog has a problem back up and start again," says Green. "When they fail, give them some success."

Evaluating Equipment and Expense

Enthusiasts say that one of the great things about tracking is that it's cheap and easy for any dog and owner to try. The only necessary equipment is a tracking harness and a 20- to 40-foot line (a length of strong clothesline will do), neither of which is particularly expensive. Other necessary items are an old pair of gloves and a few pairs of old socks as scent articles.

The cost to enter a tracking-dog test is generally $50 to $100, and higher costs may be incurred if a handler–dog team is forced to travel long distances to find an available test. In that case, you will have to factor in travel time and costs, as well as food and lodging.

Canine Competition

Tracking tests are complicated to run and require a great deal of space. For the lowest levels, 300 to 400 acres of land are needed to lay out the tracks, according to Presnall. It takes a day for judges to walk the fields, and there is enough time to test only 12 dogs in a day. For an advanced test, 800 to 1,000 acres are required to test six dogs in one day. Although these numbers seem astounding, these wide swatches of land result from the fact that much of the reserved space will not or cannot be used. The track cannot come close to heavily trafficked roads or pass through heavy vegetation or other obstacles that dogs can't track through, and it must provide ways for the person laying the track to go into and out of the area without disturbing any part of the track.

In addition, there must be ample space between the tracks laid for each dog, with extra space allowed if there is a road or other obstacle between the tracks. Craig Green recently plotted seven tracks using Google Earth for a TDX test he judged. For fun, he looked at the map and drew a rectangular boundary around it; he concluded that he used about 850 acres of the available area. Each track, including the distances between them, required between 45 and 50 acres. Although that is only about 350 acres, land not used for tracks had to be reserved in order to use the area of land they did use.

Presnall could conceivably judge up to eight dogs in one day for the variable surface tracking test, which tests dogs in urban areas across asphalt and grass, but the test requires a university campus so large that there only about six or seven in the country that will do. In reality, smaller campuses are usually used, but in that case only four dogs can be tested in one day.

TESTING IS TOUGH

Because tracking tests are few and far between, tracking is unusual in that dogs may train for a very long time, even years, before being tested on their skills. And even when a dog is ready to be tested, there is no guarantee that he will be able to get a spot in a region's occasional test. Often, only a small percentage of the people who apply for a test are actually able to test. Competitors are chosen randomly from among those who apply.

Tracking tests are pass/fail. Before being eligible to test for a title, a dog must pass a certification test, which consists of a track equivalent to the Tracking Dog (TD) track that is not judged as rigorously. If the dog passes the test, he is allowed to enter a TD test. At the time the dog passes the certification test, the handler is given four certification certificates, which are good for one year. The certificate must be presented to the judge when taking the TD test and the dog gets only four tries. If he fails the TD test four times, he must recertify.

ORGANIZATIONS

American Kennel Club The AKC is the most popular venue through which to test for tracking.

Australian Shepherd Club of America (ASCA) ASCA tests Aussies as well as other breeds and mixed breeds.

TITLES

Both the AKC and the Australian Shepherd Club of America (ASCA) award the following titles:

Tracking Dog (TD)	The dog must follow a 30-minute-old scent trail that is 440 to 500 yards long. There are at least three and not more than five turns, two of which are 90 degrees. The dog must find the scent article at the end of the trail.
Tracking Dog Excellent (TDX)	The dog must follow a scent trail that is three to five hours old and between 800 and 1,000 yards long. There are five to seven turns, three of which are 90 degrees. Along the trail there are three false scent articles and two cross tracks. The dog must find the correct scent article at the end of the trail.

The AKC also awards the following title:

Variable Surface Tracking (VST)	The dog must follow a scent trail that is three to five hours old and between 800 and 1,000 yards long. Like TDX, there are five to seven turns, three of which are 90 degrees. What makes it so difficult is that it is held in an urban environment on a variety of surfaces, including sand, grass, concrete or asphalt, and gravel.

POINT, SET, FLUSH:
FIELD TRIALS & HUNT TESTS

Living with eight large red dogs seems perfectly normal to Allen and Deb Fazenbaker, longtime Irish setter breeders. Although they once hunted extensively, nowadays they prefer field trials (both on foot and on horseback) and hunt tests. Like many breeders, the Fazenbakers have a strong commitment to maintaining the utility of their dogs.

Irish setters, who have a reputation for being airheaded, can be quite different in their field and show incarnations. This, field breeders say, is because show Irish setter lines have been heavily diluted by breeders seeking physical perfection with little to no emphasis placed on hunting skills. In fact, field-bred Irish setters are rarely registered with the AKC and are usually called red setters to distinguish them from show-bred lines.

"What differentiates field-bred setters from others is their superior intelligence and easy dispositions," says Deb Fazenbaker. "There is really nothing quite as beautiful as watching a red setter make a long cast across a field, catch scent of a bird, and suddenly slam on point — head high, tail at 12 o'clock! They are classy, stylish, and gorgeous to watch."

The Fazenbakers love to see their dogs doing the work they were meant to do. "They really live to hunt and trial," says Deb. "As soon as we get out the equipment and start to put on our boots, they start running back and forth and waiting for the signal to jump in the car and go."

Of all the uses of a dog, hunting is probably the most basic and instinctive. For thousands of years, dogs have helped humans hunt everything from lions to boars to birds. Hunting was both the first form of work for domestic dogs and the first real canine sport. Many people still hunt with dogs for sustenance or recreation, and many more, both hunters and non-hunters, participate in the sports that celebrate the hunting relationship: hunt tests and field trials, which primarily test a dog's bird skills.

The Basics of Field Trials and Hunt Tests

The differences between field trials and hunt tests can be confusing, especially as the terms mean different things to different organizations and for different types of dogs. Depending on who you talk to, field trials or hunt tests may be touted as the most difficult or best

test of a dog's hunting skills. Within the competition distinctions, there are also dividers between the sanctioning organizations, such as the AKC, North American Versatile Hunting Dog Association (NAVHDA), or Amateur Field Trial Clubs of America (AF), and the types of birds hunted, such as upland game or waterfowl. Pointer field trials differ from both retriever field trials and spaniel field trials. Participants tend to have strong allegiances regarding the organization they trial or test under.

FIELD TRIALS

Field trials are made up of one or more "stakes" — different competitions within the trial. Depending on the breed, the field trial may consist of retrieving downed waterfowl or pointing upland game birds for the gunner to shoot. Handlers may work from the ground or from horseback. Dog and handler teams compete against other dog–handler teams within their stake to earn points. The dogs with the most points are awarded ribbons for first through fourth place.

HUNT TEST

In hunt tests, dogs compete against a standard, rather than against the other dogs testing the same day. Because the dogs are being tested to see if they can do what they are bred to do, the skills

FIELD TRIAL & HUNT TEST SAFETY

As with any sport in which the dog spends long periods of time working intensely outdoors, there is the risk of exhaustion or heat stroke. During warm summer months, dogs shouldn't work during the hottest times of the day, should receive adequate rest, and must be well hydrated. Always carry adequate water for both you and your dogs.

Hunting dogs are also exposed to the various dangers inherent in working in wilderness settings: venomous and predatory animals, burrs and stickers, and stinging insects and ticks.

For those doing field trials on horseback, there are also concerns for the safety of the horses; they need to be rested and watered as often as, or more often than, the dogs. The horses themselves can be a safety threat to the dogs and hunters. Horses in field trials should be reliable and well-trained, but participants should take the necessary precautions to ensure that dogs or humans aren't kicked or trampled by a panicked horse.

If live game and guns are being used, then a number of gun safety precautions must be taken.

being tested differ depending on the breed of dog. Handlers do not compete from horseback, and many handlers prefer hunt tests to field trials because they feel the lack of competitiveness encourages a more supportive atmosphere.

Who Does Field Trials and Hunt Tests?

Field trials and hunt tests are almost exclusively the province of dogs bred to hunt birds, called sporting dogs or gun dogs depending on the sponsoring organization. Common hunting dogs are Labrador retrievers, golden retrievers, pointers, springer spaniels, and Gordon and Irish setters. Although all of these dogs were originally bred to hunt, many breeds now differentiate between show dogs and field dogs. Different breeds have been developed to specialize in certain types of birds and different styles of hunting; for example, pointers point in order to direct the hunter, while spaniels flush game out of the brush so the hunter can take a shot. Some dogs, such as German shorthaired pointers, were bred to be versatile hunters, meaning that they hunt, point, and track, and can also retrieve on land and water.

The people who do field trials and hunt tests usually can be divided into two categories: hunters who do some field trials and people who do field trials instead of hunting. Many participants don't wish to hunt but are looking for a fun sport that will allow their dogs to utilize the skills and instincts they were born with.

Talking about Training and Time

The amount of time spent training a hunting dog varies from person to person and dog to dog. Dogs with a great deal of natural ability don't require formal training as much as shaping or honing their instinctive behaviors. Other dogs can be trained intensively for years and still not be great hunters.

Most serious handlers begin training their dogs as quite young puppies, working on basic obedience as well as on specific hunting training. If a dog is going to hunt live birds, he should be introduced to birds by about three to six months of age. He should start actually hunting, or doing hunt test or field trials, by about one year of age, though he probably won't be steady until about two years of age.

Most hobbyist handlers only train their dogs in the field on birds a few times a month but do a great deal of training at home daily. This training may include using handling techniques and retrieving bumpers designed for dogs. Serious handlers may train their dogs in the field on a daily basis.

Experienced handlers highly recommend that newcomers to the sport find a mentor who is experienced in training breeds similar to yours. Some handlers go so far as to say that finding a mentor is a requirement for training a hunting dog.

Evaluating Equipment and Expense

Competing with your dog can become quite expensive, whether you are doing field trials or hunt tests.

FIELD TRIALS

Field trialing with horses is the most expensive form of competitive hunting; handlers are responsible not only for their dogs and their care, but for their horses' care and equipment. They must also train with live birds, and when training away from home or attending trials must transport dogs and horses, requiring a large truck and trailer.

HUNT TESTS

Participating in hunt tests that do not use live game is the least expensive way to compete. Dogs can train with bumpers rather than live birds, and dogs are handled from foot, so horses and their expensive upkeep and equipment are not required. As tests are often held in rural areas, however, competitors may still need to travel long distances by car to reach training areas or tests.

Canine Competition

Competition style and events differ sharply between hunt tests and field trials, among organizations, and among the different breeds of dogs. To determine which type of hunting competition makes sense for you and your dogs, contact the organizations, as well as breed-specific hunting clubs.

ORGANIZATIONS

Amateur Field Trial Clubs of America (AF) The AF is considered to be the highest level of field trialing, though no titles are awarded.

American Kennel Club (AKC) The AKC sanctions hunt tests and field trials; it's largely considered to be the least serious of the venues. In AKC, hunt-tested dogs can receive junior hunter (JH), senior hunter (SH), and master hunter (MH) titles; field trial dogs can receive field champion (FC), national field champion (NFC), amateur field champion (AFC), and national amateur field champion (NAFC) titles.

National Shoot to Retrieve Association (NSTRA) NSTRA was developed as a way for hunters and dogs to hone their skills outside of the brief hunting seasons. In NSTRA, dogs are not awarded titles but they do receive awards and championships and can be inducted into a Hall of Fame.

North American Versatile Hunting Dog Association (NAVHDA) The NAVHDA sanctions hunt tests for versatile breeds, such as pointers. It is considered a high-level venue with a high percentage of hunters in its ranks. NAVDHA dogs can receive titles for the natural ability test (NA), utility test (UT), or for versatile champion (VC).

United Kennel Club (UKC) The UKC also sanctions bird dog hunt tests and field trials, as well as hunt tests for other hunting dogs, such as coon dogs. Titles include Started Hunting Retriever (SHR), Hunting Retriever (HR), Hunting Retriever Champion (HRCH), Grand Hunting Retriever Champion (GHRCH), and Upland Hunter (UH).

DOWN & DIRTY EARTHDOG

On a serene farm on an island near Seattle, an annual earthdog test has the look of a country fair. Dogs and people lounge on the warm grass under heavily laden apple trees while they watch the tests and wait their turn. The sound of terriers barking is heard in the gentle wind that occasionally gusts through the bucolic setting.

Almost hidden in tall grass are a tiny Border terrier and a slightly larger Scottish terrier. From the viewing area about 300 or 400 yards away, the handlers and the judge are too far away to be heard, but I can see the dogs being released from their leads and instructed to find the quarry — this is called the hunt out and is the first part of the Master Earthdog test. After a few moments of sniffing, the dogs find the scent and quickly make their way across the field to a mound of brush. There the little Border terrier finds the mouth of the tunnel, where a caged rat is located.

The Border terrier begins to "work" the tunnel — barking and scratching — and the Scotty quickly joins him, looking to see what the Border terrier has found. The Scotty smells the rat and barks briefly but then runs away from the entrance, looking for another way to the rats. Although the judge could penalize the Scotty for this, she chooses not to this time. After both dogs have indicated, the steward instructs the owners to pick up their dogs and turn away from the den. As the handlers and their dogs stand facing toward us, the steward moves the rat cage to the end of the tunnel.

The Border terrier, because he was the first to work the tunnel, is now the first to enter it, while the Scotty must "honor" him as he works by standing back. The Border terrier's handler holds him briefly at the mouth of the tunnel before releasing him.

He has 90 seconds to make his way through the tunnel to the rat in the den. Along the way, he will encounter roots, narrowed tunnel walls, a false exit and false den with rat bedding, and three turns. Ninety seconds suddenly seems like a painfully long time. The Border terrier plunges into the tunnel for 10 or 20 seconds before his little head pops back out the entrance. He glances at the open sky and plunges back into the tunnel. Another 20 or 30 seconds pass, but there is no indication from the steward, who is crouched above the rat cage, that the terrier has found the quarry.

Another tense minute passes before the steward gestures for the handler to collect his dog. The Scotty is then released into the tunnel and after only a brief pause the steward motions the owner to the quarry den. After 30 seconds of working the quarry, the Scotty is pulled from the tunnel. Both handlers talk briefly with the steward and judge and then return to the spectators.

The Border terrier has not passed — although he eventually made his way to the quarry, he'd exceeded the time limitation. His handler looks grim but shrugs off the failure quickly. "Oh, well," he says, scruffing the dog's fur, "it was fun!" The Scotty's handler grins as she pumps her fist in the air. "We passed!" she shouts.

Some Words to Know

Working the quarry: Showing strong interest by scratching and barking when the quarry is found.

The Basics of Earthdog

Earthdog, also called going to ground, allows terriers to show off their distinct and specialized hunting skills. Most terrier breeds were developed in Britain during the 18th and 19th centuries when the Enclosure Movement led to the deeding of common property to wealthy landowners across the British Isles. With this new concept of private property came fences and severe restrictions on hunting. Poor people who had previously hunted on the common land could now receive long prison sentences for poaching on private property.

Because the use of large hunting dogs was now restricted to wealthy landowners, commoners began to develop their own hunting dogs — small terriers who would "go to ground," or hunt in tunnels, after fox, badgers, and rats. The little dog would chase its prey into the tunnels and then kill it by shaking it and breaking the animal's neck. This type of hunting was done for sport, for pest control, and for sustenance. As the rural poor were forced from the land and into the squalor of the cities, terriers were taken along to control rat populations and for the blood sport of killing rats in pits.

Safety Considerations

Earthdog provides a safe alternative to allowing dogs to go to ground on their own. Hunting terriers can be seriously injured by cornered prey, and they are also at risk of injury or even death if the tunnel collapses. When terriers were used regularly for hunting vermin, it was not uncommon for one to be lost in a tunnel and not find his way out.

For optimal safety, terriers shouldn't be allowed to work prey in natural tunnels, and artificial tunnels should always have wooden liners to prevent cave-ins. The prey should be safely protected from the dogs and vice versa.

As with all dog sports, testing in very hot weather can be hard on dogs and they should always have adequate water, shade, and rest.

EARTHDOG TODAY

Two hundred years later, there is little need for terriers to plunge into tunnels to eke out a small supper or to rid crops and barns of pests, but the dogs bred for this task still exist. Enter earthdog trialing, first established by the American Working Terrier Association (AWTA) in 1971. The AKC adopted the sport in 1994. Although earthdog is largely an instinctual sport, dogs are tested on their abilities to hunt up to the tunnel, track the quarry in the tunnel, and then work the quarry, meaning they scratch, bark, and whine in an attempt to get to the rats.

Most terriers today use their innate skills only in these simulated exercises and tests, but there are some handlers who still hunt fox and other vermin with terriers, and the American Working Terrier Association accords titles for actual hunting situations as well as tests.

There is a strong stigma attached to the hunting of live animals in dens, and some of this crosses over into earthdog trials. Some animal rights advocates deride earthdog as cruel because of the dogs' working the live rats. Proponents argue that "professional" earthdog rats are so nonchalant about the dogs barking at them that they often sleep through the tests, but this is a source of controversy. In addition, some earthdog trialers believe that terriers perform best if allowed to kill a rat on occasion. Other handlers vehemently disagree.

Who Does Earthdog?

Because the sport was developed to recognize a specific style of hunting, this sport is open only to small terriers. There are two organizations that oversee earthdog, the American Working Terrier Association (AWTA) and the American Kennel Club (AKC). In both AWTA and AKC dogs must be six months old to enter a test. Dogs who do well in earthdog are those who have the typical terrier drive, which is a combination of tenacity, interest in prey, and energy.

People participate in earthdog trials for many different reasons, but mostly because they enjoy seeing their dogs show off their natural instincts. Among handlers are breeders who want to show that their dogs retain their work ethic and terrier lovers who just enjoy watching their dogs work. Although there are some junior handlers involved in earthdog, most participants are adults. Both men and women are involved, and you need a team of people to practice going to ground and conduct trials, which encourages a party-like atmosphere at trials.

Talking about Training and Time

Earthdog is less about training than about instinct. To many adherents of the sport, dogs either have the necessary drive or they don't. While some handlers do train their dogs on a regular basis, most don't.

As in all canine sports, however, a little bit of obedience training goes a long way in developing a dog you can work with. Before entering your first earthdog trial, train your dog on all the basic commands, particularly a reliable recall.

You can also get your dog interested in tunnel work by building your own small tunnel out of cardboard or plywood at home. Throw kibble or a favorite toy down the tunnel to encourage your dog to go after it. Then, the next time there is an earthdog trial near your home, sign your dog up to the Introduction to Quarry, where stewards will help you and your dog to figure out the game.

Evaluating Equipment and Expense

The main reason handlers don't do a lot of training between trials is that it's difficult to find a place to practice. Unless you have access to a local club that has its own tunnels and practice sessions, it will be almost impossible to practice going to ground (although there are those devoted souls who are willing to dig up their yard to give their dogs a place to practice).

The only real equipment in earthdog is the tunnel (and the rats). In both AWTA and AKC the tunnel is nine inches by nine inches and is made of a wooden liner with three sides and a dirt floor. A tunnel is dug out of the earth and the liner is set in. The top is usually covered with debris to camouflage it from the dogs. The tunnel is scented with "rat tea," a blend of rat urine and rat bedding soaked in water. There is a live rat in a cage at one end of the tunnel. The rat is protected from the dog both by the cage and by wooden dowels placed in front of the cage.

In some high level competitions where viewing the dog is a priority, an above-ground tunnel with Plexiglas backing allows viewers to watch the proceedings.

Canine Competition

At all levels of competition, the terrier must track rat scent through a tunnel and then work, or bark at, the rat in the cage. Depending on the level of competition, the tunnel may be more complicated, the dog may have to track the rat to the tunnel, or the dog may work alongside another dog.

ORGANIZATIONS

American Kennel Club (AKC) The AKC earthdog test is popular, especially among hobbyists who do not actually hunt with their dogs. Breeds recognized are Australian terriers, Bedlington terriers, Border terriers, Cairn terriers, dachshunds, Dandie Dinmont terriers, fox terriers, Lakeland terriers, Manchester terriers, miniature bull terriers, miniature schnauzers, Norwich terriers, Norfolk terriers, Scottish terriers, and Sealyham terriers.

American Working Terrier Association (AWTA) AWTA is the oldest earthdog organization and considered by some the more authentic earthdog organization. Breeds recognized are Australian terriers, Bedlington terriers, Border terriers, Cairn terriers, dachshunds, Dandie Dinmont terriers, fox terriers (smooth and wire), Jack Russell terriers, Jagdterriers, Lakeland terriers, Norwich terriers, Norfolk terriers, Patterdale terriers, Scottish terriers, and Sealyham terriers.

TITLES & QUALIFICATIONS

American Kennel Club (AKC)	American Working Terrrier Association (AWTA)
Introduction to Quarry	**Novice Class**
The tunnel is 10 feet long and has one 90-degree turn. The dog is released 10 feet from the tunnel and has 120 seconds to find the quarry. He must then work the quarry for 30 seconds. No titles are awarded and handlers are allowed to lead their dogs to the tunnel and to show them the quarry. The judge, rather than looking for faults, is there to help guide novice dogs and owners.	The tunnel is 9 feet long with one 90-degree turn. The dog is released 10 feet from the tunnel and has 60 seconds to enter the tunnel and find the rat. He must then work the rat for 30 seconds.
Junior Earthdog (JE)	**Certificate of Gameness**
The tunnel is 30 feet long and has three 90-degree turns. After the dog is released, he has 30 seconds to find the quarry. He must then work the rat for 60 seconds. Handlers are not allowed to give commands. To earn a title, dogs must pass the JE test two times under two different judges.	A Certificate of Gameness is awarded to dogs in simulated hunting tests. The tunnel is 30 feet long and the dog must enter the tunnel and find the quarry within 30 seconds. He must then work the quarry for 60 seconds.
Senior Earthdog (SE)	**Working Certificate**
The tunnel is 30 feet long, has three 90-degree turns, a false exit, and a false den scented with rat urine. The dog is released 30 feet from the tunnel and has 90 seconds to find the quarry. He must then work the quarry for 90 seconds. To earn a title, the dog must pass this test three times with at least two different judges.	A Working Certificate can be awarded on a number of quarry types, including badger, fox, and raccoon, for natural earth work in a hunting situation. The dog must work the quarry to the tunnel and then in the tunnel. The dog must either cause the prey to bolt or draw (pull) the quarry from the tunnel. Another AWTA member must witness the hunt.
Master Earthdog (ME)	**Hunting Certificate**
The dogs run two at a time. They are released 100 feet from the tunnel and must "hunt up" to the tunnel entrance. They have 60 seconds to reach the tunnel, which is blocked to keep them from entering it. When they reach the tunnel, they must work the tunnel for 30 seconds. Once both dogs alert at the tunnel, the judge asks the handler to remove the dogs and turn away from the tunnel while she removes the grate from the entrance and moves the rats to the end of the tunnel. The dog who alerts first is released into the tunnel while the second terrier must "honor" him — or wait while the first dog works. The working terrier has 90 seconds to find the quarry. He must then work it for 30 seconds. The judge attempts to distract the dog while he works the quarry. To receive a title, a dog must pass the ME test four times under at least two different judges.	The Hunting Certificate is awarded to a dog for killing quarry in a natural hunting setting. The dog can work the prey aboveground or draw the prey from the tunnel. Another AWTA member must witness the hunt.

STRONGDOG

While the tiny terriers play, there has been unrest among the owners of the larger terriers, including American Staffordshire terriers, Glen of Imaals, Kerry terriers, Irish terriers, Airedales, and wheaten terriers. All of these long-legged terrier breeds were bred to hunt vermin and go to ground, but the dimensions of earthdog, as well as breed perceptions, have precluded them from participating in the sport.

Enter Jim Tebbits, a longtime earthdog judge and breeder of Welsh terriers. Although his own dogs can compete in earthdog, he regretted that the larger terriers couldn't join in. As he also had some experience in establishing new canine sports — he was instrumental in writing the original AKC earthdog rule book — Tebbits did some research and found an Irish program for larger terriers called strongdog, which he set out to emulate.

Over the past several years, Tebbits has arranged for a number of strongdog demonstrations, mostly on the West Coast, and has begun the process of petitioning for AKC inclusion. Once accepted as an AKC performance sport,

strongdog will allow only certain purebred terrier breeds, but for the time being any dog can show up and try out the sport at a demo or "fun match."

Strongdog is similar to earthdog in that the dogs must enter an underground tunnel in pursuit of quarry. The dimensions are larger, 11 inches by 11 inches, and the current setup is a tunnel of 30 feet with a 45-degree turn and a 90-degree turn. Instead of live prey, the quarry is a "badger," an animal skin stuffed with sand, gravel, or sand-filled plastic bottles and weighing about 30 pounds. In addition to the weight, the handlers want the filling to give the pelt some "crunch," which gets the dogs more interested. Instead of working the prey in the tunnel, the dog pulls the "badger" out of the tunnel and releases it to his owner.

Kylene and Josh Onkka own Stellar Dog Training and are the proud owners of three Staffordshire terriers, Freyja, Vespa, and Mojo. Although they participate in obedience, rally, and conformation, they were looking for other canine sports in which to show their dogs' stuff. They attended a few strongdog demos and were hooked — they're now working with Tebbits to have the sport recognized by the AKC.

In strongdog, training starts with getting the dogs excited about the stuffed badger. "The first thing you do is have a prey circle," says Josh Onkka. "Have the dogs in a circle with the badger and agitate them. In this sport, if they don't have drive and are couch potatoes, they won't do very well."

Once the dog is interested in the badger, it is thrown a short distance into the tunnel while the dog is held back. The distance is gradually increased until the dog is charging into the tunnel and pulling the badger back out.

LURE COURSING:
THE LOVE OF THE CHASE

The heavy pounding of hoofbeats reverberating over the grass is surprising. It's hard to believe that the sound comes from a slender fawn-colored greyhound, not a snorting racehorse on the straightaway.

Stephanie Wiseman adopted Walter after his racing career ended. Standing still, the young dog is, frankly, a little homely and seems ill at ease. But from the moment he sees the lure and Wiseman releases him to chase it across the grass, Walter is a different dog: confident, athletic, and magnificent to watch.

The scene, as is so often the case in the world of dog sports, is bucolic. Handlers sit on fences, watching the dogs run, and long-legged, shiny-coated dogs play in a paddock while they wait their turn to chase the lure. Carol Chittum, a longtime whippet breeder, lure courser, and president of the Cascade Lure Coursing Club, displays a no-nonsense style with the handlers but clearly has a soft spot for the dogs.

She grins as Walter dances around after his run. "Did you have fun?!" she asks him and then turns to me. "A greyhound is capable of crossing that field in six seconds flat!"

Since Chittum first started lure coursing with her whippets in the 1970s, she has titled eight AKC Field Champions. At this practice, two of her whippets relax in crates while waiting their turns. For Chittum, lure coursing is a chance to give her dogs something fun to do as well as a way to preserve the coursing instinct in her breeding stock.

In Chittum's opinion, all sight hounds should be required to title in lure coursing before being allowed to breed, as is common in Europe. "These dogs are bred to save up energy — an energy piggy bank — and use it in big bursts of speed," she says. "Lure coursing makes them happy; it satisfies their very primitive need to hunt." She laments the fact that so many whippets today are bred for looks rather than utility. "I'd love to see these dogs prove they were more than pillow puppies."

For John Parker, a veteran lure courser and greyhound rescuer, the joy of lure coursing is seeing the satisfaction his 10 greyhounds and two whippets gain from the sport. "They love the thrill of the chase," says Parker. "I love the look on their faces when they come in on the lure at the end. It's one of complete fulfillment at doing what they were bred to do — run like the wind in pursuit of prey."

The Basics of Lure Coursing

Sight hounds have been bred to course live game for thousands of years, hunting for both sustenance and entertainment. In the 1800s in the United States, live game coursing became a spectator sport when dogs were released after live game in an enclosed area. This was an extremely popular event, but after it was criminalized in the early 1900s, it was quickly replaced by greyhound racing, which sent the dogs after a mechanical lure around an oval track.

In the 1970s, a group of sight hound fanciers became interested in developing a sport that would showcase their dogs' skills in a setting more like real game coursing. This was the birth of the modern sport of lure coursing.

The equipment used in lure coursing is extremely specialized and quite complicated. The 600- to 1,000-foot course is laid out with a loop of string that runs around a series of plastic pulleys that are fixed to the ground with thin spikes. The course must have a minimum of four turns. The lure, usually just a white plastic bag, is operated by a battery-powered motor.

At the "Tallyho" signal from the hunt master, the lure operator starts the lure. The lure is always kept 10 to 30 yards ahead of the dogs, and the operator can vary the speed according to the speed of the dog running. Although not racing against one another, dogs race in groups of three to simulate a hunting pack.

"All of the breeds automatically do something called flanking because they know they can't occupy the same space," explains Chittum. "One dog is behind the game, one dog out to one side, one dog out to the other side — in a hunting situation, those flanking dogs steer the game toward the other dog. It's absolutely amazing to see!"

Who Does Lure Coursing?

Only purebred sight hounds are allowed to participate. They must be registered with either the AKC or the American Sighthound Field Association (ASFA), and only certain breeds are allowed to participate under each program. For the ASFA, these include Afghan hounds, azawakhs, basenjis, borzois, greyhounds, Ibizan hounds, Irish wolfhounds, Italian greyhounds, pharaoh hounds, Rhodesian ridgebacks, salukis, Scottish deerhounds, sloughis, and whippets.

The AKC's list is similar, although sloughis and azawakhs cannot title. The AKC also allows Portuguese podengos and Thai ridgebacks to participate, although neither of these breeds can title either. Retired racing greyhounds must submit their track racing numbers.

Of all these breeds, greyhounds have a special relationship with lure cours-ing. For greyhound rescuers, seeing their dogs on a lure course can be a mind-opening experience. Although most rescue greyhounds are the consummate couch potatoes, when they are chasing a lure, their track instincts kick in and the result can be quite spectacular.

"Greyhounds have probably the keenest chase instinct of all the sight hounds and are the fastest sight hounds," says Parker. "Their experience on the track definitely makes them more interested."

But all of these dogs clearly love the experience. As soon as they catch sight of the lure, most of them are straining for the chance to chase it. Jeanette Ennis, who owns two Rhodesian ridgebacks, Newton and Helix, points out that every lure coursing breed has its particular skills. "Each dog breed runs differently," she says. "Greyhounds are good on the long, straight stretches but they don't turn very well. Whippets will follow the bag; ridgebacks will flank it."

Dogs cannot begin lure coursing until one year of age, and most dogs don't run past the age of four. By then they have not only begun to slow down but many have also learned the game well enough to "cheat" by crossing the course to catch the lure when it comes around a turn instead of following it along the full course.

THE IMPORTANCE OF BREEDING

Chittum counsels that potential sight hound owners who want to lure course with their dogs be sure to buy a puppy from a breeder whose dogs have been titled in lure coursing. In her experience, most whippets, Ibizan hounds, and Afghan hounds will run after the lure, but many salukis, borzoi, and deerhounds have had the desire to chase the lure bred out of them. "It depends on the breeding — there are whippets that are dumb as a stump," she says. "They wouldn't know a lure if it brushed against them; the chase instinct is bred out of them and they're just pretty lawn ornaments."

In the United States, more women than men are involved in the sport, although lure operators tend to be men. Not surprisingly, a number of lure coursers are also involved in horses. Many club events, in fact, look like a spread from *Town & Country*, with well-heeled handlers chatting while their sleek dogs lounge in the backs of Audi station wagons.

Talking about Training and Time

Because lure coursing is primarily a test of instinctive behavior (and because most people can't set up a course in their backyard), there is no training that you can do to make your dog a better lure courser. Many dogs do need to be encouraged to focus on the lure, however.

Safety Considerations

The safety of the dogs is a huge issue in lure coursing. Great care is taken to keep the dogs from becoming tangled in the lure line, but there is always the chance for injury because dogs are running at top speeds on uneven ground. Greyhounds seem to be at greatest risk for injury, but all lure coursers can suffer toe or foot injuries, or even break bones. When setting up lure coursing tracks, the operators try to ensure that the ground is fairly even and that there are no gopher holes or other hazards.

When lure coursing with your dog, be choosy about fields and course plans. Look for large fields with good footing — if the turns on a course are too tight for your dog, be ready to pull him out of the event. Always keep your dog's safety in mind. This is especially true in the case of greyhounds, who run flat out and are at more risk for injury. Greyhounds are also not used to making turns, particularly right-hand ones, as they always turn to the left on oval courses. A greyhound who has not been gradually exposed to the lure-coursing terrain before entering a trial is at serious risk of injury.

Puppies should be exposed to the lure early in order to do well in the sport. You can play little cat-and-mouse type games, using faux fur on a string at the end of a stick to stimulate their interest in chasing. Although they can't compete, most clubs welcome puppies at practices. Exposure to the bustle of an event is good experience for young dogs, and simply seeing the other dogs chasing the lure is enough training for some dogs.

Although many people give up if their dogs aren't immediately attracted to the lure, Chittum encourages them to keep trying. "I have used clicker training to train older dogs to follow the lure with their eyes," she says. "Once they follow the lure with their eyes, their feet will follow. It's a question of reinforcing an instinct that has possibly been buried."

Lure coursing isn't a terribly time-consuming activity, as most handlers go to just 5 to 10 trials each year, although some handlers are more serious about it. Local clubs may meet once a month. Club members are expected to help out at practices and at meets. Every event requires a number of people on the field (a paddock master, a lure operator, a huntsman, a field secretary, a field chairman, and a field clerk), so there are always plenty of jobs to be filled.

Evaluating Equipment and Expense

Lure coursing expenses are minimal unless handlers and dogs live far from lure coursing events, in which case travel expenses can add up. Event entries are usually quite reasonable. To practice, you'll need to join a club that owns lure-coursing equipment. Because courses and equipment are portable and can be set up in any appropriate field, clubs generally meet once a month, set up the equipment and a course, and do some practice runs. Participation fees vary, depending on the club.

You will need a special collar/leash combination called a slip lead. The slip lead consists of a wide strip of cloth with rings at each end. Another strip of cloth threads through the rings to hold the collar together until the handler pulls the cloth through the rings to release the dog.

Canine Competition

Although they run singly in practice and in qualifying trials, in sanctioned trials dogs run in groups of three. Each dog wears a colored vest to identify it. The dogs are released at the same time and must follow the lure on a 600- to 1,000-foot course with at least four turns. The lure moves at 40 miles an hour directly in front of the dogs.

ORGANIZATIONS

American Kennel Club (AKC) Only pure-bred sight hounds are allowed to compete under AKC rules; many handlers say that the AKC lure-coursing trials are more serious than ASFA events. The dogs are scored individually, rather than against the other dogs, on five elements: agility, endurance, enthusiasm, follow, and speed. The judges also consider breed characteristics when judging. Each dog can receive up to 10 points in each of these areas. A score of 25 is considered a good run.

American Sighthound Field Association (ASFA) Purebred sight hounds are allowed to compete under the ASFA. This was the first lure-coursing organization in the United States and remained popular even after the AKC began sanctioning events. The dogs are judged individually and against the other dogs they are racing. In addition to a ribbon, place winners can earn a maximum of 100 points in five areas, with possible points ranging from 15 to 25: following the lure (15 points), enthusiasm (15 points), endurance (20 points), agility (25 points), and speed (25 points).

TITLES	QUALIFICATIONS
AKC	
Junior Courser (JC)	The dog must obtain a minimum score of 25 points in two competitions on a course that is at least 600 yards with a minimum of four turns.
Senior Courser (SC)	The dog must obtain a minimum score of 25 points in four competitions on a course that is at least 600 yards with a minimum of four turns.
Master Courser (MC)	The dog must obtain a minimum score of 25 points in 31 competitions on a course that is at least 600 yards long with a minimum of four turns.
Field Champion (FC)	The dog places consistently among the top scorers in his breed.
ASFA	
Field Champion (FC)	The dog must obtain 100 points and two first-place awards or one first place and two second-place awards.
Lure Courser of Merit (LCM)	The dog must obtain 300 points and four first-place awards.

WET & WOOLLY WATER RESCUE

It's a wet, rainy Sunday morning in August when I pull into a state park in Enumclaw, Washington. A collection of trucks and SUVs, several with Newfie-themed license plates, is clustered at the beach entrance, and a group of wet suit–clad men and women and large wet dogs is milling around between the cars and the beach.

The Newfs take the weather in stride, and their handlers — despite the discomfort of the rain and the prospect of taking their turn in the unseasonably cold lake water — shout and cheer enthusiastically as a Newfie slowly but purposefully tows a "drowning victim" through the water to the beach. When the pair reaches the shore, the large dog, named Jenny, looks positively pleased with herself. The water steward is happy to be out of the lake and Jenny's owner, Janet Elliott, is beaming — Jenny has just passed her Water Dog Excellent, a grueling test that usually takes several years of training to pass. While Jenny shakes the water from her giant body, slobber flying, Elliott accepts hugs from fellow club members. Although it's hard to tell with all the water, there may be a few tears falling as she repeats, "She did it! She did it!"

Standing in the rain in a full wet suit and rain jacket, Brian Hodges looks downcast, though he is pleased for Janet and Jenny. His dog Winnie was to have tested for her Water Dog Excellent immediately following Jenny, but he explains that Winnie was spooked when practicing this morning, and he and his wife, Michelle Fuqua, have decided to pull her from the event.

"For some reason, right before the test, Winnie got scared of an exercise where two 'drowners' hide behind a boat and holler for help," recounts Hodges. "She performed this exercise perfectly countless times, but something really scared her about those disembodied voices."

At a practice session, a handler would simply guide the dog into the water to work through the fear, but in a test situation you can't help your dog. Hodges and Fuqua feel their best option is to pull the dog from the event rather than compromise Winnie's training and her trust in them.

Against the disappointments, however, there are just as many triumphs. Hodges's and Fuqua's other Newfoundland, Maggie, is also competing today, for a senior title. She passes with flying colors.

The Basics of Water Rescue

Watching Newfoundland water rescue is like watching an old picture book come to life. These gentle giants have been bred for hundreds of years to rescue drowning victims, tow disabled boats, and retrieve items from the water, but they are rarely used in this capacity any more, and testing for water skills is something of an anachronism. One reason to keep those skills honed, says Marylou Zimmerman, president of the Newfoundland Club of Seattle, is on the chance that they may someday be called back into service.

Zimmerman is a breeder of Newfoundlands with a strong interest in maintaining the water skills of these dogs. Like many breeders, she feels that it's good for the breed to maintain their utility, but she also hopes that in the United States, as has happened in some European countries, Newfoundlands will once again be popularly used as lifeguards.

"The dogs love to do water work," says Zimmerman, "and it lets the breeders preserve that instinct. If we ever needed to use them as water rescue dogs, we know they could still do it. In England they are used to patrol waterways; in Italy they are used extensively in the lakes region."

In Newfoundland water rescue, the dog must be able to tow a boat, retrieve items from the water, take a life buoy to a drowning victim, and pull a drowning victim to shore, among other skills. To rescue a person, the dog generally will grab an arm, although in a test the "victim" will usually hold on to the dog. The test is designed for a "floating" victim — someone who has already inhaled water and is not conscious enough to hold on to the dog — in which case the goal is just to get them to shore or to a boat as quickly as possible.

Who Does Water Rescue?

Newfoundlands, Portuguese water dogs, and Leonbergers were once regularly used in water work, and breed clubs for these breeds conduct their own water tests. Portuguese water dogs did not do water rescue per se, but were assistants on fishing boats. They served as couriers between boats, fetched dropped lines, and even herded fish into nets. Their breed tests reflect this background.

According to Deborah Lee Miller-Riley, it's not just the dogs bred for water work who take to it. Though an active owner of Portuguese water dogs, she believes that any water-loving dog should be able to participate in a water sport, mixed breeds included. In 1999 she founded Canine Water Sports, an organization that trains and tests all breeds and breed mixes for water work. Any dog over six months of age can participate, and Miller-Riley stresses that the club welcomes physically disabled dogs and handlers.

"There is no other canine sport where handlers and dogs are communicating at an eye-to-eye level," says Miller-Riley.

"Swimming equalizes team members because swimmers lose their height advantage in the water and the dogs are literally in your face. It is totally exhilarating to connect with a canine partner while bobbing around in a summer lake."

FUN FOR THE WHOLE FAMILY

The people who participate in water tests must enjoy water as much as their dogs do. Both in training and in testing, they are going to get wet. Handlers not only train their own dogs for tests but also work as a team to help train other dogs. In doing so, they often must serve as simulated drowning victims — meaning they float in the water waiting for a Newfie to rescue them, no matter the weather. "Believe me," says Hodges, "it takes a special kind of commitment to get into the water on some days."

Although Canine Water Sports requires that handlers be 18 years old to test, the Newfoundland Club of America has no age requirements for handlers. And handlers of any age are welcome to join training sessions. Both of Zimmerman's children, ages 11 and 13, have been water stewarding for five years. "We're a very popular play date in the summer," she laughs. "You just go out there and splash and scream and the dog will come and get you."

Water work has one of the best demographic mixes of all the canine sports.

There are equal numbers of men and women, and there are singles and couples, kids and seniors. Families participate together, and team members tend to be good friends. "You can't train a water rescue dog alone," says Zimmerman. "You need someone to go out in the water and drown for you. So it really is a sport that encourages you to make friends."

Talking about Training and Time

The time spent training a water dog depends largely on access to water, personal preference, and how quickly you want your dog to test for each level. Teams that live close to water will often train three or four times a week during the summer simply because it's fun. As a rule of thumb, each level generally takes several months to train for. Tests are conducted in late summer, so if a dog fails, he may have to wait another year for the opportunity to test again.

A great deal of training must take place before the dog ever gets into the water. A dog should know his basic commands, such as *come, stay, sit,* and *down,* as well as have a strong retrieve to hand, meaning that the dog retrieves an item but does not release it until requested to do so, before beginning actual water training. During this early training, a handler should begin introducing the dog

to water. Good Newfie breeders expose their pups to water by the time they are six or seven weeks old.

Safety Considerations

Because all water activity holds inherent risks, canine water groups have firm rules for water safety. All groups require life jackets for handlers during tests. Canine Water Sports requires life jackets for both dogs and handlers during training. During tests, the handler must wear a life jacket, although it is optional for the dog. Handlers are also encouraged to wear booties to protect their feet when wading in and out of the water and wet suits to keep them warm and to protect them from sunburn and dog claws.

When working in the water, handlers should always practice as a group with at least one person on the beach acting as a lifeguard. No dog is 100 percent predictable and a panicked dog and handler in the water can easily lead to tragedy. Boats can capsize, and people can bump their heads or trip on underwater rocks. There is also a risk of hypothermia if the handler, water stewards, or dogs stay in the cold water for too long.

GETTING WET

The introduction to water is perhaps the most important step in the whole training process. A dog should never be compelled to enter the water; being forced into water that is too cold or too rough might instill a lifelong fear. This is an ongoing issue as dogs can develop fear of the water after one negative reaction, even after many wonderful experiences in the water. Rewarding curious and explorative behavior on the part of the puppy is the best way to instill confidence and build a positive perception of water.

Once a dog knows his on-land commands and is comfortable with the water, you can begin training him in water work. There are no established training protocols in water work, and methods for training the specific skills in water tests, such as retrieving a line or object, towing a victim, or towing a boat, differ from handler to handler. However, developing a strong working bond between handler and dog is essential.

For dogs with a strong water instinct, the training is more about shaping that instinct than anything else. Other dogs may take more intensive training. Joining a club can help a handler with the nuanced needs of her particular dog.

Evaluating Equipment and Expense

Training and testing for water work requires the participation of many people, as well as a range of equipment, including a 14-foot boat, oars, boat bumpers, and life rings. For this reason, it's far easier to train with a club. Clubs, of course, require dues and training fees to help offset their considerable costs.

Finding a public swimming area where dogs are welcome is usually the most challenging task in water work. Many handlers drive more than an hour each way to find a spot to exercise and train their dogs. If you are lucky enough to live close to a beach that allows dogs, your training will be considerably easier.

As an individual, you'll need a good wet suit, booties, gloves, and a life jacket. Some dogs also use life jackets.

Canine Competition

Breed organizations and Canine Water Sports have a number of types of tests. The Newfoundland Club of America water test system is the best established. During a Newfoundland Club of America water rescue test, there are two judges and multiple stewards who serve as drowning victims, row the boat, and perform other functions.

Water dog tests are pass/fail; if a dog is not able to complete any part of the test, he fails.

ORGANIZATIONS

Canine Water Sports This all-breed water sports organization is well established on the East Coast and is slowly making its way across the states.

The following breed clubs conduct breed-specific water tests and training opportunities: **Newfoundland Club of America; Leonberger Club of America; Portuguese Water Dog Club of America.**

TITLES

As an example, each test of the Newfoundland Club of America consists of six exercises.

Junior: Junior is the most basic level of water testing. When a dog passes the junior test he is awarded the Water Dog (WD) title. The test includes:

- A basic control exercise done on land

- Retrieving a bumper with the dog entering the water from the boat

- Retrieving a life jacket with the dog entering the water from the shore

- Taking a line from the shore to a "drowning victim"

- Towing a boat parallel to the shore

- Swimming with his handler and allowing his handler to hold his fur while he tows her to shore

Senior: Once a dog passes the senior test, he is awarded the Water Rescue Dog (WRD) title. The senior test has six different exercises, including:

- Retrieving two objects with the dog entering the water from the shore

- Retrieving an object with the dog entering the water from a boat

- Retrieving an object from underwater

- Rescuing three victims with the dog entering the water from the shore

- Towing a boat to the shore

- Rescuing a victim with the dog entering the water from a boat

Water Dog Excellent: The Water Dog Excellent (WDX) test also has six exercises:

- Searching for an abandoned boat and then towing it to the shore

- Rescuing multiple victims from the side of a boat

- Rescuing an unconscious victim

- Rescuing a victim from under a capsized boat

- Taking a line to shore from a stranded boat

- Taking lines to multiple drowning victims

SCHUTZHUND: A SERIOUS SPORT

Rigid with concentration, a powerful German shepherd dog lunges at a man wearing a heavy padded sleeve on his arm. The man raises a stick threateningly and the shepherd leaps into the air, grabbing the man's padded arm in one swift motion and hanging on with determination.

This is the iconic vision of Schutzhund — a dog testing his protective mettle against a menacing stranger — but this sport consists of far more than bite work. Schutzhund, also called Vielseitigkeitspruefung für Gebrauchshunde (meaning "versatility test for working dogs"), tests a dog's valor, courage, and loyalty through a series of rigorous obedience, obstacle, and tracking exercises.

One common misconception is that the goal of Schutzhund training is to produce an aggressive attack dog. To serious Schutzhund people, this couldn't be further from the truth. The ideal is to train a dog to control his aggression. A dog who can be called off when in mid-attack is a dog who can be controlled in almost any situation.

Sandi Purdy is just what you might imagine a lifelong Schutzhund competitor to be: tough as nails, smoky-voiced, and in love with her dogs. A competitor for almost 40 years, Purdy currently serves as a judge for DVG America Schutzhund, one of two North American clubs. She acknowledges that Schutzhund training is not an easy road. For some, that's the attraction. For others, the long, difficult process is worth the result: a dog who is trained down to the smallest movement.

"My first dog was a Great Dane," says Purdy. "She earned all the titles available. One time we were sitting under a tree at a trial. Big Bertha was lying on her back and a two-year-old [child] came over and sat on her. This was a dog who had just come off of the protection field with a 98 score!"

To Purdy, the story exemplifies the beauty of a well-trained Schutzhund dog: driven and loyal enough to fend off even the most threatening stranger, well-trained enough to do it only at the direction of his handler, and even-tempered enough to go from the high-adrenaline intensity of a protection test to snoozing under a tree and enduring the prodding of a curious toddler.

Purdy, like many Schutzhund competitors, enjoys tracking first and obedience second; protection is a distant third. "Protection is just something that I have to do to earn the titles," she says. Lisa Clark agrees. She has four German shepherd dogs, three of whom she is training for Schutzhund.

Clark values the importance of the protection work, especially in combination with the other two phases, but enjoys the obedience work most. Clark initially competed in AKC obedience, but found it confining. "Schutzhund looks more at the dog, its temperament, character, and drive. AKC obedience is only sport; nothing matters but correctness."

The Basics of Schutzhund

Schutzhund was developed in Germany in the early 1900s as a way of testing the working skills and temperament of German shepherd dogs. Only after titling in Schutzhund were registered shepherds permitted to breed. The program was never intended solely to produce attack dogs but rather to select the best individuals to continue the breed.

Schutzhund first came to the United States in the early 1970s through an organization called the North American Schutzhund Association (NASA). NASA tried to get AKC recognition, causing a number of members to leave the organization feeling that the sport had been dissipated through this effort. Another group, United Schutzhund Clubs of America (USA), formed in 1975, but this club also eventually diverged along philosophical lines.

In 1980, several Schutzhund purists started an American chapter of the DVG, which is the oldest established Schutzhund organization in Germany. They established DVG America, which is recognized by the Federation Cynologique Internationale (FCI), a European umbrella registry and sanctioning organization for dog breeds.

There are three levels of Schutzhund: Schutzhund Examination I, II, and III, which correspond with three titles, called degrees. Dogs can title in Schutzhund A and B phases — tracking and obedience — without competing in the C — protection — phase. All three phases are tested in a single day.

SCHUTZHUND A (TRACKING)

The dog must follow a track with scent articles; he is scored by how precisely he follows the track as well as by whether he finds the scent articles and completes the track. The length and difficulty increases with each level.

SCHUTZHUND B (OBEDIENCE)

The dog is tested on recalls, directed retrieves over a hurdle and a six-foot wall, heeling, long downs and stays, and reaction to gunshot noise. Dogs are tested in pairs, with one dog on a long down while the other performs other activities, switching places after the first dog completes his exercises. The tests increase in complexity by level.

SCHUTZHUND C (PROTECTION)

The dog is tested on his ability to protect his handler. In the protection phase, a "helper" (or decoy) plays the role of an aggressor. The dog must find the helper in a blind and indicate the find by barking. He must protect his handler by biting the sleeve of the helper but must immediately release the sleeve when asked to by his handler. Again, the complexity increases with each level.

SCHUTZHUND SAFETY

Because Schutzhund involves training dogs for protection work, there are serious safety implications both on and off the field. A dog who is properly trained and titled in Schutzhund is a dog who can be controlled under all circumstances. However, there are unethical trainers or handlers, and "knock-off" sports that promote aggression over the control and even temperament promoted in true Schutzhund. A well-trained Schutzhund dog is ideally like a well-trained police dog: a fierce protector and defender as well as an eager and friendly ambassador; as comfortable pursuing a suspect as greeting a grade-school classroom.

A dog who is incorrectly trained in Schutzhund can be extremely dangerous. Always train your dog with a recognized Schutzhund club that is affiliated with one of the two national Schutzhund organizations. If anything in the training makes you uncomfortable, walk away. If you hire a trainer, work only with a trainer who has titled her own dog in Schutzhund, preferably to a level III.

"Potential handlers need to be very, very cautious," says Purdy. "If someone says, 'I'll train your dog for $1,500,' run, don't just walk away."

Who Does Schutzhund?

Although there are no breed requirements in Schutzhund, the sport by its nature requires a dog who is large and strong enough to participate in the training and competition, particularly in the protection phase. The dogs most commonly seen in Schutzhund are German shepherds and other breeds developed as guard dogs: Rottweilers, giant schnauzers, Doberman pinschers, Belgian Malinois, Bouvier des Flandres, and Tervurens.

Some handlers have been very successful with non-German dogs, including Aussies, boxers, pit bull types, and Airedales. Purdy has seen a corgi achieve a Schutzhund II and a golden retriever and a Labrador retriever earn Schutzhund IIIs. Her Great Dane, Big Bertha, remains the only member of that breed to earn a Schutzhund III.

For the most part, however, dogs who tend to do well in Schutzhund were bred for this sport. Many Schutzhund handlers are also Schutzhund dog breeders. Good Schutzhund breeders take great pride in producing dogs with the suitable conformation and temperament for Schutzhund. They also begin training their pups for Schutzhund from when they are very young.

People who enjoy Schutzhund tend to be type-A personalities who are willing to devote huge amounts of time to their dogs' training. According to Purdy, there are only about 1,000 Schutzhund participants currently training in the United States. To be a Schutzhund dog handler is to be part of a very exclusive club.

Part of Schutzhund training involves retrieving an object over a barrier.

A number of handlers work with police dogs. Many of the dogs bought by police departments are bred and trained Schutzhund dogs, and some officers continue their training as a hobby outside of the work setting. Most Schutzhund participants are over the age of 40, and unlike many canine sports, somewhat more men than women participate. Schutzhund remains an extremely small-scale sport. USA estimates it has 4,000 members and DVG about 1,200 members, although only about a fifth of these members are actively training and testing at any one time.

Talking about Training and Time

Schutzhund is an extremely time-intensive sport. It may take several years before a dog is ready to test for his first title. Of all the dogs who participate, only a select few will make it through all three levels. It takes enormous discipline and commitment on the part of both the dog and the handler.

The training for the obedience portion of Schutzhund is similar to standard obedience, with an even greater emphasis on correctness and precision. The tracking differs from standard tracking in that Schutzhund dogs are expected to track the trail exactly as it was laid, rather than the general trail that a typical tracking dog is expected to follow. The protection training is extremely specialized and requires months of work with an experienced (and possibly expensive) trainer.

Participants emphasize the need to join a good Schutzhund club that will help you train your dog correctly. A good club emphasizes tracking and obedience over protection; some may even ban newcomers from protection until they have trained in tracking and obedience.

Within modern dog sports, Schutzhund is controversial not only for its protection phase but also for its emphasis on traditional corrections. Most trainers continue to use such methods as strong leash corrections, pinch and prong collars, and shock collars, although most combine these with positive reinforcement techniques such as toy and food treats and verbal praise.

Evaluating Equipment and Expense

The equipment, like the sport, is specialized. In tracking, participants need tracking gloves, a tracking harness, and a long line. In obedience, participants need a one-meter hurdle, a six-foot scaling wall, and dumbbells. In Schutzhund, participants need access to a blind (basically a three-sided tent), a protective sleeve (usually just called the sleeve), and other protective clothing.

Expenses to participate in Schutzhund vary. A dog bred for the sport can be quite expensive, several thousand dollars or more. Specialized equipment for training, safe kennels or crates for boarding, and training fees if you opt to work with a professional trainer can also add up.

Unlike agility or flyball, in which dogs may trial every weekend, Schutzhund dogs are tested only when they move up a level or when they need to repeat a test. Schutzhund tests are not available in every region, which means many handlers will need to travel to attend one. Anecdotally, in the United States, Schutzhund seems to be particularly popular in the Southwest.

Canine Competition

Points are awarded for each aspect of Schutzhund: 100 possible points for tracking (80 for the track and 20 for the 7 articles the dog must find); 100 possible points in protection (5 to search for helper, 10 for hold and bark, 35 for attack, and 50 for pursuit and hold); and 100 possible points for obedience. To pass, the dog must receive a minimum of 70 points in tracking and obedience each, and 80 points in protection.

ORGANIZATIONS

- **Landesverband DVG America (LV/DVG)**

- **United Schutzhund Clubs of America (USA)**

The main differences in the two clubs are ones of administration rather than in the way in which training or trialing are conducted.

CHAPTER 9

Pure Dog Power

Sledding / Skijoring / Dryland Pulling
Carting / Weight Pulling

FOR SOME DOGS, THE DRIVE TO PULL is intrinsic to their nature. For the Nordic dogs, it's the will to run — to use their great strength and agility to move across the snow into a darkening horizon. For Rottweilers and pit bulls, it's the need to please their people, to prove their worth by putting their very essence into the task they are given. The pulling sports are vastly different — some are about speed and adventure; others are about will and tenacity. Whatever the motivation, the results are spectacular.

SLEDDING: THE ULTIMATE SNOW SPORT

For mushers, it always comes back to this: the cacophony of dozens of harnessed sled dogs howling, screeching, and whining as they wait to be released and then the instant white silence that ensues when they are allowed to run. Once on the trail, the sound of paws muffled by the snow, each team is an entity, moving together instinctually as they follow the lead dogs and the occasional direction from the musher. In the woods, the only sound from a dog team is panting and the quiet jingle of harnesses.

"We all love the forest, the quiet, and the wildlife," Miriam Cooper says of mushing with her dogs in North Pole, Alaska. "That is the main reason why I got into the sport: to go farther into the woods — to chase the silence."

"As the musher, I have the privilege of running as part of the pack, traveling at their speed, seeing what they see, watching their interactions, and knowing that they are doing what they love to do," says TC Wait, who has 17 dogs in her kennel but usually runs a team of eight. "The dogs really do love to pull. Their ears are up, they have happy faces, there's sheer excitement when they see their harnesses, and there are howls of joy when it snows! I often wonder what job I might have that would get me that excited every day to go do it."

Sledding, or mushing, celebrates the use of dogs to pull sleds. In many cultures, including native Alaskan, Siberian, and Samisk, dogs have been used for thousands of years to transport both people and goods across ice and snow. With the advent of airplanes and snow machines, few people still need to maintain a sled dog team, although many do out of tradition, for sport or for hobby, or to maintain the utility of the sledding breeds.

The Basics of Sledding

Among mushers the most dramatic distinction is the divide between the competitive mushers and the hobbyists. There are those who just love the rush of the dogsled and do it for the occasional fun of spending time with their dogs in the outdoors. These mushers may not even have a full team, making one up by combining their dogs with borrowed dogs. And then there are those who do it to win, to breed stronger, faster dogs, and to gain the recognition that comes with winning a race along the lines of the Iditarod.

Most mushers fall in the middle — they are passionate about their dogs and about their sport; it is more than a hobby but not quite an obsession. They may breed an occasional litter or compete once in a while, but the emphasis is not on winning or creating a super dog — it's on enjoying the winter in a way that is simply impossible without a dogsled.

Who Does Sledding?

The best sled dogs, as is to be expected, are the ones who are born to it: Siberian huskies, Alaskan huskies, and Samoyeds. Alaskan malamutes excel in pulling heavy loads at a slower pace. Dogs who like sledding typically have boundless energy, a love of cold weather, and the inability to stay next to you on a walk. Unlike in obedience, pulling is a good thing in this sport.

Although they might not win races, other dogs such as hounds, Labs, golden

Verbal Commands

Easy: Slow down

Gee: Turn right

Haw: Turn left

Hike/Let's go: Start running (not *mush*, despite popular perception)

retrievers, and Aussies participate, too. Hounds, in fact, have proven to be such good sled dogs that a great deal of hound blood has been bred into Alaskan huskies, widely regarded as the super sledders. In fact, some Alaskan huskies look more like hounds than huskies.

Dogsledding is one of the few canine sports in which as many men are as involved as women. "You see a lot of single men sledding, as well as single women," says Steve Loper, who sleds with his Samoyeds. "There are also couples and families with children." The beauty of sledding, says Loper, is that the kids can be involved with the parents. There are plenty of sledding races open to juniors, and young children can ride on the sled while a parent mushes.

Mushers are, as a rule, outdoorsy people who savor the opportunity to get out into nature with their favorite companions. They tend to be risk takers and thrill seekers, and they are quick to point out that sledding is not a hobby; it's a lifestyle. "Mushing isn't just about training on the trail," says Cooper. "It's feeding, maintaining the dog yard, cleaning, brushing, scooping poop, socializing, and giving as much time as I have to them every day, all the while giving them all my love."

To regularly run a four-dogsled dog team, a musher needs at least six dogs. A sled dog team is a constantly changing entity; puppies grow into the sport while older dogs age out. Because few hobby mushers give up their dogs simply because they can no longer run, there are always at least a few retirees in a kennel.

KEEPING SLED DOGS

The most common way to house sled dogs is outdoors in doghouses, sometimes with a large exercise area for supervised play. It's unusual for sled dogs to live inside the house, although many modern mushers will allow one or two dogs inside the house on a rotating basis. Mushers argue that their dogs prefer to live outside, but there is controversy

over the ethics and viability of maintaining a large kennel of sled dogs. Faced with criticism from observers and animal welfare groups about keeping dogs tied out on tethers, mushers are quick to respond that their dogs generally receive far more exercise and attention than most house dogs who are crated for 9 to 10 hours a day.

That may well be the case with some dogs, but not all mushers are alike. Some provide their dogs with plenty of personal attention and exercise, humane living conditions, and a large turnout area for play when they are not tethered or kenneled. (A number of mushers are moving away from the traditional tie out and now house their dogs in less restrictive kennels.) Others keep their dogs in substandard conditions with little interaction or exercise other than sledding, and some participate in the hugely controversial practice of culling dogs who don't display excellent sledding qualities.

Talking about Training and Time

Although the thrill of running a dog team is palpable, mushers have a heavy load of responsibility. Their dogs must be cared for, fed, housed, and trained every day. This is an extremely time- and cost-intensive sport.

Pulling a dogsled is part natural instinct, part socialization, and part training. Some dogs, especially those bred for it, just take to pulling a sled right away. In fact, mushers say that experienced dogs not only train each other but also train new mushers. Often a musher will just add a new dog into a team and the dog will learn to run along with the other dogs. An Alaskan husky from a well-established sled dog breeder will probably need minimal exposure to a sled before picking it up. A Lab might need much more.

Although there is a learning curve when introducing a young dog to sledding, most sled dogs need little ongoing training; what they do need are lots of opportunities to mush and stay conditioned. During the winter season, mushers generally run their dogs every other day. During summer months, they may take time off or run their dogs on ATVs or carts during cool morning hours.

HOW TO GET STARTED

A beginning musher really needs to connect with a good mentor. The International Sled Dog Racing Association (ISDRA) Web site provides contact information for those willing to counsel new mushers. A mentor will not only help to guide you in training your dogs but will also expose you to sledding before you make the commitment to purchase a sled.

SLED DOG SAFETY

Sledding, especially long runs, can be incredibly taxing on the teams. Before running, mushers often feed their dogs a mixture of canned dog food and warm water for extra fluids and energy to sustain them through a long run. A good musher looks for signs that her dogs are faltering and knows when to turn around. In addition to exhaustion, dogs can fall, become tangled in lines, have confrontations with other dogs or wildlife, or even run into things. Mushers always carry sled bags in case their dogs are injured and need to be pulled to safety.

To ensure that dogs and handlers are safe on the trail, there are several rules of the road:

- Never allow your dog to interfere with another dog team.

- Always be conscious of your dogs' fitness and stamina.

- Always keep dogs well hydrated.

- Be aware of the trail conditions and hazards at all times.

- Tell someone where you are sledding and what trail you are using.

Dogsleds go fast — very fast — and mushers, even experienced ones, can be injured, too. Falls are an unfortunate but not unusual part of sledding. Falling off a sled at full speed and then trying to jump back on is an art form. Mushers can also run into trees if the trail turns and their dogs don't, or they can be hit by low overhanging branches. Other risks include avalanches, frostbite, storms, wildlife, getting lost, or being stranded when equipment fails.

Joining a local sledding club is another way to find mentorship opportunities. Because you need a minimum of two dogs (although four is preferable to distribute weight properly) to pull a sled, a club allows you to "share" dogs. In this way, a musher can avoid committing to "running a pack" before she is sure that this sport is for her.

Sled socialization should start slow and never be scary. Slowly introduce the harness to your dog by putting it on and then giving him lots of tasty treats. Do this often until he seems completely confident with this contraption on his back. Then, attach something light, such as empty milk jugs, to the harness for him to pull around. Again, do this for several weeks, giving him lots of positive reinforcement until he is comfortable.

If your dog is an adult, you can then start adding some weight to it. Go slowly. Once he's used to pulling weight, hook him up to the sled and walk alongside, praising him as he pulls. Don't let him stop if he becomes scared — just ask him to pull a few more steps and then take him off of the sled. Reinforcing his fear by immediately ending the session will only increase it.

Evaluating Equipment and Expense

To run a dogsled, you need at least two dogs, but preferably four. For this reason, a musher must really love dogs and have adequate space for them, or she must have friends who are willing to lend their dogs. It's not uncommon for two mushers to share a dog team. Those who become very active in sledding, however, almost always end up with their own teams.

Maintaining a kennel of dogs is expensive, and sleds, harnesses, and lines are all high-priced items. Traveling to and from races and trials takes time and can be costly. Sledding is one of the most equipment-heavy dog sports around, and mushers spend a great deal of money on the following necessities.

THE SLED

Basket sleds are light and made for racing. Toboggan sleds are heavier and made for longer distances and for hauling loads rather than for racing. Both types of sleds have baskets in the front and runners in the back where the musher stands. There is a brake, called the brake bar, that the musher can step on to slow the team. Mushers also carry a snow hook that is kicked into the snow to hold the sled in place before the race begins.

THE GANGLINE

The dogs run in front of the sled and are attached to the sled by a towline, which runs between the dogs and attaches to the sled. The dogs are attached to the towline by tuglines, which are attached to their harnesses. The dogs may also have a neckline, which attaches to the tugline at the collar and prevents the dogs from moving around too much and getting tangled in the lines. All of these lines together are called the gangline.

THE HARNESS

A well-fitting harness is an essential part of a sled dog's wardrobe. A harness that does not fit properly can lead to serious back problems. Harnesses are X-back or H-back in design. An X-back harness is used for pulling lighter loads and for racing. It's the most popular design. The H-back is a freight harness, used for pulling heavy loads on a toboggan.

THE SLED BAG

This is a bag that can be pulled behind the sled. It may be used to hold extra equipment or it can be used to carry an injured or tired dog.

DOG BOOTIES

Many mushers put neoprene booties on their dogs, especially if they are running considerable distances or on icy snow. These booties fit over the paws and are tightened with Velcro. The dogs tend to kick them off as they run, so a constant supply of replacements is necessary.

Canine Competition

The International Sled Dog Racing Association (ISDRA) sanctions most sled dog events in North America. They offer a variety of events, including races for children as young as three years old, freight races with weighted sleds for the heavy lifters such as Alaskan malamutes, and distance events that range from 50 to 1,000 miles.

Races are also divided by the number of dogs in the team:

- **Three Dog:** Two- to three-dog teams; trails are a minimum length of three miles

- **Four Dog:** Three- to four-dog teams; trails are a minimum length of four miles

- **Six Dog:** Three- to six-dog teams; trails are a minimum length of six miles

- **Eight Dog:** Five- to eight-dog teams; trails are a minimum length of eight miles

- **Ten Dog:** Seven- to ten-dog teams; trails are a minimum length of 10 miles

- **Unlimited:** Teams that are a minimum of seven dogs on a trail that is between 12 and 30 miles long

ORGANIZATIONS

International Federation for Sleddog Sports (IFSS) This is an international organization that sanctions sled dog events with an ultimate goal of Olympic participation.

International Sled Dog Racing Association (ISDRA) The ISDRA runs the lion's share of sled dog events in Alaska and the continental United States.

TITLES

The ISDRA and the IFSS do not award titles, but some breed clubs do. For example, the Siberian Husky Club of America awards the following:

SIBERIAN HUSKY CLUB OF AMERICA	
Sled Dog (SD)	Recognizes basic proficiency in sledding; awarded after completing 5 races or no less than 100 miles total
Sled Dog Excellent (SDX)	Recognizes a high level of proficiency; awarded after 5 successfully completed races and a total of 150 miles
Sled Dog Outstanding (SDO)	Recognizes an outstanding level of proficiency; awarded after 5 successfully completed races and a total of 200 miles

SKIJORING: CANINE CROSS-COUNTRY

As the skijorer turns a bend in the snow-covered forest, a long groomed trail narrows into the trees. She pushes forward on her skis as her Alaskan huskies jog ahead of her, leaning into their harnesses to keep the towline between them taut. The air is almost perfectly still but for an occasional whisper of wind that sends snow crystals sparkling into the sun. The only sound is the shush-shush-shush of skis against the snow and the panting of the dogs.

It's this stillness that makes the sport endlessly attractive to its participants. "Skijoring is my escape," says Kristen Ballard, who lives in Alaska. "It's so quiet and peaceful; you just can't get that with a snowmobile."

Skijoring captures the appeal of sledding without the expense and inconvenience. It is the sport of choice for cross-country skiers who want to include their dogs, and it is often the obvious next step for mushers who can no longer support a full dog team. One aspect that many skijorers extol is that rather than standing on the back of a sled while your team does all the work, in skijoring you actively participate in the movement.

John Thompson is a longtime skijorer who owns a Minnesota skijoring outfitting company, Skijor Now. His entry into the sport is typical. He tried dogsledding in the early 1990s and loved it. However, he wasn't in a position to maintain a four-dog team, so he turned to skijoring. "I only had one dog and that's all you need for skijoring," says Thompson. "Skijoring is the only sport in the world that engages both the dog and the handler in moving. If you just stand behind your dog [on a sled], you're not going to go very fast. You're getting a workout as much as your dog is. For the dog, it's complete freedom to run as hard as he wants to."

The Basics of Skijoring

Skijorers like to say that the only things you need for this sport are snow, skis, and a dog, and this is basically true. Long popular in Norway, skijoring began to garner interest in Alaska in the 1980s, eventually becoming known in the continental United States about 10 years later. Alaskans originally brought the sport to the lower 48, and it is rapidly growing in popularity in Minnesota and surrounding states where a lack of hills

and lots of snow provide ideal conditions. The sport is also catching on in the Northwest, where the combination of dogs and cross-country skiing has spurred interest.

In skijoring, one to three dogs run in front of a handler who glides behind them on cross-country skis. The skier wears a special belt around his waist, which is attached to a 7- to 12-foot towline. The towline attaches to the harness of the dog. With a team of three, a pair runs abreast either in front or in back of the single. Each dog has a separate towline but they are connected with neck lines that keep them from pulling too far away from one another.

In the cross-country skiing world there can be a perception that skijoring is bad for the trails. Dog footpads shouldn't put enough weight on the snow to cause any damage to a groomed trail, but dog

Verbal Commands

Easy: Slow down

Gee: Turn right

Haw: Turn left

Hike/Let's go: Pull

Line out or Tighten up: Go to the end of the line and lean into the harness

On by: Keep moving past a distraction

Whoa: Stop

waste and yellow snow can be distasteful to other Nordic skiers. Encourage your dog to relieve himself before setting out, and don't allow him to mark excessively. Always be sure to have plastic bags to pick up waste, and pick up any stray poops you see as well. Try to find multiuse trails where you won't offend anyone by taking your dog, and consider non-traditional trails, such as fire roads and paths around lakes (if you are in an area where this is safe).

"It's similar to any other organized sport; the vast majority do it for fun and fitness and then there are a few nuts who just can't get enough and train all the time and enter races every weekend," says Thompson. "Most of our customers are people who get out once or twice a week with their dog. It's primarily a recreational pursuit."

Who Does Skijoring?

At the top competitive levels, most of the dogs are Alaskan huskies or Siberian huskies; however, any dog who is physically sound and weighs more than 25 pounds can participate on a hobby level. Dogs commonly seen on skijoring trails include Labs, German shorthaired pointers, poodles, even corgis and beagles. You may not go as fast with a smaller dog, but both you and your dog will have a good time and enjoy being outdoors together.

Before beginning skijoring, your dog should be well trained and responsive to commands. He must demonstrate a willingness to run in front of his handler; some dogs aren't comfortable in that position or are too carefully trained to heel. In some ways, the perfect skijoring dog is one who has never learned not to pull on the leash. Skijoring can be a great sport for a dog with huge amounts of energy, particularly one who sometimes uses that energy for less than desirable purposes.

Both men and women participate in skijoring and tend to be fairly young, healthy, and outdoorsy individuals. They are generally the types who engage in other outdoor sports, such as canoeing, kayaking, camping, hiking, and of course, cross-country skiing. Confidence on skis is essential: You do not want to learn how to ski with a dog pulling you.

Talking about Training and Time

The amount of training needed depends on the individual handler and the dog(s). It is critical that handlers have at least some cross-country skiing background. If you are attracted to skijoring but have never skied before, or have only skied downhill, a series of cross-country ski lessons is the best place to begin your training. If you can't handle yourself on skis, you won't be able to handle your dog.

While you are perfecting your skiing skills, your dog can begin learning the essential mushing commands on dry land. As with all canine sports, your dog should respond to basic commands and have a sound recall before beginning to skijor. The recall is especially important because if you need to release him for some reason, you want to be sure he won't run off.

A good way to start training for both of you is in canicross, which is running with your dog attached to you with a towline. (See page 230.) This way he gets used to running in front of you, and you can begin training the basic commands without dealing with skis and snow. If you start canicross in summer, you and your dog may be ready to go by the first snowfall.

Typical sledding breeds, especially those that come from sledding lineages, may not need any real training. They usually know instinctively what to do when a harness is put on them. Other dogs take a bit more coaxing. Follow these steps if your dog isn't a natural skijorer.

- Start by letting your dog wear the harness around the house or yard for five minutes at a time. Don't leave a dog alone with a harness on.

- Once the dog is comfortable with the harness, attach a leash to the harness and let him walk in front of you out on a trail. If your dog isn't a puller, enlist a helper. While one of you walks behind, putting tension on the harness, the other walks next to the dog encouraging him to pull with praise and treats.

- To increase his comfort level with pulling, before getting on skis, attach a towline to the harness and fasten the other end to a skijor belt around your waist. Encourage your dog to walk in front of you — again, you may need a helper at first.

- End each session after about 15 minutes, even if the dog hasn't grasped the concept. Shorter, more frequent sessions are more effective, and you want the dog to have a positive experience each time he is on the harness.

- You can also encourage a dog to pull in a harness by taking him out with other pulling dogs. You may find that he starts pulling at the lead as soon as he sees the other dogs take off. Some dogs learn better by example.

Eventually, if your dog is going to pull, he will get the hang of it. Some dogs, however, are simply not interested in or suited to pull in a harness. If after patient and positive training over several months your dog still has not shown interest in pulling, it might be time to find a different sport for him.

SKIJORING SAFETY

This sport is almost tailor-made for accidents, so keeping safety in mind is especially important. First and foremost: take emergency provisions if you are going to ski off groomed trails — in the middle of winter, a fun day of skijoring can quickly become dangerous if the weather turns, you become lost, or you or your dog is injured. Here are some specific concerns.

EQUIPMENT

- Until you are very experienced, use only skis without metal edges, which in a fall can cause serious injury to both dog and skier.

- Dress appropriately in layers of clothing and take a coat for short- or smooth-coated dogs. Most dogs don't need an extra layer when running but might begin to shiver during breaks or if you have to stop in an emergency.

- Wear a backpack with water (enough for both/all of you) and emergency provisions, including waterproof matches, Sterno, a bowl in which to melt snow, some type of light dehydrated food, a compass, and a cell phone.

- Consider putting neoprene booties on your dog for icy or rough trails. They protect against cuts and bruises and prevent chunks of snow and ice from building up in the hair between the paw pads. These "snowballs" are uncomfortable and can lead to frostbite if left unattended. This is especially an issue for dogs with feathered hair, such as golden retrievers, spaniels, and setters.

- If traveling off groomed trails or skijoring for speed, wear a helmet, especially when conditions are bad. Trails are often narrow and falls can be dangerous.

PRECAUTIONS

- Because skijoring is almost always done on snowy trails in isolated areas, skijorers should ski in pairs. If you have to skijor alone, tell someone where you are going and when you expect to be home.

- Do not let your dog eat snow for hydration. Although it may quench his thirst, it will also dangerously lower his body temperature.

- Take breaks. Your dog might not want to stop, but enforce a rest break every half hour. Don't stop long enough to become chilled but do give your dog the chance to urinate, have a drink, and roll in the snow for a minute.

- Do not let your dog chase furry creatures or interfere with other skijoring or sledding dogs. This can be dangerous for you, your dog, and the other animals.

- Let go when you need to. There may be times when it's safer to unhook your dog and let him run down a steep hill or along a particularly rough trail.

- As with any sport, don't expect an out-of-shape dog to run 10 miles, or even two miles for that matter. If you don't train your dog year-round — scootering, bikejoring, skatejoring, canicross, drafting, and driving are all excellent off-season sports for skijoring dogs — build up strength and endurance slowly after the first snow falls.

Evaluating Equipment and Expense

The equipment for skijoring consists of cross-country skis without metal edges, light cross-country ski boots, a well-fitting harness made for skijoring, a towline, and a well-fitting padded belt. Kristen Ballard explains that different situations and conditions call for different types of equipment. Although in general skijorers are advised against wearing skis with metal edges, backcountry skijorers who go off trails will need skis with metal edges to break trails. Ballard uses telemark skis and leather boots, but most skijorers prefer lighter equipment.

Taking It to Extremes

Although skijoring has quickly gained popularity in northern climates, an offshoot of skijoring called extreme skijoring has drawn the attention of a few hardy souls. "Basically, when most people skijor they hook up their dog for an afternoon jaunt. In extreme skijoring it's long distances for an extended period of time," says extreme skijorer Kristen Ballard, who typically skijors 10 or 15 miles in a day to a backcountry cabin. Several years ago she engaged in a seven-day, 350-mile skijoring race in which she and her dogs traveled an average of 45 miles per day and camped out at night.

HARNESS

Although there are four or five different types of harnesses, most skijorers use the X-back design, which is the most commonly used design in the dog-powered sports and allows the force to be evenly distributed. Make sure the harness does not put pressure at the bottom of the neck. Pulling harnesses aren't sold in pet supply stores; you will need to look for a mushing or skijoring outfitter.

Note: Never use a regular walking or training harness in any pulling sport. Your dog could suffer injuries from a harness that isn't designed for pulling.

BELT

This is a padded belt that goes around the waist of the skijorer and attaches to the towline. Leg straps hold it in place so it doesn't ride up the torso, and there is a quick-release device that allows you to release the dogs in case of an emergency. The towline is between 7 and 12 feet long and has a length of bungee where it attaches to the belt to minimize the impact on the handler when the dog pulls.

PULK

Some skijorers use a pulk, which is a small sled that can be towed either behind the skier or between the dog and the skier. The pulk is commonly used in extreme skijoring where you will be camping with the dogs or at least need to be prepared to spend a night out in the elements.

Skijoring equipment can be expensive, although skiers will already have the basics; decent ski packages can be bought secondhand at most sports consignment stores. Skijoring belts, harnesses, and lines can be bought through skijoring outfitting companies and will cost a total of between $100 and $300 depending on the number of dogs being run at one time.

The great thing about skijoring is that it's largely a one-time expense. From then on, the only thing you pay for is gas and trail use fees.

Canine Competition

While the majority of skijorers just do it for fun, there are serious competitors out there. Racers and more serious skijorers often use skate skis instead of standard cross-country skis. Frequent competitors spend a great deal of time training their dogs and usually have a combination of sled-bred dogs, very strong skiing skills, and excellent training.

There is a host of skijor races held across the northern parts of the United States and in Alaska each year, usually in conjunction with sled dog races. Skiers can compete with one to three dogs for distances that generally range from four to eight miles.

Hobbyist skijorers, however, shouldn't be worried about an overly competitive atmosphere at a skijoring event. Thompson likens them to a marathon, where there are some elite racers but the vast majority are hobby skijorers with their pet Labs or German shepherds who are just out to have fun with their dogs.

ORGANIZATIONS

International Federation for Sleddog Sports (IFSS) This is an international organization that sanctions sled dog events with an ultimate goal of Olympic participation.

International Sled Dog Racing Association (ISDRA) The ISDRA runs the lion's share of sled dog events in Alaska and the continental United States.

DAREDEVIL DRYLAND PULLING
(Canicross, Scootering & Bikejoring)

"Line ready! Ho, ho, ho!" Suddenly, the scooter on which I've been languidly resting one foot lurches away from me as the golden dog harnessed to it begins trotting briskly in front. I just barely leap onto the scooter, and before I know it I am riding down a smooth asphalt path.

At first I'm terrified but I quickly begin to feel comfortable. As Daphne Lewis instructs me from her mountain bike, I grip the scooter handles with both hands and keep two fingers on the hand brakes at all times. For several minutes we travel along the straight and level path, Brett the dog trotting smoothly ahead and Lewis alongside us on her bike. When we approach a gravel pathway branching off of our path, however, Lewis shouts, "Gee! Brett! Gee!" Brett swerves to the right, and I hit the brakes, shouting "Whoa!" and jumping off the scooter.

I met Daphne Lewis and her two Chinook dogs, Brett and Rosy, at a park in western Washington to learn more about this relatively new sport. Chinooks are rare sled dogs who were used on Antarctic expeditions in the early part of the 20th century. Both dogs are eager and friendly and when I comment on this, Lewis tells me that Chinooks are the golden retrievers of the sledding world. Lewis is the woman behind dog scootering. She's made it a career and a life mission to introduce the sport to the thousands of dogs who love to run and pull, but who need an outlet when there is no snow.

Before we begin our session Lewis wants to see how well I can do without the dog. I push weakly with my left leg, my right leg awkwardly straight on the deck, and when I try to coast toward her I go so slowly that I teeter and begin to fall. I quickly jump off and she sighs. "Um, I think you need a little practice there."

I try various ways of standing and finally settle with a sort of moderated surfing position with my right foot straight ahead and in front and my left foot behind and angled toes out. As a surfer I'm considered a goofy foot and this appears to be the case in dog scootering as well. After some less traumatic efforts at coasting around the parking lot, Lewis clears me to add the dog to the mix. Although I'm still unsure of my capacity for this sport, she quickly hooks Brett's harness to the line and then attaches it to the scooter.

A half hour later, I've recovered from my initial panicky attempt at a right turn and am starting to get the hang of it. I run alongside the scooter while we go up a hill, and this time when I jump back on, I instruct Brett to go: "Line ready! Go! Go! Go!" Brett takes off at a trot on a loose gravel path that quickly turns to dirt with clusters of tree roots breaking up the surface.

I'm sure I'm going to wipe out at any moment, but the large mountain bike tires give a surprisingly smooth ride and I never really careen out of control. The only times I even come close to falling are when I freak out and jump off the scooter, which I do at regular intervals, especially when we come to a steep downhill incline. "This is the fun part," shouts Lewis, but I opt to run alongside the scooter instead of riding. As with surfing, however, it's when you challenge yourself that you begin to do better. About halfway into the ride, my confidence is boosted hugely by a quick but uninterrupted ride down a steep hill.

Careening behind Brett as he gallops down a steep rocky slope, my heart is beating wildly and only sheer will keeps me from jumping off the scooter in terror. Moments later we are at the bottom of the hill and at the beginning of a slight incline, and I am again coasting mildly behind the trotting dog. As soon as my heart stops racing, I can't wait for the next hill.

The Basics of Dryland Pulling

Whereas sledding has been done for thousands of years in Alaska and Siberia, and skijoring has been done for at least hundreds of years in Norway, the dryland sports are fairly new. Canicross, scootering, and bikejoring utilize the same concepts as sledding and skijoring, but without the snow. A dog (or team of dogs) is harnessed either directly to the handler or to a wheeled vehicle, and off they go. With roots firmly based in the sports of dogsledding and skijoring, these sports are often called dryland pulling.

Although canicross, scootering, and bikejoring were specifically developed for off-season training and conditioning of snow dogs, they've quickly gained popularity in their own right, attracting a large number of dog handlers from more southern climes or from urban areas. Because all of these sports are done on leash and the equipment is fairly portable, they can be done within city parks as long as there is a wide running or biking trail. Most people do these sports for recreation and to keep fit for snow season, though some organizations sponsor races and meets.

CANICROSS

Canicross is the easiest of the dog pulling sports to do; many mushers use it to begin to train their dogs in other dryland pulling sports, as well as skijoring. As in all of the dryland sports, the dog runs in front of the handler and is directed with traditional mushing commands. Although many handlers simply use canicross as a way to train their dogs to stay in front while pulling and on the proper commands, some people get hooked. There are now even canicross races.

"It's growing by leaps and bounds," says John Thompson, owner of Skijor Now, a skijoring and dryland-pulling equipment company. He gives part of the credit for the sport's recent popularity to a lack of snowfall in many areas, but also says that many canicrossers like the convenience of the sport. "You just put on your shoes and down the trail you go."

To increase or decrease the effort made by the dog, you can either "call your dog up" when going uphill and give an "easy" command when you are running downhill. Despite the risk of spills from an overeager dog and from running on icy or wet surfaces, canicross is safer than the other pulling sports because the speeds are much slower and you're not on wheels or skis. It is still important you have control over your dog at all times, especially in busy park settings.

Some canicrossers up the ante with their dogs by adding in-line skates. Once wheels are added to the mix (this is called bladejoring), speeds can get quite high, so it's important for the dogs to know mushing commands (and for bladejorers to be proficient on blades before adding the dog to the excursion).

SCOOTERING

Scootering in the United States owes much of its popularity to the advocacy of one woman: Daphne Lewis. Lewis first began scootering when she moved to the

> ## Verbal Commands
>
> Dryland racing commands are the same as those used in sledding and skijoring, but some commands are used more than others.
>
> **Easy:** Slow down (in bikejoring and scootering, used in conjunction with braking)
>
> **Gee:** Turn right
>
> **Haw:** Turn left
>
> **Line out or Line ready:** Dog walks out on the line and pulls it taut (especially used in scootering)
>
> **On by:** Go past a distraction; also used when the dog tries to mark
>
> **Pull (also hike, okay):** Go
>
> **Ready:** Be ready to go
>
> **Wait:** Stop

city in 1996 and found that it was difficult to keep up with her Rottweiler's exercise needs. She began by skating with him and then bought a child's scooter with 12-inch air-filled tube tires. Both she and Rottweiler Rubro were hooked almost instantly.

The small scooter was inadequate for her needs, so Lewis began developing her own, eventually designing a lightweight brushed-aluminum model with 16-inch studded mountain bike tires made for uneven trails and with a wide deck that provides better balance for the handler. She now sells her scooters to other fans and has written a self-published book on scootering, *My Dog Likes to Run, I Like to Ride*. Lewis points out that during the time that she was developing the sport in the States, dogs in Europe, Australia, and New Zealand were already competing in their own form of scootering.

BIKEJORING

In bikejoring, the handler rides a mountain bike while the dog (or dogs) runs ahead and pulls the bike. Alternatively, the dog can run alongside the bike, attached by the tug line to a springer that keeps the dog at a distance from the bike and prevents any accidental entanglements. Most bikejorers recommend having the dog run in front of the bike, especially if the musher plans to do other dryland sports or sledding or skijoring with the dog. It's also much safer: With the dog in front, the bicyclist has far more control than when the dog is to the side. "We like to have the dog out in front primarily because the dog is in that position for skijoring and canicross," says Thompson. "We want them listening to our commands rather than following our movements."

Bikejoring presents greater risks than the other dryland pulling sports, so you should try it only if you are experienced and confident riding a mountain bike on rough trails. Your dog must be dependable and well-trained to voice commands.

Who Does Dryland Pulling?

Because dryland pulling is usually done during fall, spring, and summer, it can be hard on the heavily furred breeds that are traditionally found in sledding and skijoring, though with careful management in hot weather, huskies and other northern breeds are naturals. Other pullers such as Rottweilers, American pit bull terriers and Staffordshire terriers, and hounds also do well. The important thing is to have a dog who likes being outdoors, loves to run, and enjoys pulling.

A prime candidate for any of the dog-powered activities is the same dog who can never seem to grasp the concept of "heel." Many rescue dogs become excellent dryland pullers because they are typically young, high-energy dogs who pull on the leash.

Dogs of any size can participate in dryland pulling, but no dog should pull any weight until he is fully grown. It's a good idea to have a potential scooter or bikejoring dog checked by a vet to ensure that there are no underlying joint or hip issues that could be exacerbated by weight-bearing exercise.

A range of people engage in dryland pulling activities, but most are athletic and have a deep love of being outdoors. Once a person tries one of the pulling sports, they often segue into one or two others. As Lewis points out, skijoring and scootering are really the same sport: "If there is no snow, you scooter; if there is snow, you skijor."

Talking about Training and Time

To get started in dryland pulling, it's best to find someone to train with. That way, you can get pointers on the right kind of equipment, borrow a scooter until you decide it really is for you, and have someone answer your questions. It's also easier to train your dog for these sports in a group because most dogs will grasp what they need to do by following the other dogs. Putting a novice into a dog team will help him understand what's being asked of him even more quickly.

Many mushers recommend that all dog-pulling sports begin with canicross. This way you can train your dog to run in

Safety Considerations

The main safety issue for dogs is over-exertion or heat exhaustion. Ideally, dogs should pull only in temperatures lower than about 50 degrees, which in many summer climates means the early morning or evening. Proper hydration is very important.

Other safety issues for dogs are being run into by the scooter or bike and damage to the paw pads. Dogs who run long distances or on very rocky surfaces may need to wear booties, which are available through skijoring outfitting companies.

The potential for injury, primarily from falling, is much higher for people than for the dogs in these sports. The gangline can become tangled in the front wheel or you might use your brakes too strongly and fly over the handlebars. A dog can turn more sharply at speed than you can on a bike, pulling you over. Anyone engaging in scootering or bikejoring should wear a bike helmet, goggles, long sleeves, long pants, and gloves.

front of you and to respond to directional commands without risking the falls that many novices experience in bikejoring, scootering, and skijoring.

Before doing anything else, train your dog to walk as you want him to run: no weaving from side to side, no running on the wrong side of fire hydrants and telephone poles, and no stopping to sniff, mark, or pee.

BEGINNING TRAINING

Once you have established that behavior as the dog walks next to you, train him to move out in front. Although many dogs will walk in front of you instinctively (that's why all those dogs who will never learn to heel are so great for these sports!), some dogs need to be taught to walk in front.

To do this, ask a friend to walk alongside your dog while you hold the tug line and walk behind. Encourage your dog to stay in front with lots of positive encouragement and treats from your friend. Another method is simply to do canicross, skijoring, or bikejoring with other dogs. The dogs will often begin running just to keep up with the pack. You can also hitch a novice dog up with an experienced dog who can show him the ropes.

The next step is making sure your dog is comfortable with the harness and moves confidently with weight behind him. Daphne Lewis recommends using a double-ended leash with one end attached to the harness and one end to the collar. "As you pull backwards on the harness and forward on the collar, the dog learns he can pull on harness and it's fine." This kind of training can begin even when your dog is still a puppy and too young to actually pull any real weight.

Evaluating Equipment and Expense

The need for equipment varies from sport to sport, but wearing a helmet is recommended for all except canicross. For any of the dryland pulling sports, a special two-dog tug line is required for running more than one dog.

CANICROSS

The equipment is minimal: a padded belt that goes around the runner's hips, a tug line, an X-back skijoring or sledding dog harness, and good running shoes. The tug line attaches to the front of the runner's belt and to the dog's harness. There is a short length of bungee cord where the tug line attaches to the belt. The setup is similar to skijoring except that a canicross line is about three feet shorter. John Thompson suggests braiding a handle into the tug line for greater control over your dog.

SCOOTERING

A good scooter can cost several hundred dollars. The dog wears an X-back skijoring or sledding harness or a harness made specifically for scootering. The tug line should be five or six feet in length for in-city scootering and about seven or eight feet for open-trail scootering. The tug line has an 8- to 10-inch bungee cord section built into it where it attaches to the scooter handlebars.

BIKEJORING

Bikejoring requires a mountain bike and one, two, or even, rarely, three dogs. The dogs are attached by an 11-foot tug line with an 8-inch length of bungee cord where it connects to the bike. The tug line is attached to the head tube (where the handlebars attach) or to the base of the handlebar stem. Attaching it to the upper end of the handlebar stem gives the dog too much control over the steering.

If your dog isn't ready to be a leader, you can use a springer that keeps the dog to the side; however, this can be dangerous if the dog pulls to the side because he can easily topple the bike.

Canine Competition

The International Sled Dog Racing Association (ISDRA) sponsors an annual dry-land racing event in Brainerd, Minnesota. Under ISDRA regulations, bikejorers ride three to five miles on an even surface consisting of gravel, sand, grass, or dirt. The line connecting the dog to the bike must be 7 to 12 feet in length. The divisions are one and two dogs, pro and novice, and adult, seniors (40-plus), and juniors (14 to 17).

The International Federation of Sleddog Sports (IFSS) hosts a Dryland World Championship, where competitors compete in canicross, bikejoring, scootering, and rig racing (dryland sledding).

ORGANIZATIONS

International Federation of Sleddog Sports (IFSS) This sledding organization places greater emphasis on skijoring and dryland racing and holds an annual Dryland World Championship.

International Sled Dog Racing Association (ISDRA) This organization is based in the United States. Its emphasis is on sledding, although they do sanction skijoring and occasional dryland racing.

CLASSES	
Classes are divided by number of dogs and the year the handler was born:	
Canicross	Handler's Year of Birth (in 2008)
Men Juniors	1992, 1993, 1994
Women Juniors	1992, 1993, 1994
Men Seniors	between 1969 and 1991 inclusive
Women Seniors	between 1969 and 1991 inclusive
Men Veterans	1968 and before
Women Veterans	1968 and before
Bikejoring	
Men Seniors	between 1969 and 1992 inclusive
Women Seniors	between 1969 and 1992 inclusive
Men Veterans	1968 and before
Women Veterans	1968 and before
Scootering	
1 dog	1992 and before
2-dog	1992 and before
Juniors	1991 and before
4-dog	1991 and before
6-dog	1991 and before
8-dog	1992, 1993, 1994

THE DELIGHTS OF CARTING
(Drafting & Driving)

The first time she hooked him up, Jennifer Hunt Brightbill knew that carting was the sport for her Bernese mountain dog, Porter. "He just lit up, as if to say, 'Why, you finally found my job. Let's go have some fun!'" she says. "Porter will take that cart up stairs, over garden beds, through play equipment at the park — anywhere! He especially likes to pull a noisy load and will go faster and faster to make more and more noise."

Darlette Ratschan is the author of *Travel at the Speed of Dog: A Guide to Driving,* a self-published book. She drives her four Portuguese water dogs for fun, but also because it fulfills a need for her dogs. "Dogs need jobs for the same reason kids need chores, games, and school," says Ratschan. "They need exercise and men- tal stimulation to be healthy and happy. Carting, whether it's draft or driving, provides challenges that are not found in any other dog sport. My dogs love to drive and find that the feeling of being out in front and assuming the responsi- bility of maneuvering the cart to be fun and rewarding."

Humans have trained dogs to pull wagons and carts for millennia. Rebecca Morris, an expert in the area of dog carting, has traced the use of draft dogs as far back as 300 BCE. Dogs have pulled garbage wagons and delivered meat, milk, and other products. Driving dogs have also been used for centuries; according to Morris, European royalty used dogs to introduce very young children to horse riding and carriage driving.

Today, drafting and driving are done recreationally — a fun way for people to spend time with their dogs, and for dogs who were bred for this work to show their stuff. For breeders of traditional drafting and driving dogs, it's also a way to maintain the ability and desire to pull in their dogs' lines.

The Basics of Carting

There are two types of carting: drafting and driving. In drafting, the dog pulls a wagon of some sort while the handler walks alongside the dog. In driving, the dog pulls a four-wheeled wagon or a two-wheeled cart called a sulky while the handler rides the cart. Like all the harness sports, carting requires a sound dog who loves to pull. Carting, although it can be competitive, really isn't for the competitive-minded. It has been called a "gentle art" — one that you should and,

perhaps can, do only with a dog who truly enjoys it.

Handlers who drive a cart or sulky may decide to get involved in fun runs or even compete in races as their dogs become more and more confident and skilled. Drafting events are held on the breed club level and may include skills such as making tight turns, going through narrow passes, moving at varying paces, and stopping quickly.

Driving events are races, along the lines of sledding or scootering races. The International Sled Dog Racing Association (ISDRA) holds driving events during their dryland pulling competitions. Under the ISDRA, dogs pull sulkies with the goal of finishing with the best time possible.

Verbal Commands

Not all carters use the same commands, but the following are typical:

Back: Back the cart up

Easy: Slow down

Go!: Increase pace

Gee/Right: Turn right

Haw/Left: Turn left

Pull/Okay/Let's go: Move forward (some carters use "pull" for "pull harder")

Whoa/Stop/Halt: Stop

Who Does Carting?

Unlike skijoring and scootering, this sport is well suited to slow but powerful pullers, such as Rottweilers, Newfoundlands, and Saint Bernards, although sulky drivers may prefer working with speedier, more traditional sled dog breeds such as huskies and Chinooks. The latter is a rare breed developed in the United States in the 1920s as a sled dog and recognized by the UKC and by the AKC as a Foundation Stock Service breed.

Plenty of other breeds may enjoy carting as well. Hounds, for example, often take to the pulling sports. Pit bull types often enjoy pulling a cart; just be cautious not to overheat a bully with a short snout, as this can lead to breathing problems.

More than breed, the key to a dog's enjoyment of carting is that he be large enough and sufficiently physically sound to pull a cart. A dog with bad hips, arthritis, or back problems should not do carting. As with other weight-bearing sports, dogs shouldn't start carting until they are at least one year old and should not be expected to pull any real weight until they are at least 18 months old for a standard-sized dog and 24 months old for a giant breed.

Soundness of temperament is also important. A dog who is skittish, afraid of loud noises, or fearful about being close to a bumping noisy cart will not like this sport. Your dog must know his basic commands and be reliable in outdoor settings. A good way to see if your dog is ready for the carting experience is to take the Canine Good Citizen test. (See page 50–51.)

As is typical with most dog sports, the majority of people involved in drafting are women. Many folks who particularly enjoy carting live in rural areas, where they have farmland and dirt roads on which to exercise their dogs. Having a barn to store the carts is also helpful. Carting is one of the few dog sports that lends itself well to families with very young children. Most drafting dogs especially enjoy having children in their wagon and many enthusiasts say their dogs take special care with small charges. It's also a sport children can grow into, moving from being a passenger to being a driver.

Equipment

Cart: A two-wheeled vehicle

Sulky: A lightweight cart for driving

Wagon: A four-wheeled vehicle

Shafts: A pole or poles that attach the vehicle to the harness by the traces

Traces: Straps that connect from the harness to the shafts; the dog pulls on the traces to pull the cart

Bridle: As with horses, the bridle attaches to the dog's head and is attached to reins, which are used by the handler for steering

CARTING SAFETY

A carting dog must be in good condition, with healthy bones and joints. Never let a dog who is not fully grown pull any significant weight. Once you begin carting with your dog, keep these safety tips in mind:

- Don't push your dog to go too fast. He might panic and injure himself.

- Do not cart in areas where there is a lot of traffic.

- Train your dog to stop dead on your command. You could both be hurt if he decided to chase a cat.

- If your dog begins to pant excessively, acts lethargic, or indicates that he wants to stop, it's time to stop.

- Stay away from hills and water's edges, and avoid slippery surfaces, such as wet grass; make sure all spaces are wide enough for both handler and cart.

Make sure that the cart is well balanced, as an unbalanced cart can tip, spooking the dog and potentially injuring dog and handler, especially when driving. It can also put too much pressure on the dog's neck, shoulders, and back. Modern sulkies are built with this balance in mind, but new carters should ask someone with experience to check their cart to ensure that it's balanced properly, neither tipping nor putting too much weight on the dog. With a sulky, it may be a matter of ensuring that you are sitting properly — not leaning forward so far that too much weight falls on the dog.

Talking about Training and Time

Training a dog for carting has two components: (1) exposing the dog to the cart, and (2) teaching the cart commands. Before beginning to learn carting commands, your dog should know the standard obedience commands: stay, sit, down, come, and leave it.

The cart itself may intimidate some dogs, and some will never become good carters because they don't enjoy it or are afraid of the cart. Carting takes a special type of dog — one who thrives on pulling and one who does not spook easily. Even more than skijoring, sledding, scootering, and bikejoring, pulling a cart is a lot for a dog to get used to. The time it takes to train a dog for carting varies greatly from dog to dog, but the one essential factor is never to push your dog beyond what he is capable of or comfortable with.

BEGINNING TRAINING

To begin training your dog, you will need a proper-fitting pulling harness. Let your dog wear the harness around the house while you supervise him. Give him lots of yummy treats, ear scratches, and jolly talk while he has his harness on. This is excellent practice while your dog is a puppy and can't do any real pulling. This way, he'll be fully comfortable in the harness by the time he's actually hitched up to a cart.

Once your dog feels comfortable in the harness, begin to familiarize him with the feeling of traces brushing against him by attaching the traces and allowing them to drag behind. (The traces are the straps that attach the dog's harness to the cart.) Once he's used to the traces, he can began pulling something behind him. To start, tie two empty milk jugs to the traces. Encourage your dog to walk around with the milk jugs dragging behind him, all the while giving him lots of treats and praise. As he becomes accustomed to the jugs, gradually fill them with water or pebbles so he feels more weight and noise behind him. Once he is comfortable dragging the full weight of the jugs, it's time to expose him to the cart.

Ask a friend to pull the cart alongside the two of you while you walk your dog on his harness, giving out treats and happy talk. Once the dog is comfortable walking next to the cart, hitch him up and let him pull it for a few steps. Even if you plan to do driving with him, at first just have your dog pull the cart while you lead him. It's helpful to have a friend on the other side of the cart in case your dog becomes frightened and tries to buck or run away from the cart. Keep training sessions short, low-key, and full of encouraging treats and positive reinforcement. Clicker training can be very useful while training your dog for carting.

Evaluating Equipment and Expense

Carting is an investment. A simple drafting cart is fairly inexpensive and can even be homemade. A cart made specifically for dog pulling can cost several hundred dollars, though, and a lightweight racing sulky is even more.

Most carters have several carts and wagons that they use for different purposes. So unless you like to throw money around, you will want to make sure your dog actually enjoys this sport before buying a cart of your own. Since training is a long, slow process, find some like-minded people to share this hobby with, and ideally they'll lend you a cart while you're learning.

Dogs must use a harness specifically made for pulling. Most harnesses run less than $100. Other expenses are minimal, as many drafters do not compete but rather draft on their own time as a casual hobby.

Canine Competition

There are a number of dryland pulling events in which a dog and musher can demonstrate their abilities. Draft dog events are held by breed clubs and have varying expectations. In general, however, the dog is expected to demonstrate that he follows basic commands and responds to his handler's directions, is willing to pull a cart, and is able to pull the cart through a course, with added weight, and with distractions.

ORGANIZATIONS

Drafting is mainly overseen by breed organizations. Some will accept other breeds into their competitions or will at least let them participate in demos. The AKC is planning to begin drafting tests in the near future. The following breed clubs host drafting tests:

- **American Working Collie Association**
- **Bernese Mountain Dog Club of America**
- **Newfoundland Club of America**
- **North American Working Bouvier Association**
- **Saint Bernard Club**

Sulky driving is considered part of the other dryland pulling sports, and the International Federation of Sleddog Sports sanctions races.

TITLES

Although the AKC is in the process of developing draft testing regulations, currently draft tests are still done at the breed club level. Several offer titles. Dogs competing in the Newfoundland Club of America test, for example, can earn a draft dog title (DD) and a team draft dog title (TDD).

HEAVY-DUTY WEIGHT PULLING

Head ducked almost to the ground, a tan-and-white
American pit bull terrier strains against the harness that connects him to the cart
behind him. The wheeled cart stands on a metal track and is stacked with concrete
bricks weighing nearly 1,000 pounds. The dog's handler stands 16 feet away at the
end of the track, calling enthusiastically. Inch by inch, the dog pulls the cart to the
end of the rails amid great cheers.

The sport of weight pulling, long the realm of freight dogs such as Alaskan malamutes and drafting dogs such as Bernese mountain dogs, has recently been taken over by dogs of all kinds, from heavyweight pit bull types to toy poodles. "They call us the shorthair people and we call them the longhair people," says Dan Riddle, who competes with four American pit bull terriers (APBT). His dogs compete in weight pulls exclusively for APBTs, as well as open breed pulls against the "longhair dogs."

Sue Ferrari has participated in weight pulling for more than seven years. Two of her Alaskan malamutes are regional gold medalists and have placed nationally as well. One of her main motivations is to continue the legacy that has been bred into her dogs. "It has to do with having working dogs and keeping their heritage alive," she explains. "Pulling is what these dogs are bred for. If you have a water dog and you don't work with it in a water sport, it kind of defeats the purpose, I think."

Weight-pulling handlers are quite aware that some members of the public cast a less-than-positive shadow on their sport. In particular, there has been ongoing suspicion that weight pulling is related to dogfighting, perhaps because of the large number of pit bull–type dogs participating or because of a similarity in conditioning methods (the use of treadmills, for example). Participants claim unequivocally that weight pulling has nothing to do with dogfighting, and most animal welfare advocates are quick to agree.

Inga Gibson of the Humane Society of the United States points out that for one thing, the bully dogs who do weight pulling are far too big for dogfighting. Dogmen, as professional pit bull fighters are called, use light, athletic dogs, not the burly, muscular types that compete in weight pulling.

People who do weight pulling want to put their sport in the best light possible, says Riddle. "It's a family fun sport that can be enjoyed by anybody."

The Basics of Weight Pulling

In weight pulling, dogs pull on three different surfaces: dirt, rails, and snow. In dirt, a cart on four wheels is pulled on a dirt track. In rails, the cart wheels are placed on a rail system, while the dog pulls the cart from between the rails. On snow, the dogs pull a sled. The track for all surfaces is 10 feet wide and 16 feet long.

The methods for pulling depend on the surface. On snow, the sled runners are typically frozen to the ground, so the dog must jerk the cart loose from the snow. When pulling a wheeled vehicle, the dog is encouraged to pull the cart slowly and steadily. In wheels and rails, dogs pull straight down the middle of the track, while on snow the dogs usually pull to one side or the other in order to get traction.

Whether the dog pulls on snow, wheels, or track, he wears a freight harness, which is attached by a towline to the cart or sled. The dog stands at the start line while the handler stands at the finish line. Once the handler calls the dog, he must complete the pull within

Some Words to Know

Bully dogs: Pit bull types, as well as other short-faced breeds a set period of time, usually 60 seconds. He is disqualified if he stops pulling before the finish line. During the pull, the handler is not allowed to touch the dog, the line, or the cart, although she can (and most people do) call the dog and encourage him. In most weight-pulling organizations the handler isn't allowed to use bait, such as food or a toy.

Every dog starts his heat with the same weight — usually the weight of the cart. Weight is added in increments; a dog moves on to the next weight level if he pulls the cart the length of the track in the required 60 seconds. Experienced dogs may skip two weights in order to conserve their energy. Dogs compete only against other dogs in their own weight class. As Riddle points out, "That means a toy poodle can be a champion just as much as a 150-pound malamute."

Who Does Weight Pulling?

With dogs separated by weight, there really are 150-pound malamutes and 6-pound toy poodles competing in the same venues. On the larger end, you might see mastiffs, Saint Bernards, and Newfoundlands, while the smallest classes may feature rat terriers, Patterdale terriers, and poodles. In the middle are the bully breeds such as boxers and pit bull types that have heavily infiltrated this sport that was once the bastion of Alaskan malamutes and other drafting dogs. A good candidate is a highly driven dog who loves to pull. If your dog constantly leans on the leash on walks no matter how much training you do, this might be just the sport for him.

The human handlers vary as widely as the dogs. Most are between the ages of 20 and 50, but there are a number of junior handlers and quite a few elderly handlers as well. An average International Weight Pulling Association (IWPA) weight pull will attract handlers ranging in age from 10 to 70. For what is considered something of a macho sport, a surprisingly large number of women and families compete.

If you are interested in learning more, attend a weight-pulling event. The International Weight Pulling Association (IWPA) is the most widely recognized and respected weight-pulling organization. Dogs of any breed are allowed to participate and safety standards are stringent.

Pulls are good places to meet people who have a great deal of experience, and many of them are eager to introduce newcomers to their sport. You can ask questions and even take your dog along to see how he reacts. There is often a chance for neophytes to give weight pulling a try. It's a good opportunity to try a harness on your dog and find out whether he has a natural affinity for it.

WEIGHT PULLING SAFETY

IWPA restricts dogs from competing before one year of age because pulling large weights can have serious long-term effects on joint development in young dogs. However, other weight-pulling organizations allow dogs to compete at six months. Despite the fact that you can do it, don't. Waiting another six months to begin competing and serious training won't make any difference in your dog's ability and will protect him from the serious injuries that can occur when dogs pull before their growth plates are closed.

There is a perception among other dog people that weight pulling poses more risk of injury than other sports, but weight-pull handlers disagree. In the three and a half years that Riddle has been doing weight pulling, he's seen one dog injured during a competition and that was a broken nail. He concedes though that the greatest chance of injury is during training, when humans are pushing dogs too hard and dogs develop repetitive-use injuries.

While IWPA weight pulling is mostly safe for dogs as long as they are handled responsibly, the extreme weight-pulling competitions sometimes seen at pit bull events are more likely to lead to injuries. Some of the riskier competitions are the ones where weight is added suddenly or treadmill events where dogs are asked to run as far and as hard as they can.

Pit bull types are at special risks for injuries in weight pulling because the breeds have been bred to work till they drop. Nordic breeds, on the other hand, are far more independent and will stop pulling when they feel like it rather than when their owners tell them to.

Talking about Training and Time

Like the other pulling sports, weight pulling is largely an instinctive sport in which the dog is not so much trained as socialized. Because pulling heavy weight can have severe orthopedic effects on growing dogs, early training is limited to conditioning the dog to wearing a harness and pulling a small amount of weight behind him. A good foundation of obedience training is extremely important in weight pulling, a sport in which you can't touch the dog while he's pulling. The dog must not only understand and be willing to follow your commands from a distance but also respect you enough to want to work for you.

The first step in weight-pull training is to accustom the dog to wearing the harness. Many handlers will just let the dog hang out in harness while receiving lots of attention and tasty treats until they are very used to it. Weight can be added starting with empty milk jugs, which are light but make noise when dragged on the ground. Gravel is gradually added to the jugs to make them both heavier and noisier. Lengths of heavy chain can also be used: Dan Riddle started training his 7-month-old APBT puppy, Rage, with a 10-pound chain that she dragged around while doing laps in the park. While getting used to the feeling of weight behind her, the puppy also learns where to place her feet as she pulls.

DIFFERENT TECHNIQUES

Once you introduce your dog to the cart or sled and begin to train with real weight, techniques vary. In sledding, the dog needs to break the sled from the ice by pulling in hard, quick movements. With carts on wheels and tracks, the pull is begun gradually. Every handler teaches the dog to pull a little differently depending on the surface and the dog's individual temperament. A mentor can be very helpful at this stage of training.

Another important part of weight-pull training is figuring out how best to motivate your dog to come to you: a high, excited voice; a low, urgent voice; clapping and cheering; or a sing-songy "Come here!" This is a sport where the rapport between dog and handler is particularly

between dog and handler is particularly important, as there is distance between them, no contact is allowed, and treats and rewards aren't permitted during competition. Your dog has to really want to please you in order to move that much weight.

A final component of weight-pulling training is preventing the dog from becoming discouraged or bored or burned out. Successful handlers recommend spotting your dog as the weight increases so that you can help him before he fails. If he tries and can't pull the weight, get behind the cart and help him. If you do a good job of that over and over and over again, your dog will never feel like quitting.

The duration and amount of training in weight pulling largely depends on the breed and the individual dog, but also somewhat on the time of year. Nordic dog handlers usually do not train at all during the summer because of the heat, and IWPA offers weight pulls only during fall through spring. Nordic dogs rarely have a temperament that suits them to constant training, while pit bull types seem to thrive on activity. Most American pit bull terriers and Staffies compete and train year-round.

Evaluating Equipment and Expense

The key piece of equipment is a properly fitted weight-pulling harness. A weight-pull harness is designed to distribute the weight evenly so the dog won't be injured. It is padded to prevent chafing and has spreader bars on either side of the hind legs to prevent the straps from rubbing against the dog's legs.

Weight-pull harnesses are often available for sale at weight-pulling events and can also be purchased online through links on the IWPA Web site. This is typically the biggest expense and may cost $60 to $100.

Other expenses include competition entry fees, which are usually minimal, and travel. If your dog is successful and you become enthusiastic, you may find yourself spending more money in entry fees, on training equipment, and on driving long distances to regional and national championships. Many serious weight pullers purchase treadmills to exercise their dogs, which range from about $300 to more than $1,000, and they may even set up their own cart-and-rail systems in their backyards.

Warning!

Your dog absolutely cannot pull in a standard dog-walking or sledding harness.

Canine Competition

Weight-pull trials are held throughout the United States by several sanctioning organizations. IWPA pulls are held only from September through March. Other organizations hold pulls year-round.

Before each competition, the dogs are weighed and placed in one of six weight divisions: 20 pounds or less, 21 to 40 pounds, 41 to 60 pounds, 61 to 80 pounds, 81 to 100 pounds, 101 to 125 pounds, 126 to 150 pounds, and Unlimited — dogs weighing more than 151 pounds

Each dog begins with the same amount of weight on the cart or sled and must pull it 16 feet in 60 seconds. The dog who pulls the most weight wins. Experienced weight-pull dogs can bypass the first two pulls in order to save their strength for the heavier weights.

Dogs earn points based on what place they take, as well as on how many dogs they compete against. Each dog's five best pulls are tallied at the end of the season. Each year, the top three dogs in each weight class from each of IWPA's 10 regions are invited to a national pull-off.

ORGANIZATIONS

American Dog Breeders Association (ADBA) This organization is for purebred American pit bull terriers registered with the ADBA only.

International Weight Pulling Association (IWPA) The IWPA is open to any dog, purebred or mixed breed. This organization is widely considered to be the most legitimate, safest, and most established weight-pulling organization.

United Kennel Club (UKC) The UKC is a purebred organization that allows mixed breeds to compete.

A number of breed clubs hold their own weight pulls, including the **Alaskan Malamute Club of America** and the **Saint Bernard Club of America**.

TITLES	QUALIFICATIONS
International Weight Pulling Association (IWPA)	
In IWPA, dogs can compete against themselves by earning titles for the amounts of weight pulled.	
Working Dog (WD)	Dog pulls 12 times his weight (5 times his weight on snow) at 4 weight pulls.
Working Dog Excellent (WDX)	Dog pulls 18 times his weight (10 times his weight on snow) at 4 weight pulls.
Working Dog Superior (WDS)	Dog pulls 23 times his weight (15 times his weight on snow) at 3 weight pulls.
United Kennel Club (UKC)	
United Weight Puller (UWP)	
United Weight Pull Champion (UWPCH)	
United Weight Pull Champion Excellent (UWPCHX)	
United Weight Pull Champion Versatile (UWPCHV)	
United Weight Pull Champion Outstanding (UWPCHO)	
United Weight Pull Champion Supreme (UWPCHS)	

Appendix A: Canine Sports Organizations

The best way to get involved with a canine sport is to join an organization or club for the sport that interests you.

AGILITY
American Kennel Club (AKC)
919-233-9767
www.akc.org

Australian Shepherd Club of
America (ASCA)
979-778-1082
www.asca.org

North American Dog Agility
Council (NADAC)
info@nadac.com
www.nadac.com

United Kennel Club (UKC)
269-343-9020
www.ukcdogs.com

United States Dog Agility
Association (USDAA)
972-487-2200
www.usdaa.com

CANINE FREESTYLE
Canine Freestyle Federation (CFF)
directors@canine-freestyle.org
www.canine-freestyle.org

Musical Dog Sport Association
(MDSA)
www.musicaldogsport.org

World Canine Freestyle
Organization (WCFO)
718-332-8336
www.worldcaninefreestyle.org

CARTING
American Working Collie
Association
www.awca.net

Bernese Mountain Dog Club of
America
admin@bmdca.org
www.bmdca.org

International Federation of
Sleddog Sports (IFSS)
www.sleddogsport.com

Newfoundland Club of America
secretary@newfdogclub.org
www.ncanewfs.org

North American Working
Bouvier Association
830-755-9006
www.nawba.biz

Saint Bernard Club of America
correspondingsecretary@saint-
bernard.org
www.saintbernardclub.org

CONFORMATION
American Kennel Club (AKC)
919-233-9767
www.akc.org

American Rare Breed
Association (ARBA)
301-868-5718
www.arba.org

Mixed Breed Dog Clubs of
America (MBDCA)
740-259-3941
http://mbdca.tripod.com

United Kennel Club (UKC)
269-343-9020
www.ukcdogs.com

DISC DOG
Ashley Whippet International
alex@ashleywhippet.com
www.ashleywhippet.com

International Disc Dog Handlers'
Association
770-735-6200
www.iddha.com

Skyhoundz
770-751-3882
www.skyhoundz.com

UFO
www.ufoworldcup.org

U.S. Disc Dog Nationals
(USDDN)
www.usddn.com

DOCK JUMPING
DockDogs
330-241-4975
www.dockdogs.com

Splash Dogs
925-783-6149
www.splashdogs.com

DRYLAND PULLING
International Federation of
Sleddog Sports (IFSS)
www.sleddogsport.com

International Sled Dog Racing
Association (ISDRA)
218-765-4297
www.isdra.org

EARTHDOG
American Kennel Club (AKC)
919-233-9767
www.akc.org

American Working Terrier
Association (AWTA)
530-796-2278
www.dirt-dog.com/awta

FIELD TRIALS AND HUNT TESTS

Amateur Field Trial Clubs of America (AFTCA)
901-465-1556
www.aftca.org

American Kennel Club (AKC)
919-233-9767
www.akc.org

National Shoot to Retrieve Association (NSTRA)
317-839-4059
www.nstra.org

North American Versatile Hunting Dog Association (NAVHDA)
847-253-6488
www.navhda.org

United Kennel Club (UKC)
269-343-9020
www.ukcdogs.com

FLYBALL

North American Flyball Association (NAFA)
(800) 318-6312
www.flyball.org

HERDING

American Herding Breed Association (AHBA)
www.ahba-herding.org

American Kennel Club (AKC)
919-233-9767
www.akc.org

Australian Shepherd Club of America (ASCA)
979-778-1082
www.asca.org

LURE COURSING

American Kennel Club (AKC)
919-233-9767
www.akc.org

American Sighthound Field Association (ASFA)
724-586-6158
www.asfa.org

OBEDIENCE

American Kennel Club (AKC)
919-233-9767
www.akc.org

Australian Shepherd Club of America (ASCA)
979-778-1082
www.asca.org

Mixed Breed Dog Clubs of America (MBDCA)
740-259-3941
http://mbdca.tripod.com

United Kennel Club (UKC)
269-343-9020
www.ukcdogs.com

RALLY

American Kennel Club (AKC)
919-233-9767
www.akc.org

Association of Pet Dog Trainers (APDT)
800-738-3647
www.apdt.com

SCHUTZHUND

LV/DVG America
972-617-2988
www.dvgamerica.com

United Schutzhund Clubs of America (USA)
314 638-9686
www.germanshepherddog.com/schutzhund

SKIJORING

See Dryland Pulling

SLEDDING

See Dryland Pulling

TRACKING

American Kennel Club (AKC)
919-233-9767
www.akc.org

Australian Shepherd Club of America (ASCA)
979-778-1082
www.asca.org

WATER SPORTS

Canine Water Sports
K9watersports@aol.com
www.caninewatersports.com

Leonberger Club of America
978-808-2620
www.leonbergerclubofamerica.com

Newfoundland Club of America
secretary@newfdogclub.org
www.ncanewfs.org

Portuguese Water Dog Club of America
www.pwdca.org

WEIGHT PULLING

American Dog Breeders Association (ADBA)
801-936-7513
www.adbadog.com

International Weight Pull Association (IWPA)
970-352-0083
www.iwpa.net

United Kennel Club (UKC)
269-343-9020
www.ukcdogs.com

Appendix B: Traveling with Your Canine Athlete

One of the challenges that serious canine athletes and their handlers face is how to get to trials and championships. Often, national and regional championships require traveling long distances, even cross-country.

There are really only two feasible options when traveling with your dogs: airplanes and cars. Dogs are not allowed to travel by Greyhound bus (ironically!), nor by Amtrak train. Some boat lines allow dogs but almost uniformly require that they be kenneled throughout the trip.

BY CAR

Traveling by car is the most common and convenient way to travel with dogs. Most dogs, especially those involved in sports, are used to the car and will be comfortable riding even for long distances. It also saves you the hassle of renting a car when you arrive at your destination and allows you more flexibility as far as arrivals and departures.

Traveling by car isn't always easy, however, and does require safety considerations.

- Never leave your dog in the car when it's hot outside, even for a few minutes. Even with the windows rolled down, the heat can rise rapidly, putting your dog at risk for heat stroke.

- Always restrain your dog when driving. Hook him up to an approved doggy seat belt, have him ride in a crate (which, if he loves his crate, he will probably prefer), or drive a station wagon with a dog barrier separating the back seat from the luggage area.

- Never let your dog off his leash while on the road. It's tempting to get in a game of Frisbee when stopping at a rest stop, but it's very unsafe. Even very predictable dogs can get spooked at highway rest stops and run off. Once a dog is loose on a highway, it can be incredibly difficult to get him back, not to mention dangerous for the dog and fellow motorists.

BY PLANE

Traveling by airplane may not be a handler's first choice, but at times it may be a necessity. If, for example, your dog makes the Worlds and you need to get to Atlanta from Seattle, an airplane is probably going to be the way to go.

Unless your dog is small enough to fit in a crate under an airplane seat, he will have to travel by cargo. Over the years, there has been a great deal of concern about pets' safety when traveling in the cargo hold of an airplane. Although it appears that the risks were overstated, there are still reasons to be concerned.

Dogs have escaped from their crates during travel and have been lost when the baggage door opens.

Dogs have also died during a flight due to breathing problems. Most vets recommend against flying with brachycephalic dogs (dogs with short snouts) because they are more prone to breathing problems. Dogs should never be tranquilized before flying, because again, their breathing can be compromised.

Although the cargo compartment in a plane is pressure- and temperature-controlled while the plane is in the air, it is not temperature-controlled when the plane is on the ground. This means that if it's very warm and your plane sits on the tarmac for several hours, your dog will suffer. It's important to remember that many airlines will cancel flights if it is too hot or too cold, so plan accordingly. Some airlines do not transport dogs at all during the summer.

When flying with your dog, there are some basic rules to fly by.

- Follow the airline's guidelines. This usually means affixing a sticker with name and contact information on the front of the crate, putting "Live Animal" stickers on each side of the crate and "This Side Up" stickers as appropriate, taping a plastic bag with one meal's worth of food to the side of the crate, and providing a water dish that clips onto the inside of the metal grate. It's a good idea to freeze the dish full of water the night before leaving so the water will melt gradually without spilling. Also, fasten a photograph of your dog to the crate in the event that he is lost.

- Use zip ties to doubly secure the door; it won't pop open, and the ties can be easily cut in case of an emergency.

- If possible, take a direct route with no airplane transfers. The majority of problems when flying with dogs happen when the dog is transferred from one plane to another. Book your flights in the early hours before sunrise or after dark so your dog will not be subjected to very warm weather.

- To keep your dog comfortable during the flight, provide him with a mat or blanket in the bottom of the crate. This will soak up any accidents plus it will keep him cozy. Also provide several toys to keep him busy and comforted.

- Let your dog relieve himself after arriving at the airport and before checking in.

- Wait outside the plane until you see your dog boarded. You can also wait and watch him being unloaded from the plane. If you do not see your dog being boarded or unloaded, or notice anything that makes you uncomfortable, inform the flight desk attendant. Let everyone on the plane know that your dog is flying in cargo — the more people who know he is there, the better they will be able to assist you in the event of a problem.

- Request a window seat in the right forward part of the cabin; that way you will be able to see the baggage compartment door.

LODGING

When on the road, you will have to find someplace to stay where your dog is welcome. Fortunately, in many parts of the country dog-friendly motels and even high-end hotels are now common.

For the best possible experience, it is good to follow some guidelines.

- Book your motel or hotel before leaving home. Although many hotels accept dogs, not all do, and if you're attending a large event the rooms will book up quickly.

- Ask whether your dog is welcome in all of the hotel rooms or just in special dog-friendly rooms. If the hotel has set aside rooms for dogs, expect them to be the least desirable. If you don't expect your dog to exhibit perfect behavior, this may not be a concern, but if you're sensitive to doggy smells, you might seek another place to lodge.

- If possible, book a kitchenette. Although dog-friendly hotels are increasingly popular, dog-friendly restaurants are nonexistent or rare. If you're traveling in the summer, you'll probably be able to find a few spots that welcome dogs on the patio, but during winter travel, you will likely be eating a lot of takeout without a kitchenette.

- Avoid leaving your dog alone in your room. Unattended barking dogs are a huge nuisance, and even a calm dog may bark in a strange place.

- If you leave your dog in the room, keep him in his crate. Dogs often act unpredictably when they are left alone in a strange place and a normally mellow dog may have an accident.

- Be a good ambassador. That means don't allow your dog on the furniture, or if that's impossible, at least drape it with a sheet you take with you. Keep food and water bowls in the bathroom.

- Do not allow your dog to bark at or harass other visitors. Keep your dog on a leash, even if he's perfectly reliable. Take him to a private spot to relieve himself and always clean up after him.

There's nothing like being on the open road with your faithful dog companion. Be prepared for some extra logistical issues, but don't let that scare you away from what will likely be one of your best doggy memories. Traveling with your dog will open doors for you wherever you go and allow you to see the world with a whole new point of view.

Index

Page numbers in **bold** indicate charts.